TOEFL® MAP
ACTUAL TEST

New TOEFL® Edition

Listening **2**

TOEFL® MAP
ACTUAL TEST New TOEFL® Edition
Listening 2

Publisher Chung Kyudo
Editors Cho Sangik, Zong Ziin
Authors Michael A. Putlack, Stephen Poirier, Angela Maas,
Maximilian Tolochko
Designers Park Narae, Chung Kyuok

First published in April 2022
By Darakwon, Inc.
Darakwon Bldg., 211, Munbal-ro, Paju-si, Gyeonggi-do 10881
Republic of Korea
Tel: 82-2-736-2031 (Ext. 250)
Fax: 82-2-732-2037

ISBN 978-89-277-8011-3 14740
978-89-277-8007-6 14740 (set)

www.darakwon.co.kr

Photo Credits
Shutterstock.com

Components Main Book / Translation Book
8 7 6 5 4 3 2   23 24 25 26 27

TOEFL MAP

ACTUAL TEST

New TOEFL Edition

Listening **2**

INTRODUCTION

Studying for the TOEFL® iBT is no easy task and is not one that is to be undertaken lightly. It requires a great deal of effort as well as dedication on the part of the student. It is our hope that, by using *TOEFL Map Actual Test Listening* as either a textbook or a study guide, the task of studying for the TOEFL® iBT will become somewhat easier for the student and less of a burden.

Students who wish to excel on the TOEFL® iBT must attain a solid grasp of the four important skills in the English language: reading, listening, speaking, and writing. The Darakwon *TOEFL Map* series covers all four of these skills in separate books. There are three different levels in all four topics. In addition, there are *TOEFL Map Actual Test* books that contain a number of actual tests that students can use to prepare themselves for the TOEFL® iBT. This book, *TOEFL Map Actual Test Listening*, covers the listening aspect of the test by providing conversations and lectures in the TOEFL® iBT actual test format.

TOEFL Map Actual Test Listening has been designed for use both in a classroom setting and as a study guide for individual learners. It contains a total of seven full-length listening actual tests. Each test contains a varying number of conversations and lectures. Every conversation and lecture are the same length as those found on the TOEFL® iBT. The conversations and lectures also have the same numbers and types of questions that appear on actual TOEFL® iBT listening section passages. In addition, the changes that were made to the TOEFL® iBT in August 2019 have been incorporated into this book. By studying these conversations and lectures, learners should be able to prepare themselves to take and, more importantly, to excel on the TOEFL® iBT.

TOEFL Map Actual Test Listening has a great amount of information and should prove to be invaluable as a study guide for learners who are preparing for the TOEFL® iBT. However, while this book is comprehensive, it is up to each person to do the actual work. In order for *TOEFL Map Actual Test Listening* to be of any use, the individual learner must dedicate him or herself to studying the information found within its pages. While we have strived to make this book as user friendly and as full of crucial information as possible, ultimately, it is up to each person to make the best of the material in the book. We wish you luck in your study of both English and the TOEFL® iBT, and we hope that you are able to use *TOEFL Map Actual Test Listening* to improve your abilities in both of them.

Michael A. Putlack
Stephen Poirier
Angela Maas
Maximilian Tolochko

TABLE OF CONTENTS

HOW IS THIS BOOK DIFFERENT

CONTAINS CONVERSATIONS AND LECTURES MOST RECENTLY PRESENTED

- Has 18 conversations and 25 lectures in total
- Reconstructs the most frequently asked questions after analyzing real TOEFL® iBT questions
- Reflects the changes made to the TOEFL® iBT in August 2019

CONSISTS OF VARIOUS TOPICS

- Deals with academic topics such as the humanities, sciences, and arts
- Handles all types of conversations regarding campus life

PROVIDES AN EXPLANATION FOR EVERY QUESTION

- Shows the question types and provides detailed explanations
- Presents tips for getting a higher score

PRESENTS TRANSLATIONS OF THE CONVERSATIONS AND LECTURES

- Contains translations for all conversations and lectures

OFFERS FREE MP3 FILES

- Provides MP3 files for free at www.darakwon.co.kr
- Includes QR codes for listening to the MP3 files instantly

HOW TO USE THIS BOOK

QUESTION

This book contains every type of question that appears on the TOEFL® iBT. The difficulty level of the questions is the same as those on the actual TOEFL® iBT.

SCRIPT AND EXPLANATION

Every question has its own detailed explanation, so readers can learn why some answer choices are correct while others are not. Readers can also check their listening ability by consulting the scripts. The scripts are word-for-word reproductions of the recordings of the conversations and lectures.

TRANSLATION

In case some Korean readers cannot fully understand the script, a translation section has been attached to the book. This section can help readers grasp the meanings of certain conversations and lectures.

WORD REMINDER

Words and expressions that frequently appear on the actual TOEFL® iBT are listed in this section. In addition, readers can learn key words related to specific topics.

ABOUT THE TOEFL® iBT

TOEFL® iBT Test Sections

Section	Tasks	Time Limit	Questions
Reading	Read 3-4 passages from academic texts and answer questions.	54 – 72 minutes	30 – 40 questions
Listening	Listen to lectures, classroom discussions, and conversations and then answer questions.	41 – 57 minutes	28 – 39 questions
Break 10 minutes			
Speaking	Express an opinion on a familiar topic and also speak based on reading and listening tasks.	17 minutes	4 tasks
Writing	Write essay responses based on reading and listening tasks and support an opinion in writing.	50 minutes	2 tasks

TOEFL® iBT Test Contents

The TOEFL® iBT test is a test given in English on an Internet-based format. The TOEFL® iBT has four sections: reading, listening, speaking, and writing. The test requires approximately three and a half hours to take.

Combining All Four Skills: Reading, Listening, Speaking, and Writing

During the test, learners must use more than one of the four basic skills at the same time. For instance, learners may have to:

• listen to a question and then speak a response

• read and listen and then speak a response to a question

• read and listen and then write a response to a question

What Is the TOEFL® iBT Test?

The TOEFL® iBT test measures how well learners understand university-level English. The test requires students to use a combination of their reading, listening, speaking, and writing skills to do various academic tasks.

Which Learners Take the TOEFL® iBT Test?

Around one million people take the TOEFL® iBT test every year. The English abilities of most people taking the test are anywhere from intermediate to advanced. The following types of people most commonly take the TOEFL® iBT test:

• students who will study at institutes of higher learning

• students who wish to gain admission to English education programs

• individuals who are applying for scholarships or certificates

• learners who want to determine the level of their English ability

• students and other individuals who are applying for visas

Who Accepts TOEFL® iBT Test Scores?

In more than 130 countries around the world, over 8,000 colleges, universities, agencies, and other institutions accept TOEFL® iBT scores. In addition, the following places utilize TOEFL® iBT scores:

• immigration departments that use the scores when issuing visas

• medical and licensing agencies that award various certificates

• individuals who are trying to determine the level of their English ability

ABOUT THE LISENING QUESTION TYPES

Type **1**   Gist-Content Questions

Gist-Content questions cover the test taker's basic comprehension of the listening passage. While they are typically asked after lectures, they are sometimes asked after conversations as well. These questions check to see if the test taker has understood the gist of the passage. They focus on the passage as a whole, so it is important to recognize what the main point of the lecture is or why the two people in the conversation are having a particular discussion. The test taker should therefore be able to recognize the theme of the lecture or conversation in order to answer this question correctly. On occasion, the test taker is asked to identify two correct answers to a single question.

Type **2**   Gist-Purpose Questions

Gist-Purpose questions cover the underlying theme of the passage. While they are typically asked after conversations, they are sometimes asked after lectures as well. Because these questions focus on the purpose or theme of the conversation or lecture, they begin with the word "why." They focus on the conversation or lecture as a whole, but they are not concerned with details; instead, they are concerned with why the student is speaking with the professor or employee or why the professor is covering a specific topic.

Type **3**   Detail Questions

Detail questions cover the test taker's ability to understand facts and data that are mentioned in the listening passage. There questions most commonly appear after lectures; however, they also come after conversations, especially when the conversations are about academic topics. Detail questions require the test taker to listen for and remember details from the passage. The majority of these questions concern major details that are related to the main topic of the lecture or conversation rather than minor ones. However, in some cases when there is a long digression that is not clearly related to the main idea, there may be a question about the details of the digression. On occasion, the test taker is asked to identify two correct answers to a single question. These questions may also appear as charts.

Type 4 Understanding the Function of What Is Said Questions

Understanding the Function of What Is Said questions cover the test taker's ability to determine the underlying meaning of what has been said in the passage. This question type often involves replaying a portion of the listening passage. There are two types of these questions. Some ask the test taker to infer the meaning of a phrase or a sentence. Thus the test taker needs to determine the implication—not the literal meaning—of the sentence. Other questions ask the test taker to infer the purpose of a statement made by one of the speakers. These questions specifically ask about the intended effect of a particular statement on the listener.

Type 5 Understanding the Speaker's Attitude Questions

Understanding Attitude questions cover the speaker's attitude or opinion toward something. These questions may appear after both lectures and conversations. This question type often involves replaying a portion of the listening passage. There are two types of these questions. Some ask about one of the speaker's feelings concerning something. These questions may check to see whether the test taker understands how a speaker feels about a particular topic, if a speaker likes or dislikes something, or why a speaker might feel anxiety or amusement. The other category asks about one of the speaker's opinions. These questions may inquire about a speaker's degree of certainty. Others may ask what a speaker thinks or implies about a topic, person, thing, or idea.

Type 6 Understanding Organization Questions

Understanding Organization questions cover the test taker's ability to determine the overall organization of the passage. These questions almost always appear after lectures. They rarely appear after conversations. These questions require the test taker to pay attention to two factors. The first is the way that the professor has organized the lecture and how the professor presents the information to the class. The second is how individual information given in the lecture relates to the lectures as a whole. To answer these questions correctly, the test taker should focus more on the presentation and the professor's purpose in mentioning the facts rather than the facts themselves.

Type 7   Connecting Content Questions

Connecting Content questions almost exclusively appear after lectures, not after conversations. These questions measure the test taker's ability to understand how the ideas in the lecture relate to one another. These relationships may be explicitly stated, or the test taker may have to infer them from the words that are spoken. The majority of these questions concern major relationships in the passage. These questions also commonly appear in passages in which a number of different themes, ideas, objects, or individuals are being discussed.

Type 8   Making Inference Questions

Making Inferences questions cover the test taker's ability to understand implications made in the passage and to come to a conclusion about what these implications mean. These questions appear after both conversations and lectures. These questions require the test taker to hear the information being presented and then to make conclusions about what the information means or what is going to happen as a result of that information.

TOEFL® MAP

ACTUAL TEST Listening 2

01

Listening Section Directions

🎧 00-01

This section measures your ability to understand conversations and lectures in English.

The Listening section is divided into separately timed parts. In each part, you will listen to 1 conversation and 1 or 2 lectures. You will hear each conversation or lecture only **one** time.

After each conversation or lecture, you will answer some questions about it. The questions typically ask about the main idea and supporting details. Some questions ask about a speaker's purpose or attitude. Answer the questions based on what is stated or implied by the speakers.

You may take notes while you listen. You may use your notes to help you answer the questions. Your notes will not be scored.

If you need to change the volume while you listen, click on the **Volume** at the top of the screen.

In some questions, you will see this icon: 🎧 This means that you will hear, but not see, part of the question.

Some of the questions have special directions. These directions appear in a gray box on the screen.

Most questions are worth 1 point. If a question is worth more than 1 point, it will have special directions that indicate how many points you can receive.

A clock at the top of the screen will show you how much time is remaining. The clock will not count down while you are listening. The clock will count down only while you are answering the questions.

PART 1

Listening Directions

 00-02

In this part, you will listen to 1 conversation and 1 lecture.

You must answer each question. After you answer, click on **Next**. Then click on **OK** to confirm your answer and go on to the next question. After you click on **OK**, you cannot return to previous questions.

You may now begin this part of the Listening Section. You will have **7 minutes** to answer the questions.

Click on **Continue** to go on.

01-01

1   What are the speakers mainly discussing?

   Ⓐ A class that the student is taking

   Ⓑ A book that the student needs to purchase

   Ⓒ An item that the student wants to return

   Ⓓ A price that the student thinks is too high

2   Why does the bookstore manager explain one of her store's policies to the student?

   Ⓐ To inform the student that he can get his money back

   Ⓑ To tell the student that he has arrived too late

   Ⓒ To let the student know that a deadline has passed

   Ⓓ To ask the student why he took the plastic wrapping off the book

3   According to the student, why is he dropping the class?

   Ⓐ He finds the material in the class to be too difficult.

   Ⓑ He received a low grade on the midterm exam.

   Ⓒ He has decided not to major in philosophy.

   Ⓓ The professor is expecting too much work in it.

4   What will the student probably do next?

   Ⓐ Ask the bookstore manager another question

   Ⓑ Receive his money from the bookstore manager

   Ⓒ Sign a form to drop his philosophy class

   Ⓓ Search for another book to purchase

5   Listen again to part of the conversation. Then answer the question.

What does the bookstore manager imply when she says this: 🎧

   Ⓐ The price of the student's philosophy book is reasonable.

   Ⓑ She agrees with the student that book prices are too high.

   Ⓒ It is easy to get in contact with the book's publisher.

   Ⓓ She does not determine the prices of any books.

01-02

Biology

6 What is the lecture mainly about?

    Ⓐ The life of Norman Borlaug

    Ⓑ Genetically modified foods

    Ⓒ Changes that have been made to wheat

    Ⓓ The advantages of modifying some crops

7 According to the professor, why do people try to modify wheat?

Click on 2 answers.

    ① To have it use less water

    ② To let it resist certain diseases

    ③ To enable it to grow more quickly

    ④ To make it more productive

8 What is the professor's opinion of Norman Borlaug?

    Ⓐ The work that he did was of great importance.

    Ⓑ He should not have genetically modified some plants.

    Ⓒ His work came at the end of the Green Revolution.

    Ⓓ It is possible that people overstate his influence.

9 Why does the professor mention dwarf wheat?

   Ⓐ To emphasize that it is a highly productive form of wheat

   Ⓑ To state that it is mainly grown by farmers in Japan

   Ⓒ To describe how it is able to resist many harmful diseases

   Ⓓ To note how it was crossbred with another type of wheat

10 What can be inferred about the Green Revolution?

   Ⓐ It occurred thanks to improvements in farm machinery.

   Ⓑ It would not have happened without Norman Borlaug.

   Ⓒ Many people have protested the way that it started.

   Ⓓ It only took place in Mexico and India.

11 What will the professor probably do next?

   Ⓐ Give the students a short reading assignment

   Ⓑ Discuss some modifications to another crop

   Ⓒ Talk about some changes made to barley

   Ⓓ Continue his discussion on Norman Borlaug

PART 2

Listening Directions

🎧 00-02

In this part, you will listen to 1 conversation and 1 lecture.

You must answer each question. After you answer, click on **Next**. Then click on **OK** to confirm your answer and go on to the next question. After you click on **OK**, you cannot return to previous questions.

You may now begin this part of the Listening Section. You will have **7 minutes** to answer the questions.

Click on **Continue** to go on.

00:07:00 ⊖ HIDE TIME

🎧 01-03

1 Why did the woman ask to see the student?

    Ⓐ To let her know about an academic scholarship

    Ⓑ To talk about her student loan application

    Ⓒ To discuss a few problems with some paperwork

    Ⓓ To find out about her grades the previous semester

2 What is the first error that the woman points out?

    Ⓐ A missing transcript

    Ⓑ The lack of a signature

    Ⓒ A mistaken date

    Ⓓ An unanswered question

3 What can be inferred about the student's GPA?

    Ⓐ It was lower than normal during the past semester.

    Ⓑ It will be her highest ever after the current semester.

    Ⓒ It has been consistently high in recent semesters.

    Ⓓ It is good enough for her to graduate with honors.

4 What does the woman imply about the student's mistakes?

    Ⓐ They are all ones that can be solved.

    Ⓑ They will stop her from getting a scholarship.

    Ⓒ They could have been easily avoided.

    Ⓓ They should not be made again in the future.

5 Listen again to part of the conversation. Then answer the question.

    What can be inferred about the student when she says this: 🎧

    Ⓐ She thinks the woman is lying to her.

    Ⓑ She has a copy of her transcript with her.

    Ⓒ She can fix that mistake with no problem.

    Ⓓ She is surprised by the woman's comment.

01-04

Aqueducts

6 In the lecture, the professor describes a number of facts about Roman aqueducts. Indicate whether each of the following is a fact or not.

Click in the correct box for each statement.

	Fact	Not a Fact
1 Some of them could carry water uphill.		
2 They took water to large population centers.		
3 Many of them were found underground.		
4 They were made from a variety of materials.		

7 What can be inferred about the water system in Rome?

Ⓐ It was only connected to a few private homes.

Ⓑ It suffered many breakdowns over the years.

Ⓒ It was the most expensive public works project in the city.

Ⓓ It required thousands of laborers to maintain.

8 Why does the professor discuss the aqueduct system in Rome?

Ⓐ To point out its disadvantages

Ⓑ To emphasize how large it was

Ⓒ To show how it was easily destroyed

Ⓓ To talk about its enormous costs

9 According to the professor, what happened to Rome's aqueduct system when Germanic tribes invaded?

(A) It continued to work as expected.

(B) It suffered a great amount of damage.

(C) It was rebuilt by the invaders.

(D) It was taken apart in its entirety.

10 Listen again to part of the lecture. Then answer the question.

Why does the professor say this: 🎧

(A) He feels that aqueducts are impressive structures.

(B) He is not eager to provide an explanation.

(C) The students should have done their reading on time.

(D) Some students may not know what aqueducts are.

11 Listen again to part of the lecture. Then answer the question.

What does the professor imply when he says this: 🎧

(A) Aqueducts were seldom used after Roman times.

(B) Humans are easily susceptible to some diseases.

(C) Human civilization reached a high point in the Roman Empire.

(D) The Romans built aqueducts all throughout Europe.

PART 3

Listening Directions

 00-03

In this part, you will listen to 1 conversation and 2 lectures.

You must answer each question. After you answer, click on **Next**. Then click on **OK** to confirm your answer and go on to the next question. After you click on **OK**, you cannot return to previous questions.

You may now begin this part of the Listening Section. You will have **10 minutes** to answer the questions.

Click on **Continue** to go on.

01-05

1 Why did the professor ask to see the student?

Ⓐ To go over the presentation she just gave

Ⓑ To talk about her midterm exam

Ⓒ To discuss some work that she turned in

Ⓓ To tell her about the most recent lecture

2 According to the professor, what happened during the Middle Ages?

Click on 2 answers.

1 Rome entered a period when it expanded in Europe.

2 Monasteries helped save knowledge from Greece.

3 Charlemagne became the Holy Roman Emperor.

4 There were no advances that helped with farming.

3 What does the professor tell the student to do?

Ⓐ Prepare for her presentation

Ⓑ Read the class material again

Ⓒ Join a study group

Ⓓ Rewrite her outline

4 What can be inferred about the student?

Ⓐ She has some mistaken ideas about history.

Ⓑ She has already written most of her paper.

Ⓒ She is planning to change her major to history.

Ⓓ She frequently asks questions during class.

5 Listen again to part of the conversation. Then answer the question.

Why does the professor say this: 🎧

Ⓐ The student needs to read some more books about the Middle Ages.

Ⓑ Some mistakes regarding dates were made by the student.

Ⓒ He knows more about the Middle Ages than the student does.

Ⓓ Scholars no longer believe the student's explanation is correct.

01-06

Zoology

6   What is the lecture mainly about?

   Ⓐ How animals take care of and protect their offspring

   Ⓑ Child-rearing behavior in reptiles and mammals

   Ⓒ Animals' instincts to protect themselves from danger

   Ⓓ The need for all animals to engage in reproduction

7   According to the professor, what is a uniparental species?

   Ⓐ One in which both parents look after their offspring

   Ⓑ One in which no parents look after their offspring

   Ⓒ One in which only the mother looks after her offspring

   Ⓓ One in which only the father looks after his offspring

8   Why does the professor mention that mother deer clean their fawns after giving birth?

   Ⓐ To prove that deer possess motherly instincts

   Ⓑ To show how they protect their fawns from predators

   Ⓒ To mention that fawns need parental assistance for a year

   Ⓓ To state why many fawns survive their early years

9 What comparison does the professor make between penguins and alligators?

   Ⓐ The animals' methods of protecting their offspring

   Ⓑ The manners in which they feed their babies

   Ⓒ The ways in which they watch their eggs before they hatch

   Ⓓ Their styles of fighting predators that attack their young

10 What does the professor imply about baboons?

   Ⓐ They make sounds when predators attack them.

   Ⓑ They may fight animals that attack their young.

   Ⓒ They travel in herds that let them guard their babies.

   Ⓓ They engage in uniparental behavior.

11 Listen again to part of the lecture. Then answer the question.

What does the professor mean when she says this: 🎧

   Ⓐ The students should pay close attention to the video.

   Ⓑ She wants someone to turn off the lights.

   Ⓒ The video she will show will be entertaining.

   Ⓓ The room is not yet dark enough.

01-07

Harriet Irwin

12 What is the main topic of the lecture?

    Ⓐ The lives of female architects

    Ⓑ New trends in home architecture

    Ⓒ A house designed by Harriet Irwin

    Ⓓ The advantages of hexagonal houses

13 Why does the professor describe Harriet Irwin's childhood?

    Ⓐ To explain why she decided to design a hexagonal house

    Ⓑ To stress the fact that she was often sick at that time

    Ⓒ To mention how she became educated in so many fields

    Ⓓ To give the reason that she never formally studied architecture

14 Based on the information in the lecture, indicate whether the statements refer to the problems that led to the design of the hexagonal house or the solutions that Harriet Irwin provided.

Click in the correct box for each statement.

	Problem	Solution
① The rooms were circular in shape.		
② The number of fireplaces increased the amount of soot.		
③ Dust tended to gather in the corners of square rooms.		
④ The many windows enabled air to circulate.		

15 What can be inferred about Harriet Irwin?

 Ⓐ Her first application for a patent was rejected.

 Ⓑ She became wealthy by selling the design of her house.

 Ⓒ Her lack of a college education kept her from becoming famous.

 Ⓓ She was not a particularly influential architect.

16 What is the professor's opinion of Harriet Irwin?

 Ⓐ It was unfortunate that she received little fame and fortune.

 Ⓑ She designed a house that was very strange looking.

 Ⓒ Her house was ideal for people with physical limitations.

 Ⓓ Many architects would benefit from studying her work.

17 Listen again to part of the lecture. Then answer the question.

 What can be inferred about the professor when he says this: 🎧

 Ⓐ He would like for the students to make a guess.

 Ⓑ He thinks the students failed to do the reading.

 Ⓒ He will test the students on this material later.

 Ⓓ He expected someone to answer his question.

TOEFL® MAP

ACTUAL TEST Listening **2**

02

Listening Section Directions

🎧 00-01

This section measures your ability to understand conversations and lectures in English.

The Listening section is divided into separately timed parts. In each part, you will listen to 1 conversation and 1 or 2 lectures. You will hear each conversation or lecture only **one** time.

After each conversation or lecture, you will answer some questions about it. The questions typically ask about the main idea and supporting details. Some questions ask about a speaker's purpose or attitude. Answer the questions based on what is stated or implied by the speakers.

You may take notes while you listen. You may use your notes to help you answer the questions. Your notes will not be scored.

If you need to change the volume while you listen, click on the **Volume** at the top of the screen.

In some questions, you will see this icon: 🎧 This means that you will hear, but not see, part of the question.

Some of the questions have special directions. These directions appear in a gray box on the screen.

Most questions are worth 1 point. If a question is worth more than 1 point, it will have special directions that indicate how many points you can receive.

A clock at the top of the screen will show you how much time is remaining. The clock will not count down while you are listening. The clock will count down only while you are answering the questions.

PART 1

 🎧 00-02

Listening Directions

In this part, you will listen to 1 conversation and 1 lecture.

You must answer each question. After you answer, click on **Next**. Then click on **OK** to confirm your answer and go on to the next question. After you click on **OK**, you cannot return to previous questions.

You may now begin this part of the Listening Section. You will have **7 minutes** to answer the questions.

Click on **Continue** to go on.

🎧 02-01

1   Why does the student visit the professor?

    Ⓐ To go over his notes with the professor

    Ⓑ To discuss the topic of his paper

    Ⓒ To talk about the Realist Movement

    Ⓓ To get the location of an art gallery

2   What does the professor imply about the *Mona Lisa*?

    Ⓐ It is the most famous painting in the world.

    Ⓑ It looks better when it is viewed in person.

    Ⓒ The student should consider writing about it.

    Ⓓ It used to be a little-known painting.

3   What does the professor suggest the student write about?

    Ⓐ The Naturalist Movement

    Ⓑ The life of Vincent van Gogh

    Ⓒ The work of Jean-Francois Millet

    Ⓓ The *Mona Lisa*

4   What does the professor give the student?

    Ⓐ A brochure

    Ⓑ A ticket to an art gallery

    Ⓒ An art book

    Ⓓ A print of the *Mona Lisa*

5   What will the student probably do next?

    Ⓐ Visit the school's art gallery

    Ⓑ Submit his paper to the professor

    Ⓒ Leave the professor's office

    Ⓓ Ask the professor another question

🎧 02-02

Urban Development

6 What is the main topic of the lecture?

Ⓐ The advantages of building cities near water

Ⓑ Factors involved in modern urban planning

Ⓒ The differences between cities and suburbs

Ⓓ How pollution and transportation affect cities

7 In the lecture, the professor describes a number of facts about the geographical locations of cities. Indicate whether each of the following is a fact or not.

Click in the correct box for each statement.

	Fact	Not a Fact
① Many cities are built in the mountains.		
② Cities are no longer built in areas that get earthquakes.		
③ A large number of cities are founded near sources of water.		
④ Soil is one factor that must be considered when building a city.		

8 What does the professor imply about airports?

Ⓐ They can be expensive construction projects for most cities.

Ⓑ They are more popular than port facilities for most modern-day cities.

Ⓒ They must be connected to highways and railways to be efficient.

Ⓓ They are not currently built inside the city limits of large urban centers.

9 How does the professor organize the lecture?

    Ⓐ By focusing on the advantages of building cities

    Ⓑ By discussing various factors one by one

    Ⓒ By engaging the students in discussion

    Ⓓ By asking questions and then answering them

10 According to the professor, how are most suburbs built nowadays?

    Ⓐ With approval from the nearby cities

    Ⓑ With little planning

    Ⓒ With virtually no forethought

    Ⓓ With great attention to detail

11 Listen again to part of the lecture. Then answer the question.

    What does the professor imply when she says this: 🎧

    Ⓐ Urban heat island is of relatively little importance.

    Ⓑ There are few people who know about urban heat island.

    Ⓒ She will discuss urban heat island in that day's lecture.

    Ⓓ There is a connection between urban heat island and pollution.

Listening Directions

🎧 00-03

In this part, you will listen to 1 conversation and 2 lectures.

You must answer each question. After you answer, click on **Next**. Then click on **OK** to confirm your answer and go on to the next question. After you click on **OK**, you cannot return to previous questions.

You may now begin this part of the Listening Section. You will have **10 minutes** to answer the questions.

Click on **Continue** to go on.

1 Why does the student visit the librarian?

   Ⓐ To request that the library purchase more books for its collection

   Ⓑ To discuss some plans concerning the future of the library

   Ⓒ To complain about the inadequate seating in the library

   Ⓓ To present the librarian with a petition from the student body

2 According to the student, how do many students feel about the proposed renovations to the library?

   Ⓐ They believe that the renovations will cost too much.

   Ⓑ They are pleased because the library will be enlarged.

   Ⓒ They are looking forward to the changes that will be made.

   Ⓓ They think that the library should spend less money.

3 How does the student want the library to spend the money it has to use?

   Ⓐ By painting the exterior of the library

   Ⓑ By adding more study rooms to the library

   Ⓒ By subscribing to more academic journals

   Ⓓ By expanding the physical size of the library

4 What is the librarian's attitude toward the student?

   Ⓐ He acts like the student is unimportant.

   Ⓑ He treats the student in a polite manner.

   Ⓒ He acts as though the student is well informed.

   Ⓓ He is abrupt when speaking with the student.

5 Listen again to part of the conversation. Then answer the question.

What does the student imply when she says this: 🎧

   Ⓐ She wants the library to purchase fewer computers.

   Ⓑ She rarely uses the library's audio-visual machinery.

   Ⓒ She believes the library's computers are inadequate.

   Ⓓ She thinks buying audio-visual machinery is a waste of money.

Environmental
Science

6 What is the lecture mainly about?

    Ⓐ The nutrients plants need to survive

    Ⓑ The importance of crop rotation

    Ⓒ Ancient methods of farming

    Ⓓ The role of nitrogen in the soil

7 Based on the information in the lecture, indicate whether the statements refer to macronutrients or micronutrients.

Click in the correct box for each statement.

	Macronutrients	Micronutrients
1 Are used by plants in fairly small quantities		
2 Include nitrogen, phosphorus, and potassium		
3 May be divided into primary and secondary nutrients		
4 Can be easily depleted from the soil		

8 According to the professor, what does nitrogen do for plants?

    Ⓐ It enables their roots to develop.

    Ⓑ It strengthens their cell walls.

    Ⓒ It helps them grow more rapidly.

    Ⓓ It lets them fight diseases.

9   Why does the professor discuss crop rotation?

    Ⓐ To claim that it was first practiced hundreds of years ago

    Ⓑ To talk about a method that can restore nutrients to fields

    Ⓒ To explain how the Native Americans once used it

    Ⓓ To point out the problems that this method of growing crops has

10 Listen again to part of the lecture. Then answer the question.

    Why does the professor say this: 🎧

    Ⓐ To apologize for stuttering

    Ⓑ To correct an error that he made

    Ⓒ To ask the student to repeat herself

    Ⓓ To express regret for sneezing

11 Listen again to part of the lecture. Then answer the question.

    What does the professor imply when he says this: 🎧

    Ⓐ Micronutrients are crucial to the survival of plants.

    Ⓑ The students should have brought their books to class.

    Ⓒ He will not lecture on the roles of micronutrients.

    Ⓓ There will probably be a quiz on the material soon.

⌒ 02-05

Geology

Fall Lines

12 According to the professor, what causes a fall line to occur?

Click on 2 answers.

☐1 The presence of running water

☐2 The bending of the ground

☐3 The eroding of an area

☐4 The existence of volcanic rock

13 What can be inferred about cliff-like fall lines?

Ⓐ They are not uniform in appearance.

Ⓑ They typically appear in large mountain chains.

Ⓒ They almost always have waterfalls.

Ⓓ They took millions of years to form.

14 Why does the professor mention Niagara Falls?

Ⓐ To give its precise geographical location in North America

Ⓑ To point out a place that is an obvious example of a fall line

Ⓒ To prove that it was formed hundreds of millions of years ago

Ⓓ To claim that it is a part of the Appalachian Mountain fall line

15 Why does the professor explain the importance of waterfalls on fall lines?

   Ⓐ To claim that some ships could sail upriver past them

   Ⓑ To note why towns and cities were built near them

   Ⓒ To name the main impediment to exploring further inland

   Ⓓ To say that they were crucial to early American industries

16 Listen again to part of the lecture. Then answer the question.

Why does the professor say this: 🎧

   Ⓐ To show the relevance of mountain building

   Ⓑ To emphasize a point to the class

   Ⓒ To provide an answer to the student

   Ⓓ To correct himself after misspeaking

17 Listen again to part of the lecture. Then answer the question.

What is the purpose of the professor's response to the student: 🎧

   Ⓐ To encourage her to rethink her answer

   Ⓑ To get her to guess again

   Ⓒ To pay her a compliment

   Ⓓ To admit that she is partially correct

TOEFL® MAP

ACTUAL TEST

Listening **2**

03

Listening Section Directions

 00-01

This section measures your ability to understand conversations and lectures in English.

The Listening section is divided into separately timed parts. In each part, you will listen to 1 conversation and 1 or 2 lectures. You will hear each conversation or lecture only **one** time.

After each conversation or lecture, you will answer some questions about it. The questions typically ask about the main idea and supporting details. Some questions ask about a speaker's purpose or attitude. Answer the questions based on what is stated or implied by the speakers.

You may take notes while you listen. You may use your notes to help you answer the questions. Your notes will not be scored.

If you need to change the volume while you listen, click on the **Volume** at the top of the screen.

In some questions, you will see this icon: 🎧 This means that you will hear, but not see, part of the question.

Some of the questions have special directions. These directions appear in a gray box on the screen.

Most questions are worth 1 point. If a question is worth more than 1 point, it will have special directions that indicate how many points you can receive.

A clock at the top of the screen will show you how much time is remaining. The clock will not count down while you are listening. The clock will count down only while you are answering the questions.

PART 1

Listening Directions

🎧 00-02

In this part, you will listen to 1 conversation and 1 lecture.

You must answer each question. After you answer, click on **Next**. Then click on **OK** to confirm your answer and go on to the next question. After you click on **OK**, you cannot return to previous questions.

You may now begin this part of the Listening Section. You will have **7 minutes** to answer the questions.

Click on **Continue** to go on.

03-01

1   Why did the professor ask to see the student?

   (A) To recruit her for graduate school

   (B) To speak with her about her presentation

   (C) To encourage her to stop majoring in English

   (D) To tell her about an upcoming art exhibition

2   What does the professor say about the student's recent work?

   (A) It received the highest grade in the class.

   (B) The idea for it was copied from a website.

   (C) He would like for her to do it again.

   (D) Her homework could have been a little better.

3   What does the professor imply about the student?

   (A) She is wasting her time by majoring in English literature.

   (B) She should apply for a job at a local art gallery.

   (C) She needs to take more classes to major in art history.

   (D) She is better at art history than some graduate students.

4   Why does the professor tell the student about the art history minor being offered?

   (A) To encourage her to consider doing it

   (B) To let her know that she has qualified for it

   (C) To ask her why she has not heard of it

   (D) To show her how it could help her career

5   Listen again to part of the conversation. Then answer the question.

   What can be inferred from the professor's response to the student: 🎧

   (A) The student is late for their meeting.

   (B) He has to leave his office in a few minutes.

   (C) He was not expecting the student until the next day.

   (D) Their meeting time needs to be changed.

🎧 03-02

Anthropology

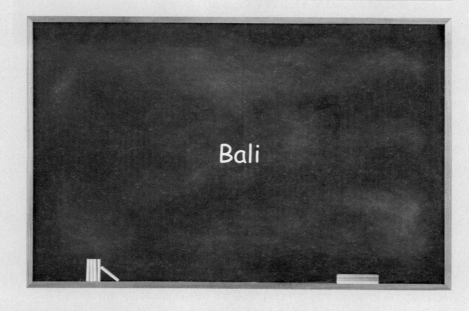

6   What aspect of Bali does the professor mainly discuss?

   Ⓐ The humanoids and humans that lived there

   Ⓑ The dominant religions on the island

   Ⓒ The technological developments of the early Balinese

   Ⓓ The Austronesians and their accomplishments

7   Why does the professor mention Java Man?

   Ⓐ To explain how humanoids similar to him arrived in Bali

   Ⓑ To describe some of his most important physical characteristics

   Ⓒ To comment on his relationship with the first humanoids on Bali

   Ⓓ To tell the class about some artifacts unearthed with him

8   What does the professor imply about agriculture on Bali?

   Ⓐ Rice is the most common crop grown.

   Ⓑ It began around 5,000 years ago.

   Ⓒ The soil there is bad for farming.

   Ⓓ The land has three growing seasons.

ACTUAL TEST 03

9 Based on the information in the lecture, indicate whether the statements refer to primitive humanoids or the Austronesians.

Click in the correct box for each statement.

	Primitive Humanoids	Austronesians
1 Introduced agriculture to Bali		
2 Made use of bronze tools and weapons		
3 Went to Bali when sea levels were low		
4 Had light skin and straight hair		

10 Why does the professor tell the students about Buddhism and Hinduism?

Ⓐ To stress that they had their origins in India

Ⓑ To compare their beliefs with those of Islam

Ⓒ To tell the students about foreign influences on Bali

Ⓓ To claim they were responsible for teaching writing to the Balinese

11 Listen again to part of the lecture. Then answer the question.

What does the professor mean when she says this: 🎧

Ⓐ She wants to stop lecturing to the students for the day.

Ⓑ She feels bad that they did not have a class discussion.

Ⓒ She wants the students to make more in-class contributions.

Ⓓ She believes she has covered all the necessary information.

Listening Directions

🎧 00-03

In this part, you will listen to 1 conversation and 2 lectures.

You must answer each question. After you answer, click on **Next**. Then click on **OK** to confirm your answer and go on to the next question. After you click on **OK**, you cannot return to previous questions.

You may now begin this part of the Listening Section. You will have **10 minutes** to answer the questions.

Click on **Continue** to go on.

03-03

1 Why does the student visit the guidance counselor?

Ⓐ To discuss a behavioral problem

Ⓑ To get some advice on graduate schools

Ⓒ To talk about looking for a job

Ⓓ To schedule an interview

2 Why does the student tell the guidance counselor about himself?

Ⓐ To provide her with some background information

Ⓑ To brag about his relatively high grades

Ⓒ To answer a question that she asks him

Ⓓ To explain why he is not interested in graduate school

3 What kind of job is the student interested in finding?

Click on 2 answers.

1 One related to his major

2 One in the financial sector

3 One with an engineering firm

4 One at a consulting company

4 Listen again to part of the conversation. Then answer the question.

What does the student mean when he says this: 🎧

Ⓐ He will not attend the larger job fair.

Ⓑ He needs some more information.

Ⓒ He is qualified to be a computer programmer.

Ⓓ He has already applied for a position.

5 Listen again to part of the conversation. Then answer the question.

What does the student imply when he says this: 🎧

Ⓐ He lacks enough money to buy a suit.

Ⓑ He is going to skip both job fairs.

Ⓒ He has accepted the woman's advice.

Ⓓ He is not interested in his appearance.

ACTUAL TEST **03**

03-04

ACTUAL TEST **03**

6 According to the professor, what is an example of an in-store survey?

Ⓐ A taste test

Ⓑ A coupon

Ⓒ A free sample

Ⓓ A rebate

7 Why does the professor explain telephone surveys?

Ⓐ To answer a student's question

Ⓑ To discuss one kind of survey

Ⓒ To tell a story about his youth

Ⓓ To name the ideal type of surveying method

8 Based on the information in the lecture, indicate which type of marketing survey the statements refer to.

Click in the correct box for each statement.

	Telephone Survey	Mail Survey	Online Survey
1 Can have slow response times			
2 Does not represent all demographics			
3 Has become more popular recently			
4 Can be cheap to conduct			

9   What comparison does the professor make between telephone surveys
    and online surveys?

   (A) The complexity of the questions

   (B) The ease of analyzing the data

   (C) The honesty of the respondents

   (D) The number of people who answer questions

10 What will the professor probably do next?

   (A) Tell the students some typical survey questions

   (B) Let the students go home for the day

   (C) Answer the question that the student asked

   (D) Provide the students with a handout

11 Listen again to part of the lecture. Then answer the question.

   What does the professor imply when he says this: 🎧

   (A) There is plenty of time to talk about surveys.

   (B) He will not talk about every kind of survey.

   (C) The students are welcome to offer their opinions.

   (D) He thinks that surveys are invaluable to marketers.

03-05

Zoology

12 What is the main topic of the lecture?

    Ⓐ The ideal way for animals to consume their food

    Ⓑ Various types of feeding behavior animals have

    Ⓒ Herbivores, carnivores, and omnivores

    Ⓓ Different food sources that animals rely upon

13 According to the professor, why are fish, reptiles, birds, and amphibians rarely herbivores?

    Ⓐ They have evolved over time to depend on meat.

    Ⓑ Their predatory habits make them unsuitable as herbivores.

    Ⓒ Their bodies cannot digest large amounts of vegetation.

    Ⓓ They can only get enough energy by eating meat.

14 What comparison does the professor make between owls and snakes?

    Ⓐ The time of day when they are most active

    Ⓑ The type of food that they mostly consume

    Ⓒ The amount of time in which they hibernate

    Ⓓ The methods they use to see in the dark

15 Why does the professor mention TV documentaries?

Ⓐ To give an example of animals eating food where they kill it

Ⓑ To let the students know about a program they need to watch

Ⓒ To say that many of them show the activities of nocturnal animals

Ⓓ To talk about one that recently was about the lives of koalas

16 What does the professor imply about bears?

Ⓐ They prefer eating fish to other types of food.

Ⓑ They can adapt to live in cold climates.

Ⓒ They live in many different environments.

Ⓓ They were herbivores but evolved to become omnivores.

17 Why does the professor tell the students about hibernating animals?

Ⓐ To respond to an inquiry that a student makes

Ⓑ To focus on how many mammals become inactive in winter

Ⓒ To explain why some animals hibernate while others do not

Ⓓ To describe how the process works in animals

PART 3

Listening Directions

 00-02

In this part, you will listen to 1 conversation and 1 lecture.

You must answer each question. After you answer, click on **Next**. Then click on **OK** to confirm your answer and go on to the next question. After you click on **OK**, you cannot return to previous questions.

You may now begin this part of the Listening Section. You will have **7 minutes** to answer the questions.

Click on **Continue** to go on.

🎧 03-06

1   What are the speakers mainly discussing?

Click on 2 answers.

☐1 Some possible uses of solar energy

☐2 Alternative energy sources versus fossil fuels

☐3 Some disadvantages of solar energy

☐4 The effectiveness of solar cells

2   Why does the student visit the professor?

Ⓐ To discuss a project that he is working on

Ⓑ To talk about the content of her recent lecture

Ⓒ To ask her about the reading material for the course

Ⓓ To describe a problem with his class project

3   What will the student probably do next?

Ⓐ Ask the professor another question

Ⓑ Leave the professor's office

Ⓒ Go over his midterm exam with the professor

Ⓓ Attend class with the professor

4   Listen again to part of the conversation. Then answer the question.

What does the student imply when he says this: 🎧

Ⓐ He does not believe it is possible to make solar roads.

Ⓑ He recently read an interesting work of science fiction.

Ⓒ He thinks many unlikely things will happen in the future.

Ⓓ He wants to know how strong solar power really is.

5   Listen again to part of the conversation. Then answer the question.

Why does the professor say this: 🎧

Ⓐ To refute the student's argument

Ⓑ To state that solar roads are difficult to build

Ⓒ To express her opinion to the student

Ⓓ To support the student's thesis

6   What is the main topic of the lecture?

    Ⓐ The effectiveness of product placement in certain stores

    Ⓑ Psychological factors that make people buy items on impulse

    Ⓒ The types of stores that rely on marketing gimmicks to sell products

    Ⓓ How businesses get shoppers to make impulse purchases

7   What does the professor imply about many stores?

    Ⓐ They will go out of business if they get no impulse shoppers.

    Ⓑ They advertise almost exclusively to people who buy on impulse.

    Ⓒ They employ the methods to attract shoppers that he describes.

    Ⓓ They make the majority of their profits from impulse shoppers.

8   According to the professor, how do stores create environments that make shoppers want to purchase items?

  Click on 2 answers.

    1 By devising easy ways for customers to buy on credit

    2 By increasing the number of products sold in them

    3 By keeping the stores open for longer periods of time

    4 By encouraging shoppers to exchange items they buy

ACTUAL TEST 03

9   Why does the professor discuss product placement?

    Ⓐ To name some of the products that are often sold thanks to it

    Ⓑ To claim that department stores and supermarkets use it the most

    Ⓒ To prove why many people purchase jewelry and cosmetics

    Ⓓ To comment on how effective it is in comparison to other methods

10   Listen again to part of the lecture. Then answer the question.

    What does the professor imply when he says this: 🎧

    Ⓐ The students should pay more attention while shopping.

    Ⓑ It is easy for some people to be convinced by slogans.

    Ⓒ The slogan that he mentioned is commonly used.

    Ⓓ He does not want to have to repeat himself again.

11   Listen again to part of the lecture. Then answer the question.

    What can be inferred about the professor when he says this: 🎧

    Ⓐ He thinks the student may be correct.

    Ⓑ The student's idea is better than his own.

    Ⓒ Product placement is crucial at checkout counters.

    Ⓓ He agrees with what the student says.

TOEFL® MAP

ACTUAL TEST

TEST Listening 2

04

Listening Section Directions

🎧 00-01

This section measures your ability to understand conversations and lectures in English.

The Listening section is divided into separately timed parts. In each part, you will listen to 1 conversation and 1 or 2 lectures. You will hear each conversation or lecture only **one** time.

After each conversation or lecture, you will answer some questions about it. The questions typically ask about the main idea and supporting details. Some questions ask about a speaker's purpose or attitude. Answer the questions based on what is stated or implied by the speakers.

You may take notes while you listen. You may use your notes to help you answer the questions. Your notes will not be scored.

If you need to change the volume while you listen, click on the **Volume** at the top of the screen.

In some questions, you will see this icon: 🎧 This means that you will hear, but not see, part of the question.

Some of the questions have special directions. These directions appear in a gray box on the screen.

Most questions are worth 1 point. If a question is worth more than 1 point, it will have special directions that indicate how many points you can receive.

A clock at the top of the screen will show you how much time is remaining. The clock will not count down while you are listening. The clock will count down only while you are answering the questions.

PART 1

Listening Directions

 00-03

In this part, you will listen to 1 conversation and 2 lectures.

You must answer each question. After you answer, click on **Next**. Then click on **OK** to confirm your answer and go on to the next question. After you click on **OK**, you cannot return to previous questions.

You may now begin this part of the Listening Section. You will have **10 minutes** to answer the questions.

Click on **Continue** to go on.

04-01

1 What are the speakers mainly discussing?

Ⓐ A test that the student will take

Ⓑ The subject of the student's paper

Ⓒ The professor's most recent lecture

Ⓓ The student's upcoming presentation

2 What did the student originally plan to write about?

Ⓐ The American Revolution

Ⓑ George Washington and diplomacy

Ⓒ The American presidency

Ⓓ The life of George Washington

3 What is the professor's attitude toward the student?

Ⓐ She is eager to listen to the student's idea.

Ⓑ She is a little short tempered.

Ⓒ She is helpful to the student.

Ⓓ She is complimentary of the student's topic.

4 What will the professor probably do next?

Ⓐ Hold her office hours

Ⓑ Go to her next class

Ⓒ Attend a lunch event

Ⓓ Meet the head of the department

5 Listen again to part of the conversation. Then answer the question.

What is the purpose of the student's response: 🎧

Ⓐ To accept the professor's apology

Ⓑ To provide an explanation

Ⓒ To request that the professor do something

Ⓓ To answer the professor's question

ACTUAL TEST **04**

04-02

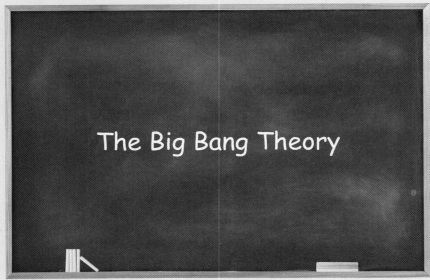

The Big Bang Theory

6   What does the professor imply about the class?

   Ⓐ It will focus on the history of astronomy.

   Ⓑ It is meeting for the first time.

   Ⓒ It requires some knowledge of advanced math.

   Ⓓ It is for upper-level students.

7   According to the professor, what did Georges Lemaitre propose?

   Ⓐ The universe is expanding.

   Ⓑ Dark matter and dark energy exist.

   Ⓒ The galaxies are creating more stars.

   Ⓓ The universe formed from hydrogen and helium.

8   Why does the professor explain the discovery made by Edwin Hubble that galaxies are moving away from Earth?

   Ⓐ To explain why Edwin Hubble is more famous than Georges Lemaitre

   Ⓑ To credit Edwin Hubble with the formulating of the Big Bang Theory

   Ⓒ To note that it meant that the universe must have started at a single point

   Ⓓ To point out that this discovery was made possible with advanced telescopes

9 Why does the professor mention cosmic microwave background radiation?

Ⓐ To claim that it was first recognized by Edwin Hubble

Ⓑ To prove that it came into existence billions of years ago

Ⓒ To compare it with dark matter and dark energy

Ⓓ To say that its presence supports the Big Bang Theory

10 What is the professor's opinion of the Big Bang Theory?

Ⓐ It will likely never be proven to be correct.

Ⓑ It is a good model, yet it has some problems.

Ⓒ It should be reconstructed to account for some errors in it.

Ⓓ It is the best theory that humans will ever have.

11 What does the professor imply about dark matter and dark energy?

Ⓐ The scientists who believe they exist are mistaken.

Ⓑ Their discovery would help support the Big Bang Theory.

Ⓒ It should be a simple process to prove that they exist.

Ⓓ They will be utilized as energy sources in the future.

04-03

Art History

12 What aspect of miniature portrait painting does the professor mainly discuss?

Ⓐ The materials used

Ⓑ Its history

Ⓒ Its similarity to photography

Ⓓ Painting techniques

13 What does the professor imply about the origin of miniature portrait painting?

Ⓐ Art historians do not agree on how it started.

Ⓑ It may have been practiced by the ancient Greeks.

Ⓒ No one knows when the first miniature portrait was made.

Ⓓ It developed as a reaction against early photography.

14 According to the professor, who often commissioned miniature portraits?
Click on 2 answers.

1 Kings and queens

2 Sailors

3 Suitors

4 Colonists

15 What does the professor say about the materials that were used to make miniature portraits?

    Ⓐ It was simple to make miniature portraits on a copper background.

    Ⓑ They varied depending upon the country and artist.

    Ⓒ Ivory was the most expensive material people used.

    Ⓓ The most popular of all materials was enamel.

16 What will the professor probably do next?

    Ⓐ Show the students some real miniature portraits

    Ⓑ Demonstrate how miniature portraits were made

    Ⓒ Begin to lecture on the advent of photography

    Ⓓ Let the students start giving their class presentations

17 Listen again to part of the lecture. Then answer the question.

    What does the professor mean when she says this: 🎧

    Ⓐ She wants the student to clarify his statement.

    Ⓑ The student's explanation is incorrect.

    Ⓒ The student has permission to continue.

    Ⓓ She fully agrees with what the student said.

TOEFL® MAP
ACTUAL TEST

PART 2

Listening Directions

00-02

In this part, you will listen to 1 conversation and 1 lecture.

You must answer each question. After you answer, click on **Next**. Then click on **OK** to confirm your answer and go on to the next question. After you click on **OK**, you cannot return to previous questions.

You may now begin this part of the Listening Section. You will have **7 minutes** to answer the questions.

Click on **Continue** to go on.

04-04

1   Why did the student ask to meet the man?

   Ⓐ To request that she be permitted to take an extra class

   Ⓑ To talk about an obligation all university students have

   Ⓒ To find out where she can submit some forms she has

   Ⓓ To learn about some opportunities to work around campus

2   What does the man imply about the student's request?

   Ⓐ She is making a request that he has not heard before.

   Ⓑ He is not in a position to approve or reject it.

   Ⓒ It is too late in the semester for him to assist the student.

   Ⓓ Ones that are similar to hers are not often approved.

3   Why does the student tell the man about her roommate?

   Ⓐ To complain about her roommate's actions

   Ⓑ To inform the man of her need to drop a class

   Ⓒ To explain why she has to make a change

   Ⓓ To tell the man why she needs a new dormitory room

4   According to the student, what is her roommate going to do?

   Ⓐ She is going to attend a different school.

   Ⓑ She is going to take a job at an elementary school.

   Ⓒ She is going to apply to graduate school.

   Ⓓ She is going to move to another dormitory.

5   What will the man probably do next?

   Ⓐ Send an email to a school principal

   Ⓑ Make a telephone call

   Ⓒ Give the student a form

   Ⓓ Record the student's personal information

ACTUAL TEST 04

04-05

Biofuels

6 What is the lecture mainly about?

   Ⓐ The way to make biofuels

   Ⓑ Differences between biofuel and biodiesel

   Ⓒ The advantages of biofuels

   Ⓓ Various types of biofuels

7 What does the professor imply about sugarcane?

   Ⓐ It is better than corn for making biofuel.

   Ⓑ It should be grown in more countries around the world.

   Ⓒ It requires a large amount of water to cultivate.

   Ⓓ It has a relatively short growing season.

8 Based on the information in the lecture, indicate whether the statements refer to corn or sugarcane.

Click in the correct box for each statement.

	Corn	Sugarcane
1 Can produce 600-800 gallons of ethanol per acre		
2 Has been increasing in price recently		
3 Has more than 50% fewer harmful emissions than gasoline		
4 Can make ethanol with just a little more energy than the energy used to make it		

9   According to the professor, why do few people currently use biodiesel?

 (A) It is not available in most countries.

 (B) There are few cars equipped to use it.

 (C) It is more expensive than regular diesel.

 (D) Not many people are aware that it exists.

10   Why does the professor discuss algae?

 (A) To note that it could be an ideal source of biofuel

 (B) To show how easily it can be grown almost anywhere

 (C) To explain the process of converting it into biofuel

 (D) To stress that people are starting to learn about its uses

11   Listen again to part of the lecture. Then answer the question.

 What does the professor mean when she says this: 🎧

 (A) She doubts that Brazil relies on ethanol that much.

 (B) More countries need to produce sugarcane ethanol.

 (C) The amount of ethanol produced in Brazil is very large.

 (D) She wishes that sugarcane ethanol were easier to produce.

TOEFL® MAP

ACTUAL TEST

Listening **2**

05

Listening Section Directions

🎧 00-01

This section measures your ability to understand conversations and lectures in English.

The Listening section is divided into separately timed parts. In each part, you will listen to 1 conversation and 1 or 2 lectures. You will hear each conversation or lecture only **one** time.

After each conversation or lecture, you will answer some questions about it. The questions typically ask about the main idea and supporting details. Some questions ask about a speaker's purpose or attitude. Answer the questions based on what is stated or implied by the speakers.

You may take notes while you listen. You may use your notes to help you answer the questions. Your notes will not be scored.

If you need to change the volume while you listen, click on the **Volume** at the top of the screen.

In some questions, you will see this icon: 🎧 This means that you will hear, but not see, part of the question.

Some of the questions have special directions. These directions appear in a gray box on the screen.

Most questions are worth 1 point. If a question is worth more than 1 point, it will have special directions that indicate how many points you can receive.

A clock at the top of the screen will show you how much time is remaining. The clock will not count down while you are listening. The clock will count down only while you are answering the questions.

Listening Directions

00-03

In this part, you will listen to 1 conversation and 2 lectures.

You must answer each question. After you answer, click on **Next**. Then click on **OK** to confirm your answer and go on to the next question. After you click on **OK**, you cannot return to previous questions.

You may now begin this part of the Listening Section. You will have **10 minutes** to answer the questions.

Click on **Continue** to go on.

05-01

1 What does the student speak with the man about?

Click on 2 answers.

☐1 How she can run for club president

☐2 How to get more students to join the club

☐3 How often the club should meet

☐4 How to reserve a room for her club

2 What is the man's opinion on having a club meeting every week?

Ⓐ He believes that it is a good idea.

Ⓑ He thinks the club should meet more often.

Ⓒ He is strongly against doing that.

Ⓓ He is neutral concerning that matter.

3 What will the man probably do next?

Ⓐ Show the student where she needs to go

Ⓑ Continue speaking with the student

Ⓒ Leave his office to attend a meeting

Ⓓ Give the student a form to fill out

4 Listen again to part of the conversation. Then answer the question.

What does the student imply when she says this: 🎧

Ⓐ She wants some assistance from the man.

Ⓑ She is doing a poor job as club president.

Ⓒ Her duties as club president are overwhelming.

Ⓓ She has considered resigning from her role as president.

5 Listen again to part of the conversation. Then answer the question.

What does the man mean when he says this: 🎧

Ⓐ The student should think a little longer.

Ⓑ There is nothing that he can do to help.

Ⓒ It is necessary for her to follow his advice.

Ⓓ He agrees with the student's decision.

05-02

Physics

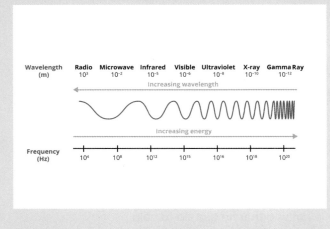

6 What aspect of the electromagnetic spectrum does the professor mainly discuss?

(A) The various types of radio waves that exist

(B) The frequencies where visible light is found

(C) The importance of blackbody radiation to it

(D) The different types of waves that are on it

7 How does the professor organize the lecture?

(A) By showing slides of the various types of waves that he discusses

(B) By providing the students with a handout that he refers them to

(C) By encouraging the class to follow along in their textbooks

(D) By describing the waves on the electromagnetic spectrum from left to right

8 According to the professor, what is a characteristic of the waves that are on the right-hand side of the electromagnetic spectrum?

Click on 2 answers.

1 They are visible to the human eye.

2 Their frequencies are low.

3 They have long wavelengths.

4 They can harm living creatures.

9　What is a hertz?

　　Ⓐ A system of measurement for the frequency of waves

　　Ⓑ An instrument that can determine how harmful waves are

　　Ⓒ A tool that lets people see waves invisible to the human eye

　　Ⓓ A navigational signal that is often used by submarines

10　What does the professor imply about radio waves?

　　Ⓐ They penetrate rock more easily than water.

　　Ⓑ They can be dangerous to humans in large doses.

　　Ⓒ They can move on the Earth but not in outer space.

　　Ⓓ They have a limited number of uses.

11　Listen again to part of the lecture. Then answer the question.

　　What can be inferred from the professor's response to the student: 🎧

　　Ⓐ He enjoys when students ask insightful questions.

　　Ⓑ He had not intended to discuss that topic yet.

　　Ⓒ He feels that her question is rather important.

　　Ⓓ He dislikes being interrupted during his lectures.

05-03

Ancient Greek Music

12 What aspect of ancient Greek musical instruments does the professor mainly discuss?

Ⓐ How they sounded

Ⓑ When they were invented

Ⓒ How they were played

Ⓓ What they looked like

13 How does the professor organize the information about ancient Greek musical instruments that he presents to the class?

Ⓐ By showing slides of the instruments while talking about them

Ⓑ By describing what the primary Greek instruments looked like

Ⓒ By focusing primarily on the wind instruments the Greeks played

Ⓓ By talking about the instruments in their order of their popularity

14 In the lecture, the professor describes a number of facts about ancient Greek music. Indicate whether each of the following is a fact or not.

Click in the correct box for each statement.

	Fact	Not a Fact
① It involved three basic kinds of instruments.		
② It was seldom monophonic.		
③ It was played for a number of reasons.		
④ It can be replicated by modern musicians.		

15 Why does the professor discuss Pythagoras?

    Ⓐ To credit him with inventing a stringed instrument

    Ⓑ To say that he developed certain aspects of Greek music

    Ⓒ To note his influence on the philosophy of music

    Ⓓ To claim that he wrote down some music in note form

16 What does the professor imply about Plato?

    Ⓐ His influence on ancient Greek music was greater than Pythagoras's.

    Ⓑ He dedicated some of his dialogues to writing about Greek musicians.

    Ⓒ He is an important source of information about ancient Greek music.

    Ⓓ He most likely knew how to play several different musical instruments.

17 Listen again to part of the lecture. Then answer the question.

    Why does the professor say this: 🎧

    Ⓐ To give examples of places where the Greeks often played music

    Ⓑ To defend his statements about Greek stringed instruments

    Ⓒ To comment on the importance of the lyre in ancient Greece

    Ⓓ To mention that Greek musicians played solo and also in groups

ACTUAL TEST **05**

PART 2

Listening Directions

 00-02

In this part, you will listen to 1 conversation and 1 lecture.

You must answer each question. After you answer, click on **Next**. Then click on **OK** to confirm your answer and go on to the next question. After you click on **OK**, you cannot return to previous questions.

You may now begin this part of the Listening Section. You will have **7 minutes** to answer the questions.

Click on **Continue** to go on.

05-04

1   Why does the student visit the theater manager?

    Ⓐ To change her group's rehearsal time

    Ⓑ To ask about an upcoming performance

    Ⓒ To try to solve a problem her group has

    Ⓓ To ask about the location of the storage area

2   Where does the theater manager tell the student her group can put their props?

    Ⓐ Behind the stage

    Ⓑ In his storage room

    Ⓒ In their dormitory rooms

    Ⓓ In an empty classroom

3   What will the student probably do next?

    Ⓐ Go with the theater manager

    Ⓑ Begin rehearsing for her play

    Ⓒ Try to memorize her lines

    Ⓓ Remove her props from storage

4   Listen again to part of the conversation. Then answer the question.

    What does the theater manager imply when he says this: 🎧

    Ⓐ He will contact the group advisor for the students.

    Ⓑ There is nothing he can do to help the student.

    Ⓒ The students should have asked for help earlier.

    Ⓓ It might be possible to find another professor.

5   Listen again to part of the conversation. Then answer the question.

    What does the theater manager mean when he says this: 🎧

    Ⓐ He has a solution to the student's problem.

    Ⓑ He has a good imagination.

    Ⓒ He agrees with the student.

    Ⓓ He will watch the students perform.

ACTUAL TEST **05**

05-05

Zoology

6   What is the main topic of the lecture?

  Ⓐ The life of the western scrub-jay

  Ⓑ Long-term and short-term memories

  Ⓒ Episodic memory in humans and other animals

  Ⓓ The possibility that animals have memories

7   According to the professor, how do human and animal memories differ?

  Ⓐ Animals cannot remember as many events as humans can.

  Ⓑ Most animal memories are short term while most human ones are long term.

  Ⓒ Long-term human memories last longer than those of animals.

  Ⓓ It is easier for humans to recall memories lasting more than twenty seconds.

8   What was a result of the experiments conducted on western scrub-jays?

  Ⓐ Many birds ignored both types of food they were given.

  Ⓑ The birds began choosing the nuts instead of the worms.

  Ⓒ Most birds consumed the worms and buried the nuts.

  Ⓓ Some birds buried more worms than they did nuts.

9 Why does the professor discuss the thieving behavior of western scrub-jays?

Ⓐ To explain why they steal food from other birds

Ⓑ To show how it proves they possess memories

Ⓒ To focus on the untrusting nature of the birds

Ⓓ To mention why the birds often hide their food

10 What is the professor's opinion of animal memories?

Ⓐ She believes that animals clearly have memories.

Ⓑ She thinks only western scrub-jays possess memories.

Ⓒ She says that only mammals are able to remember events.

Ⓓ She states that very few animals have clear memories.

11 What will the professor probably do next?

Ⓐ Talk about memories in other animals

Ⓑ Show some slides to the students

Ⓒ Give some handouts to the students

Ⓓ Ask the students for their opinions

Listening Directions

🎧 00-02

In this part, you will listen to 1 conversation and 1 lecture.

You must answer each question. After you answer, click on **Next**. Then click on **OK** to confirm your answer and go on to the next question. After you click on **OK**, you cannot return to previous questions.

You may now begin this part of the Listening Section. You will have **7 minutes** to answer the questions.

Click on **Continue** to go on.

🎧 05-06

1 What problem does the student have?

    Ⓐ She is currently receiving a failing grade in a class.

    Ⓑ She has not signed up for the professor's course yet.

    Ⓒ She has not completed some assigned work.

    Ⓓ She does not understand the class material.

2 What is the student's original opinion of lab reports?

    Ⓐ There is no need to write them.

    Ⓑ They can help her understand an experiment.

    Ⓒ She has learned a lot by writing them.

    Ⓓ They are too difficult to write.

3 What does the professor tell the student she is not permitted to do?

    Ⓐ Get extra time to prepare for an exam

    Ⓑ Conduct an experiment with another student

    Ⓒ Redo an experiment in the laboratory

    Ⓓ Submit her missing lab reports

4 According to the professor, how can writing lab reports benefit the student?

    Click on 2 answers.

    ① By helping her organize the thoughts she has

    ② By improving her reading comprehension skills

    ③ By making her skills as a writer get better

    ④ By teaching her how to ask important questions

5 What can be inferred about the professor?

    Ⓐ He is unwilling to change the student's final grade.

    Ⓑ He tries to change the student's mind on lab reports.

    Ⓒ He believes the student can get an A in his class.

    Ⓓ He will help the student conduct her next experiment

ACTUAL TEST **05**

05-07

Mayan Art

6   What is a stela?

Ⓐ A Mayan mural

Ⓑ A type of sculpture

Ⓒ A form of ceramics

Ⓓ A kind of stucco

7   What does the professor imply about Mayan sculptures?

Ⓐ They were the works of art that were the least valued by the Mayan nobility.

Ⓑ The ones that the Mayans made required a great amount of skill.

Ⓒ It was difficult for the Mayans to make large sculptures due to a lack of stone.

Ⓓ Those from the same time period sometimes had different characteristics.

8   What is the professor's opinion of Mayan paintings?

Ⓐ The majority of them lack sophistication.

Ⓑ They are not particularly colorful at all.

Ⓒ Most of them are inferior to Mayan sculptures.

Ⓓ It is unfortunate that few have survived.

ACTUAL TEST **05**

9   According to the professor, what is Maya Blue?

   Ⓐ The color most frequently used on stucco

   Ⓑ A kind of paint that the Mayans made

   Ⓒ A valuable stone used to make jewelry

   Ⓓ Turquoise that the Mayans decorated artwork with

10   How does the professor organize the lecture?

   Ⓐ By discussing various aspects of Mayan art individually

   Ⓑ By focusing on individual works of art and discussing them in detail

   Ⓒ By describing Mayan art in order of its modern-day relevance

   Ⓓ By detailing some of the most accepted theories on Mayan art

11   Listen again to part of the lecture. Then answer the question.

   What does the professor imply when she says this: 🎧

   Ⓐ She has a couple of ceramics to show the students.

   Ⓑ There are few intact examples of Mayan pottery.

   Ⓒ Most Mayan artists worked with ceramics.

   Ⓓ The pictures on Mayan ceramics were creative.

TOEFL MAP

ACTUAL
TEST Listening 2

Listening Section Directions

🎧 00-01

This section measures your ability to understand conversations and lectures in English.

The Listening section is divided into separately timed parts. In each part, you will listen to 1 conversation and 1 or 2 lectures. You will hear each conversation or lecture only **one** time.

After each conversation or lecture, you will answer some questions about it. The questions typically ask about the main idea and supporting details. Some questions ask about a speaker's purpose or attitude. Answer the questions based on what is stated or implied by the speakers.

You may take notes while you listen. You may use your notes to help you answer the questions. Your notes will not be scored.

If you need to change the volume while you listen, click on the **Volume** at the top of the screen.

In some questions, you will see this icon: 🎧 This means that you will hear, but not see, part of the question.

Some of the questions have special directions. These directions appear in a gray box on the screen.

Most questions are worth 1 point. If a question is worth more than 1 point, it will have special directions that indicate how many points you can receive.

A clock at the top of the screen will show you how much time is remaining. The clock will not count down while you are listening. The clock will count down only while you are answering the questions.

PART 1

Listening Directions

🎧 00-02

In this part, you will listen to 1 conversation and 1 lecture.

You must answer each question. After you answer, click on **Next**. Then click on **OK** to confirm your answer and go on to the next question. After you click on **OK**, you cannot return to previous questions.

You may now begin this part of the Listening Section. You will have **7 minutes** to answer the questions.

Click on **Continue** to go on.

06-01

1   What are the speakers mainly discussing?

    Ⓐ An engineering project the student is doing

    Ⓑ The student's grade on the most recent exam

    Ⓒ Some work the student has to complete for the class

    Ⓓ An extra project that the student wants to do

2   What can be inferred about the student?

    Ⓐ He is in danger of losing his A in the class.

    Ⓑ He is showing initiative in talking to the professor.

    Ⓒ He is going to graduate at the end of the semester.

    Ⓓ He is in need of a new academic advisor.

3   What will the student probably do next?

    Ⓐ Visit the school library

    Ⓑ Do some research on his project

    Ⓒ Attend his next class

    Ⓓ Go to an engineering laboratory

4   Listen again to part of the conversation. Then answer the question.

    What does the professor imply when she says this: 🎧

    Ⓐ The student should stop asking questions.

    Ⓑ The student needs to submit his work.

    Ⓒ The student has a high grade in her class.

    Ⓓ The student failed to do the assignment in time.

5   Listen again to part of the conversation. Then answer the question.

    What is the purpose of the professor's response: 🎧

    Ⓐ To grant the student permission to do the assignment

    Ⓑ To indicate that she will not answer the student's question

    Ⓒ To let the student know that she is disappointed in him

    Ⓓ To give the student an important hint about the project

ACTUAL TEST **06**

00:04:00 ⊖ HIDE TIME

06-02

Physiology

6　What is the lecture mainly about?

 Ⓐ How humans are able to perceive colors

 Ⓑ The colors of the electromagnetic spectrum

 Ⓒ How the eye sends signals to the brain

 Ⓓ The trichromatic and opponent process theories

7　Why does the professor mention Sir Isaac Newton?

 Ⓐ To criticize his interpretation of white light

 Ⓑ To claim he was an important figure in science

 Ⓒ To talk about his experiment with a prism

 Ⓓ To explain that his conclusions on light were faulty

8　What is scotopic vision?

 Ⓐ The perceiving of color in bright light

 Ⓑ The perceiving of only black and white

 Ⓒ The perceiving of light in dim conditions

 Ⓓ The perceiving of light by the rods

9 Based on the information in the lecture, indicate whether the statements refer to the trichromatic theory or the opponent process theory.

<u>Click in the correct box for each statement.</u>

	Trichromatic Theory	Opponent Process Theory
1 It was first promulgated in the 1800s.		
2 It states that each cone is attuned to a different wavelength of color.		
3 It claims that the cone receptors have some overlap in the colors they perceive.		
4 It is interpreted by retinal ganglion cells.		

10 Why does the professor tell the students about the class website?

Ⓐ To tell them to download some files from it

Ⓑ To assign some homework to them

Ⓒ To make sure they view the film on it

Ⓓ To ask them to log on to it soon

11 What will the professor probably do next?

Ⓐ Hand out the midterm exams

Ⓑ Return to his office

Ⓒ Show the students a diagram

Ⓓ Continue his lecture

PART 2

Listening Directions

 00-03

In this part, you will listen to 1 conversation and 2 lectures.

You must answer each question. After you answer, click on **Next**. Then click on **OK** to confirm your answer and go on to the next question. After you click on **OK**, you cannot return to previous questions.

You may now begin this part of the Listening Section. You will have **10 minutes** to answer the questions.

Click on **Continue** to go on.

🎧 06-03

1 What are the speakers mainly discussing?

   Ⓐ The work the student will do next semester

   Ⓑ The student's duties as cafeteria manager

   Ⓒ The number of hours the student needs to work

   Ⓓ The salary that the student currently receives

2 What can be inferred about the cafeteria manager?

   Ⓐ He has known the student for a long time.

   Ⓑ He is going to take a trip during winter break.

   Ⓒ He likes to plan ahead for the future.

   Ⓓ He recently received a promotion.

3 What does the cafeteria manager say about the student's schedule for the next semester?

Click on 2 answers.

   1 He will mostly work during the evening.

   2 He must work on the weekend sometimes.

   3 He needs to work some lunch shifts.

   4 He has to work at least twenty hours a week.

4 Why does the cafeteria manager ask the student about his plans for winter break?

   Ⓐ To find out if he can train to be a manager then

   Ⓑ To see if he will be able to work during it

   Ⓒ To determine how much he needs to be paid

   Ⓓ To ask how many shifts he can work then

5 Listen again to part of the conversation. Then answer the question.

What does the cafeteria manager mean when he says this: 🎧

   Ⓐ The student will work some longer shifts.

   Ⓑ The student is going to earn a lot of money.

   Ⓒ The student does not work enough hours.

   Ⓓ The student had better improve his behavior.

ACTUAL TEST **06**

06-04

History of Science

6 What is the main topic of the lecture?

Ⓐ The scientific discoveries of Sir Isaac Newton

Ⓑ The life and research of Gottfried Leibniz

Ⓒ The controversy over the development of calculus

Ⓓ The state of science during the seventeenth century

7 How is the lecture organized?

Ⓐ The professor focuses on primary texts from the 1600s.

Ⓑ The professor looks at the facts from a modern viewpoint.

Ⓒ The professor examines the problem from Newton's point of view.

Ⓓ The professor describes important events in chronological order.

8 What does the professor imply about calculus?

Ⓐ It was developed due to the actions of many people.

Ⓑ It has a number of uses, especially in advanced mathematics.

Ⓒ It is solely a creation of individuals from Europe.

Ⓓ It should have been developed prior to the 1700s.

9 Based on the information in the lecture, indicate whether the statements refer to Sir Isaac Newton or Gottfried Leibniz.

   Click in the correct box for each statement.

	Sir Isaac Newton	Gottfried Leibniz
1 Was credited with creating calculus by the Royal Society		
2 Was considered the greatest scientist in Europe		
3 Was the first to publish his work on calculus		
4 Was accused of plagiarism in 1699		

10 According to the professor, why is it hard to determine how Sir Isaac Newton developed calculus?

   Ⓐ He wrote his notes in a code that has not yet been broken.

   Ⓑ He left little information on how he reached his conclusions.

   Ⓒ All of the work he did on calculus has been lost over time.

   Ⓓ There are many mistakes in the work he originally published.

11 Listen again to part of the lecture. Then answer the question.

   What does the professor mean when she say this: 🎧

   Ⓐ Newton was a better scientist than Leibniz.

   Ⓑ Newton and Leibniz did research in different fields.

   Ⓒ Leibniz lacked the facilities to engage in advanced research.

   Ⓓ Leibniz was the equal of Newton as a mathematician.

06-05

Geology

Open-Pit Copper Mining

12 What is the lecture mainly about?

    Ⓐ Practical uses for copper

    Ⓑ Environmental damage caused by mines

    Ⓒ Open-pit copper mines

    Ⓓ The economics of mining

13 According to the professor, what is the overburden?

    Ⓐ The steep slope inside an open-pit copper mine

    Ⓑ The soil and the rock located above copper ore

    Ⓒ The network of roads in an open-pit copper mine

    Ⓓ An individual level in an open-pit copper mine

14 What does the professor imply about copper mines?

    Ⓐ The majority of them are profitable ventures.

    Ⓑ Dynamite is used by miners to make the mines deeper.

    Ⓒ They require numerous permits before they can open.

    Ⓓ Some are in operation twenty-four hours a day.

15 What is the professor's opinion of the environmental damage caused by copper mines?

Ⓐ It is much less than it used to be during the past.

Ⓑ It is acceptable for the water table to get contaminated.

Ⓒ It is too great to justify more mines being opened.

Ⓓ It may take years for some local areas to recover.

16 According to the professor, what is a big problem with modern-day open-pit copper mining?

Click on 2 answers.

1 The local landscape becomes scarred.

2 The overburden is unpleasant to look at.

3 The economy is harmed when a mine closes.

4 Few trees grow in areas with mines.

17 Listen again to part of the lecture. Then answer the question.

Why does the professor say this: 🎧

Ⓐ To acknowledge the student's comment

Ⓑ To correct her misstatement

Ⓒ To suggest another alternative

Ⓓ To make a comparison

TOEFL® MAP
ACTUAL
TEST Listening 2

Listening Section Directions

🎧 00-01

This section measures your ability to understand conversations and lectures in English.

The Listening section is divided into separately timed parts. In each part, you will listen to 1 conversation and 1 or 2 lectures. You will hear each conversation or lecture only **one** time.

After each conversation or lecture, you will answer some questions about it. The questions typically ask about the main idea and supporting details. Some questions ask about a speaker's purpose or attitude. Answer the questions based on what is stated or implied by the speakers.

You may take notes while you listen. You may use your notes to help you answer the questions. Your notes will not be scored.

If you need to change the volume while you listen, click on the **Volume** at the top of the screen.

In some questions, you will see this icon: 🎧 This means that you will hear, but not see, part of the question.

Some of the questions have special directions. These directions appear in a gray box on the screen.

Most questions are worth 1 point. If a question is worth more than 1 point, it will have special directions that indicate how many points you can receive.

A clock at the top of the screen will show you how much time is remaining. The clock will not count down while you are listening. The clock will count down only while you are answering the questions.

Listening Directions

 00-02

In this part, you will listen to 1 conversation and 1 lecture.

You must answer each question. After you answer, click on **Next**. Then click on **OK** to confirm your answer and go on to the next question. After you click on **OK**, you cannot return to previous questions.

You may now begin this part of the Listening Section. You will have **7 minutes** to answer the questions.

Click on **Continue** to go on.

07-01

1 Why did the professor ask to see the student?

    Ⓐ To go over his midterm exam with him

    Ⓑ To find out when he will turn in a paper he is writing

    Ⓒ To discuss some work he has not submitted yet

    Ⓓ To let him know that his grade is going down

2 What can be inferred about the student?

    Ⓐ He has never spoken with the professor in private before.

    Ⓑ He believes that he is getting a good grade in the class.

    Ⓒ He is considering dropping the professor's class.

    Ⓓ He does not understand all of the material in the class.

3 Why does the student explain the history of Aspen?

    Ⓐ To let the professor know about his hometown

    Ⓑ To describe a city that he feels is very unique

    Ⓒ To tell the professor about the topic of his paper

    Ⓓ To note why he enjoys going skiing there at times

4 Listen again to part of the conversation. Then answer the question.

What can be inferred about the professor when she says this: 🎧

    Ⓐ She has some doubts about the student's honesty.

    Ⓑ She wants to give the student a second chance.

    Ⓒ She is familiar with both the student and his work.

    Ⓓ She believes the student should change his major.

5 Listen again to part of the conversation. Then answer the question.

Why does the professor say this: 🎧

    Ⓐ To dismiss the student from her office

    Ⓑ To ask if the student has any more questions

    Ⓒ To encourage the student to try harder

    Ⓓ To give the student some more time

ACTUAL TEST **07**

143

LISTENING

History

6 What is the main topic of the lecture?

Ⓐ Railroads in the United States during the 1800s

Ⓑ The building of railroad lines in the United States

Ⓒ The most famous railroads in the United States

Ⓓ The reasons railroads were popular in the United States

7 Why does the professor explain about the size of the United States?

Ⓐ To stress that the country needed thousands of miles of railroad track

Ⓑ To state how long it took to travel from one side of the country to the other

Ⓒ To explain why railroads were appealing to many Americans

Ⓓ To compare the size of the country with other nations in Europe

8 According to the professor, what important events in the history of American railroads happened in the 1860s?

Click on 2 answers.

1️⃣ The country finally reached 100,000 miles of railroad lines.

2️⃣ Work on the first transcontinental railroad began.

3️⃣ The speed that trains could travel greatly increased.

4️⃣ Trains were used during a war for the first time.

ACTUAL TEST **07**

9 What is the professor's opinion of American railroads in the nineteenth century?

- Ⓐ They should have been ignored in favor of other methods of transportation.
- Ⓑ The country would not have grown so quickly without them.
- Ⓒ It was the best period for them in the country's history.
- Ⓓ Trains were more influential on the economy than anything else.

10 How is the lecture organized?

- Ⓐ The professor focuses on the major people involved in railroads.
- Ⓑ The professor speaks while showing the students a film.
- Ⓒ The professor asks questions and then answers them himself.
- Ⓓ The professor discusses historical events in chronological order.

11 Listen again to part of the lecture. Then answer the question.

What does the professor imply when he says this: 🎧

- Ⓐ The government forced railroad operators to standardize their tracks.
- Ⓑ Standard tracks were larger than those most trains ran on.
- Ⓒ There was little competition between railroad owners.
- Ⓓ Trains could not run on some tracks prior to standardization.

Listening Directions

🎧 00-02

In this part, you will listen to 1 conversation and 1 lecture.

You must answer each question. After you answer, click on **Next**. Then click on **OK** to confirm your answer and go on to the next question. After you click on **OK**, you cannot return to previous questions.

You may now begin this part of the Listening Section. You will have **7 minutes** to answer the questions.

Click on **Continue** to go on.

00:07:00 ● HIDE TIME

07-03

1   Why did the orchestra conductor ask to see the student?

   Ⓐ To let her have some time off from practice

   Ⓑ To ask her to attend practice more regularly

   Ⓒ To give her a new role in the student orchestra

   Ⓓ To find out if there is something wrong with her

2   What does the orchestra conductor say about the student's performance?

   Ⓐ It has been below average for a while.

   Ⓑ It is steadily improving over time.

   Ⓒ It is good enough to take part in the concert.

   Ⓓ It should get better if she keeps trying.

3   What does the student imply about her grades?

   Ⓐ They are good enough for her to get into an elite graduate school.

   Ⓑ They are below the standard for Dean's List this semester.

   Ⓒ They are the lowest in her class after her midterm exams.

   Ⓓ They are currently the highest that they have ever been.

4   How does the orchestra director suggest that the student solve her problem?

Click on 2 answers.

   1 By attending fewer practice sessions

   2 By rehearsing her part during her free time

   3 By taking the rest of the week off

   4 By quitting the orchestra next semester

5   What is the student's opinion of the orchestra director?

   Ⓐ She thinks he does not understand her situation.

   Ⓑ She believes his advice is unsatisfactory.

   Ⓒ She respects the way that he is treating her.

   Ⓓ She offers no opinion about him.

ACTUAL TEST **07**

07-04

Environmental
Science

Urban Heat Island

6 What aspect of urban heat island does the professor mainly discuss?

(A) How to prevent it

(B) How it is caused

(C) Where it mostly happens

(D) When it was first noticed

7 How does the professor organize the information about urban heat island that he presents to the class?

(A) By giving a handout to the students and going over the information on it

(B) By explaining the process of urban heat island formation by using one city as a model

(C) By contrasting rural and urban areas to show how urban heat islands form

(D) By focusing mostly on how modern civilization has created urban heat islands

8 Based on the information in the lecture, indicate whether the statements refer to causes or effects of urban heat island.

Click in the correct box for each statement.

	Cause	Effect
1 The wind is blocked from blowing by manmade structures.		
2 Rainwater is washed away into drainage systems.		
3 Temperatures are higher than they are in rural places.		
4 Buildings retain much of the heat from the sun's rays.		

9   According to the professor, when does maximum heat island effect take place?

  Ⓐ At sunrise

  Ⓑ Around noon

  Ⓒ A few hours after sunset

  Ⓓ After midnight

10   According to the professor, what is a negative effect of urban heat island?

  Ⓐ People can succumb to the increased temperatures.

  Ⓑ Some machines can fail to work well in hot weather.

  Ⓒ The amount of water that people use increases in summer.

  Ⓓ Cities may suffer blackouts from the overuse of electricity.

11   Listen again to part of the lecture. Then answer the question.

  What does the student imply when she says this: 🎧

  Ⓐ She prefers cool weather to hot weather.

  Ⓑ She rarely goes back to her hometown.

  Ⓒ Farm life is harder than city life.

  Ⓓ Her school is located within a city.

PART 3

Listening Directions

🎧 00-03

In this part, you will listen to 1 conversation and 2 lectures.

You must answer each question. After you answer, click on **Next**. Then click on **OK** to confirm your answer and go on to the next question. After you click on **OK**, you cannot return to previous questions.

You may now begin this part of the Listening Section. You will have **10 minutes** to answer the questions.

Click on **Continue** to go on.

07-05

1   Why did the student ask to see the dean of students?

    Ⓐ To describe what she has already done on campus

    Ⓑ To tell him about her plans for a volunteer group

    Ⓒ To talk about how much she likes the school campus

    Ⓓ To ask about some special events the school is planning

2   Why does the dean of students tell the student about the Maintenance Department?

    Ⓐ To provide her with information on what the department does

    Ⓑ To give her directions on how to get to that department

    Ⓒ To explain why one of her proposals will be rejected

    Ⓓ To tell her who in that department she needs to speak with

3   Which part of the campus would the student like to improve?

Click on 2 answers.

    ① The area around the lake

    ② The library

    ③ The art building

    ④ The student center

4   What does the dean of students offer to do for the student?

    Ⓐ Arrange a meeting between her and a university executive

    Ⓑ Speak to the university president on her behalf

    Ⓒ Approve her request for extra funding for her organization

    Ⓓ Introduce her to someone in the Maintenance Department

5   What can be inferred about the dean of students?

    Ⓐ He believes that the student's ideas are all practical.

    Ⓑ He does not believe the student was prepared for their meeting.

    Ⓒ He will be promoted to vice president in the near future.

    Ⓓ He is happy to arrange a meeting with the school president.

ACTUAL TEST **07**

07-06

Musicology

6 What aspect of the violin does the professor mainly discuss?

Ⓐ The sounds it makes

Ⓑ Its origin and structure

Ⓒ How it is made

Ⓓ Where the best ones are from

7 What does the professor imply about the lira?

Ⓐ It was invented before the violin.

Ⓑ People first played it in Western Europe.

Ⓒ The lira was an easy instrument to play.

Ⓓ Few people ever made music with it.

8 According to the professor, where did the modern violin originate?

Ⓐ The Byzantine Empire

Ⓑ Northern Italy

Ⓒ Western Europe

Ⓓ The Middle East

9 How does the professor organize the information about the schematic of the violin that she presents to the class?

Ⓐ By pointing out its features on a real violin

Ⓑ By going over a handout she gave to the students

Ⓒ By focusing on some drawings in the textbook

Ⓓ By showing pictures while lecturing on it

10 What is the bridge of the violin?

Ⓐ The place where the strings create an arch over the body

Ⓑ The area on the violin that contains the fingerboard

Ⓒ The decorative scroll-shaped piece on the violin

Ⓓ The part of the violin with two S-shaped openings

11 Listen again to part of the lecture. Then answer the question.

Why does the professor say this: 🎧

Ⓐ To make a joke about violins to the class

Ⓑ To indicate that her lecture is about to end

Ⓒ To emphasize how valuable the violins are

Ⓓ To point out the main feature of a Stradivari violin

07-07

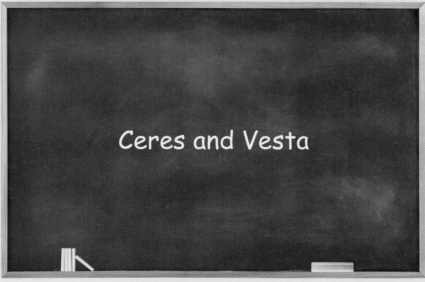

Ceres and Vesta

12 How does the professor present the information about the discovery of asteroids that he presents to the class?

   Ⓐ By focusing only on the four largest asteroids

   Ⓑ By discussing the lives of the astronomers who found them

   Ⓒ By referring to the ongoing search for Pluto at that time

   Ⓓ By describing the events in chronological order

13 Where is the asteroid belt?

   Ⓐ In between the orbits of Earth and Mars

   Ⓑ In between the orbits of Jupiter and Saturn

   Ⓒ In between the orbits of Mars and Jupiter

   Ⓓ In between the orbits of Earth and Venus

14 Why does the professor explain that Ceres is now considered a dwarf planet?

   Ⓐ To respond to a student's question

   Ⓑ To make a comparison with Pluto

   Ⓒ To emphasize how large Ceres is

   Ⓓ To note Ceres's unique composition

15 What is the professor's opinion on the possibility that life exists on
Ceres?

Ⓐ There is a strong likelihood of that.

Ⓑ Some reports indicate that there may be life.

Ⓒ It is highly unlikely that anything lives there.

Ⓓ There is no chance that life exists there.

16 Based on the information in the lecture, indicate whether the statements
refer to Ceres or Vesta.

Click in the correct box for each statement.

	Ceres	Vesta
① Has an iron inner core		
② May contain subsurface liquid water		
③ Was discovered before the other		
④ Is responsible for many meteorites on the Earth		

17 Listen again to part of the lecture. Then answer the question.

Why does the professor say this: 🎧

Ⓐ To let the students know that several of them are failing the class

Ⓑ To encourage the students to listen more carefully to his lectures

Ⓒ To indicate his displeasure with the work some students did before

Ⓓ To make sure the students know the importance of their upcoming
exam

ACTUAL TEST **07**

TOEFL MAP

ACTUAL TEST Listening 2

Answers, Scripts, and Explanations

Answers

1 Ⓒ	2 Ⓐ	3 Ⓓ	4 Ⓑ	5 Ⓓ
6 Ⓒ	7 ②,④	8 Ⓐ	9 Ⓓ	10 Ⓑ
11 Ⓑ				

1 Ⓒ	2 Ⓑ	3 Ⓒ	4 Ⓐ	5 Ⓓ
6 Fact: ②,③,④ Not a Fact: ①		7 Ⓐ		8 Ⓑ
9 Ⓑ	10 Ⓓ	11 Ⓐ		

1 Ⓒ	2 ②,③	3 Ⓓ	4 Ⓐ	5 Ⓓ
6 Ⓐ	7 Ⓒ	8 Ⓑ	9 Ⓐ	10 Ⓑ
11 Ⓑ	12 Ⓒ	13 Ⓐ	14 Problem: ②,③	
Solution: ①,④		15 Ⓓ	16 Ⓒ	17 Ⓓ

Scripts & Explanations

Conversation 🎧 01-01

p.16

W Bookstore Manager: Excuse me, but I heard you speaking with one of my employees about returning a book you bought. I hope you don't mind my listening in on your conversation. But I'm the manager here, so why don't you explain your problem to me? Perhaps I'll be able to take care of it and give you a hand.

M Student: Oh, yeah. Sure. Well, I bought this textbook here for a philosophy class, but I dropped the class today, so, I don't need this book anymore.

W: That makes sense. Go on.

M: I dropped a huge amount of money on books this semester. I think I spent a total of more than three hundred dollars on all my textbooks. [5]You know, the prices of books have been rising a lot ever since I've been here. You really ought to do something about that.

W: I sympathize with you, but I'm just the manager here. **If you want to get the prices of the books changed, you'd be much better off complaining to the publishers that print them than me.** Anyway, how much did that philosophy book run you?

M: It cost me . . . hmm, hold on a second . . . sixty-five dollars. This was my most expensive book.

W: And you want to return it, right?

M: Yes, I do. But the employee I was just speaking with told me that the deadline for returning books has already passed. That would be really depressing because I only bought this book three days ago. I've barely even opened it.

W: All right. Let me explain a couple of things.

M: Sure.

W: As a general rule, the deadline for returning books has passed. It was yesterday.

M: Oh, no.

W: Hold on a second. I'm not finished yet. I've got some possible good news for you if you'll just let me talk.

M: Sorry about that.

W: Now, you said that you bought this book three days ago. Is that correct?

M: Yes, it is. You see, I only signed up for the class four days ago. I went to the first class and then came right here and bought the book after the class ended.

W: You signed up for a class four days ago, but you're already dropping it?

M: Uh, yeah. You know, I took a closer look at the syllabus and realized that the professor is expecting way too much work for that class. I mean, it's an elective. I don't have time to write three papers and to take two tests. That's why I'm dropping it.

W: Okay. It's none of my business anyway. So assuming that you have the receipt and that you purchased this book three days ago, then, uh, yes, you can return the book for a full refund.

M: Excellent. Thank you so much. Oh, uh, one more question . . . The book came wrapped in plastic, but, as you can see, uh, I opened it. You'll still take this back, right?

W: As long as there's no damage to the book, then we'll give you a complete refund.

M: That's music to my ears. Where do we go to process this return?

1 **Gist-Content Question** | Throughout the conversation, the student and the bookstore manager talk about a book that the student purchased earlier but now wants to return.

2 **Gist-Purpose Question** | The bookstore manager tells the student, "So assuming that you have the receipt and that you purchased this book three days ago, then, uh,

yes, you can return the book for a full refund."

3 **Detail Question** | The student says, "I don't have time to write three papers and to take two tests. That's why I'm dropping it."

4 **Making Inferences Question** | The manager tells the student that she will give him "a complete refund." The student then asks where they can "process this return." So the student will probably get his money from the bookstore manager next.

5 **Understanding Function Question** | The bookstore manager tells the student he would be better off complaining to the publishers than her when he is talking about the high prices of the books. So she implies that she does not determine the prices of any books; the publishers do.

Lecture 🎧 01-02   p.18

M Professor: Today, cereal crops such as corn, rice, oats, barley, and wheat account for around fifty percent of the calories that humans consume. Right now, I'd like to take a look at each of these cereal crops and show you how humans have changed them so that, uh, over time, they've actually improved in quality. We'll begin with wheat.

The wheat grown today originated from several strains of wild wheat in the Fertile Crescent region about 10,000 years ago. The Fertile Crescent is the area that comprises the modern-day nation states of Israel, Lebanon, Syria, Jordan, and Iraq. Since that time, wheat has been modified to grow larger grains and to survive in different conditions. These modifications were done through patient trial-and-error processes over several millennia. However, in the modern era, wheat has been subjected to intense examination. Scientists have learned how to enhance its properties a great deal through the selective crossbreeding of different strains of wheat.

The two main goals of the people who create modified wheat . . . or any modified food for that matter . . . are to produce more food per plant and to make the plant more resistant to diseases. Throughout the long history of agriculture, farmers have been doing this. Yet only in recent centuries has this process been elevated to the level of science. Through scientific experiments involving thousands of instances of crossbreeding, agricultural scientists are now producing plants that can survive in various climates, resist numerous diseases, and produce

larger fruits or grains to result in higher crop yields. Wheat is no exception as it has undergone certain changes. However, until the middle of the 1900s, wheat yields remained similar to those in the past, and it was still being devastated by diseases.

This changed in the 1950s due to the efforts of one man: Norman Borlaug. I honestly don't think it's possible to say too many good things about the man and his work. Here, uh, let me tell you what he did. Borlaug was an American scientist who specialized in plant genetics. He was responsible for two major innovations during his more than twelve years of research in Mexico. First, through crossbreeding, he developed strains of wheat that could resist rust, which is a major disease. Rust was responsible for major crop losses in Mexico and elsewhere. Second, Borlaug managed to create a strain of wheat that produced larger, heavier grains. Larger grains meant more food per wheat stalk and higher food production per acre planted.

However, there was a slight problem. The stalks were too thin, so, as the wheat grew, they collapsed under the weight of the heavier grains. Wheat stalks have an evolutionary trait in which they compete against one another by growing as high as possible so that they can get more sunlight than the surrounding wheat stalks. Borlaug, fortunately, had a solution to this problem. He imported a strain of dwarf wheat from Japan. This dwarf wheat had short, strong stalks. By crossbreeding this with his large-grained wheat, he was able to produce a strain of wheat that had strong, short stalks and produced larger, heavier grains of wheat.

The end result of Borlaug's experiments is what is now termed the Green Revolution. Mexico's wheat production practically doubled. Borlaug subsequently worked in Pakistan and India, and the strains of wheat he developed in those countries produced plenty of food for their exploding populations. Many experts suggest that without Borlaug's modified wheat, large numbers of people in those nations would have starved to death. Mostly through Borlaug's efforts, worldwide wheat production has tripled in the past fifty years. For his efforts, Borlaug received the Nobel Peace Prize and many other awards and is considered the father of the modern food revolution.

W Student: Wasn't he creating genetically modified food? I've heard that it's harmful to people.

M: I believe you're referring to crops that have been modified through the direct manipulation of their genes. That's something we're going to touch on later. And that's also something Borlaug never did. His work merely involved crossbreeding various strains of wheat. There's absolutely nothing harmful in what he did. In fact, the evidence is clear since millions of people—maybe even billions—worldwide have been consuming food products made from his wheat ever since the 1950s. I suppose it's true that some critics claim crossbreeding is unnatural, but let's remember that farmers have been crossbreeding crops for thousands of years. In fact, uh, every grain you eat originally had a different wild form. And consider Borlaug's work through the eyes of those whom he has aided. Millions of people now have a steady food supply thanks to him. I think we can all agree that modified wheat has benefitted mankind.

Borlaug even thought that his work benefitted the environment. By being able to produce more food per acre, he said that fewer forests needed to be cleared for farmland and that fewer chemical fertilizers needed to be added to the soil. That's definitely something to consider. Okay, that's enough about wheat. Let's move on to rice next.

6 **Gist-Content Question** | The professor mostly talks about the ways in which wheat has been changed.

7 **Detail Question** | The professor says, "The two main goals of the people who create modified wheat . . . or any modified food for that matter . . . are to produce more food per plant and to make the plant more resistant to diseases."

8 **Understanding Attitude Question** | About Norman Borlaug, the professor remarks, "This changed in the 1950s due to the efforts of one man: Norman Borlaug. I honestly don't think it's possible to say too many good things about the man and his work."

9 **Understanding Organization Question** | The professor states, "He imported a strain of dwarf wheat from Japan. This dwarf wheat had short, strong stalks. By crossbreeding this with his large-grained wheat, he was able to produce a strain of wheat that had strong, short stalks and produced larger, heavier grains of wheat." So he focuses on how dwarf wheat was crossbred with another strain of wheat.

10 **Connecting Content Question** | The professor states, "The end result of Borlaug's experiments is what is now termed the Green Revolution." In saying this, the professor implies that the Green Revolution would not have happened without Norman Borlaug.

11 **Making Inferences Question** | At the end of the lecture, the professor tells the students, "Okay, that's enough about wheat. Let's move on to rice next."

Conversation 🎧 01-03   p.22

W1 Student: Ms. Marrone, I came here as soon as I got your message. Am I too late?

W2 Financial Aid Office Employee: Er . . . Sorry, but I'm not quite sure who you are.

W1: Oh, yeah. Right. My name is Katie Alderson. You left a voicemail message for me around two o'clock in the afternoon. I was in class at the time, so my phone was off. I didn't get the message until about five minutes ago, so I ran halfway across campus to get here.

W2: Ah, Katie. Okay. I remember now. Sorry, but I deal with so many students that it's hard to keep track of everyone. I remember your case though.

W1: Good. So, um, how much trouble am I in?

W2: I don't know if "trouble" is the word that I would use.

W1: Well, in your voicemail message, you mentioned that I was in danger of losing my scholarship next semester because I hadn't done some paperwork properly. Since it's a rather large scholarship, I'd call losing it being in big trouble.

W2: Yes, you may have a good point there. Okay. Let me tell you what's going on so that you'll know the issue.

W1: Sure.

W2: First, you're supposed to complete some paperwork every semester in order to keep your scholarship. You've done that with no mistakes for the past three semesters, but there were a couple of problems with your paperwork this semester. Hold on . . . I've got your file right here on my desk. Let me show you what you did wrong.

W1: I did something wrong? Hmm . . . I guess the instructions must have been too complicated or something.

W2: Well, your first mistake wasn't a complicated one. Look here . . . You forgot to sign the document on page three.

W1: Oh, my goodness. I can't believe that. Do you have a pen . . . ?

W2: Here you are.

W1: Okay . . . That solves that problem. What's the next one?

W2: Since your scholarship is an academic one, you are supposed to provide us with a copy of your transcript each semester. [5]That way, we can make sure your GPA is at least the minimum required according to the terms of your scholarship. But, um, we never got a copy of your transcript this time.

W1: **You didn't?** But I went to the Registrar's office, uh . . . two or three weeks ago and requested that they send you a copy. Wait . . . I've got the receipt here in my purse . . . See . . . I made that request already. But I'll go down there as soon as we're done and ask someone there what happened.

W2: That's good. Since the receipt shows you requested the transcript a while ago, I won't hold its absence against you. The fault for that definitely lies with the Registrar's office.

W1: Is there, uh, anything else?

W2: Those are the two major issues with your application. Since we've cleared them up, you don't have anything to worry about. But there are a couple of other mistakes on your paperwork that we need to go over immediately. Once we fix them, there won't be any problems at all.

W1: That's exactly what I was hoping to hear.

W2: Okay. Take a look here at page five now. Look at the third line from the bottom . . .

1 **Gist-Purpose Question** | The student states, "Well, in your voicemail message, you mentioned that I was in danger of losing my scholarship next semester because I hadn't done some paperwork properly."

2 **Detail Question** | The woman says, "Well, your first mistake wasn't a complicated one. Look here . . . You forgot to sign the document on page three."

3 **Making Inferences Question** | The woman notes that the student receives her scholarship only if her GPA is a certain level, so it can be inferred that the student's GPA has been high in recent semesters.

4 **Understanding Attitude Question** | The woman says, "Since we've cleared them up, you don't have anything to worry about. But there are a couple of other mistakes on your paperwork that we need to go over immediately. Once we fix them, there won't be any problems at all."

5 **Understanding Attitude Question** | When the student asks, "You didn't?" in response to the woman's comment that she never received a copy of the student's transcript, she is expressing her surprise. Here, the student's tone of voice is important. She is clearly surprised by the woman's statement.

Lecture 🎧 01-04   p.24

M1 Professor: [10]Another important aspect of Roman engineering was the marvelous aqueducts the Romans built. **I suppose I should explain what they are first.** An aqueduct is a structure that allows water to flow from one place to another. Typically, the water is taken from a remote area and brought to a place where people live in large numbers, such as a city. An aqueduct does this through the force of gravity. So it's like running water downhill. Gravity carries the water through a system of aboveground or belowground pipes or channels. More modern ones use pumps to transport water, but in Roman times, it was all accomplished by gravity.

As you can probably surmise, the hard part was getting the right gradient, or angle, of the aqueduct during the construction process. If it was too steep, the water flowed too quickly and might cause damage or overflow at its endpoint. On the other hand, if the gradient wasn't steep enough, the water flowed too, um, slowly or sometimes didn't even flow at all. The Romans managed to overcome these engineering challenges and built aqueducts all over their empire. And in case you're curious, the word "aqueduct" comes from two Latin words: the word *aqua*, which means "water," and the word *ductus*, which means "channel."

The purpose of aqueducts was twofold. Firstly, they brought clean drinking, cooking, and bathing water to towns and cities. [11]Secondly, the water was also used to remove waste from a region's sewage system. This helped the Romans cut down on the number of diseases that affected people in their crowded urban centers. **In fact, the system of aqueducts was so effective that Roman towns and cities rarely suffered from the mass outbreaks of diseases that were so common in Europe after the fall of the Roman Empire.**

Now, the aqueducts had to be built strongly and be well protected. Most were constructed of bricks, stones, and a special type of cement the Romans made from volcanic material. The channels through which the water flowed were masonry, clay, and lead pipes. Most of the construction work was done by slaves, paid laborers, and Roman soldiers working in the distant provinces of the empire. Naturally, the laborers were supervised by engineers who were skilled in the building of aqueducts. In addition, to protect the water from dirt, dead animals, and attacks by enemies, the aqueducts were primarily built underground.

M2 Student: Underground? But what about those huge

aqueducts with the arches that are still standing in parts of Europe?

M1: Well, yes, they were sometimes built above the ground. But those aqueducts were just minor parts of an enormous system. Actually, the Romans didn't like building those tall, arched aqueducts and pretty much only erected them when they had to cross valleys to keep the gradient of the aqueduct steady so as not to interrupt the flow of water. The reasons they didn't like them were that those arched sections were vulnerable to weathering as well as enemy attacks, so they had to be repaired frequently and patrolled at all times. Underground channels, meanwhile, were better protected and didn't get damaged as easily.

So, um, once the water reached a city or town, it went into large cisterns so that a steady supply of water was maintained. Then, a system of more pipes—mostly made of lead—moved the water to bathhouses, large private homes, and public places from which people could get drinking water. This water wasn't free though. In Rome, for instance, a person had to pay to have his home connected to the water supply. Those funds often went to the building and maintaining of the aqueduct system.

To give you an idea of how extensive the entire system was, let's look at the Roman Empire's largest city, Rome. During a period of around 500 years, the Romans constructed eleven different aqueducts to bring water to their capital. The first was completed in 312 B.C. and followed the route of the Via Appia. You probably know it as the Appian Way. The last aqueduct was completed in 226 A.D. The longest of the aqueducts leading to Rome was nearly 100 kilometers long. It's estimated that, um, at its best, Rome's water system could supply up to one million people a day with at least one cubic meter of water.

Sadly, the aqueduct system didn't last and fell apart when the empire itself fell. Germanic tribes invading Italy damaged most of the aqueducts leading to Rome in order to cut off the city's water supply. Only one aqueduct, which ran entirely underground, survived the onslaught untouched. In other parts of the empire, aqueducts were also either damaged or completely destroyed. Some, however, remained in use for centuries after the end of the empire. But as the populations in some places decreased, so too did the need for lots of fresh water, so, um, many aqueducts fell into disrepair. It wasn't until the Renaissance nearly a thousand years after the fall of Rome that European cities began to seriously plan water and sewage systems again.

6 **Detail Question** | According to the lecture, Roman

aqueducts transported water to large population centers such as Rome. In addition, the Romans built many of them underground, and they were made from many different materials, such as "bricks, stones, and a special type of cement the Romans made from volcanic material." However, Roman aqueducts relied on gravity, so they did not carry water uphill.

7 **Making Inferences Question** | The professor states, "Then, a system of more pipes—mostly made of lead— moved the water to bathhouses, large private homes, and public places from which people could get drinking water." Since he just mentions "large private homes," it can be inferred that only a few private homes were connected to the water system in Rome.

8 **Understanding Organization Question** | The professor comments, "To give you an idea of how extensive the entire system was, let's look at the largest city, Rome."

9 **Detail Question** | The professor tells the students, "Germanic tribes invading Italy damaged most of the aqueducts leading to Rome in order to cut off the city's water supply. Only one aqueduct, which ran entirely underground, survived the onslaught untouched."

10 **Understanding Function Question** | When the professor states, "I suppose I should explain what they are first," when talking about aqueducts, he is indicating that some of his students might not know what an aqueduct is.

11 **Making Inferences Question** | When the professor says, "In fact, the system of aqueducts was so effective that Roman towns and cities rarely suffered from the mass outbreaks of diseases that were so common in Europe after the fall of the Roman Empire," he implies that people did not often use aqueducts after Roman times, which is one reason that there were mass outbreaks of diseases in Europe.

PART 3

Conversation 🎧 01-05   p.28

M Professor: Janet, thank you for agreeing to come here before I go home for the day. I hope you're having a good day.

W Student: I am, sir. I got your email and arrived as soon as I could. I'm not, uh, I'm not keeping you from leaving, am I?

M: Not at all. I normally leave around this time, but I can always make some time to speak with a student.

W: Thank you, sir. So, um . . . what do you need to speak with me about?

M: I want to chat about the outline for your final paper you submitted this Monday. I've been going through them, and yours stood out enough that I felt it was important to contact you.

W: Um . . . I'm not sure if that's a good or bad thing.

M: Well, let's take a look.

W: Okay.

M: You see, uh . . . some of the terminology you use isn't appropriate.

W: What terminology?

M: I'm specifically referring to you calling the Middle Ages the Dark Ages. Now, uh, would you mind telling me why you used the term Dark Ages?

W: Not at all. Uh, I learned that the Dark Ages were the time in Europe after the fall of Rome and up until, uh, the Renaissance. Basically, people called this period the Dark Ages because there was a big step back from the Roman Empire. [5]By that, I mean knowledge from Rome was lost, society and technology didn't advance, and the overall culture of Europe declined during the Dark Ages.

M: Um . . . **Those are rather outdated notions on what happened during that time period.**

W: Really?

M: Yes, really. It's true that some historians thought that a few decades ago, but research has revealed that this period was quite dynamic. Now, uh, what you're calling the Dark Ages is typically said to begin in 476 A.D., which is when the Roman Empire fell. Historians today call this period the Middle Ages. It lasted until the Renaissance began around 1400 A.D. We can also divide the Middle Ages into the early, middle, and high periods. As a general rule, the early Middle Ages as said to have ended in the year 800, when Charlemagne was crowned the Holy Roman Emperor. Most people who use the term Dark Ages consider them to have lasted from 476 to 800.

W: Okay, but why did people call them the Dark Ages then?

M: When Rome fell, there was no more central authority over most of Europe. There was also a decline because a lot of knowledge was lost. But the early Middle Ages were not a backward time.

W: How so?

M: The Church became the strongest power during this time. Monasteries were established and became great centers of learning. They preserved a great amount of

knowledge from ancient Greece and Rome. Basically, you could say that they saved Western civilization.

W: What else?

M: There were other advances in technology, so farming benefitted. There were outstanding scholars and theologians who lived during this time as well. So, uh, I think you'd better rework your outline. Why don't you focus on mistaken ideas about the Dark Ages? How does that sound?

W: I can do that. Can I resubmit my outline after class two days from now?

M: That's fine with me.

1   **Gist-Purpose Question** | The professor asked to see the student to talk about an outline for a paper that she turned in.

2   **Detail Question** | The professor says, "As a general rule, the early Middle Ages as said to have ended in the year 800, when Charlemagne was crowned the Holy Roman Emperor," and, "Monasteries were established and became great centers of learning. They preserved a great amount of knowledge from ancient Greece and Rome. Basically, you could say that they saved Western civilization."

3   **Detail Question** | The professor tells the student, "So, uh, I think you'd better rework your outline."

4   **Making Inference Question** | The professor informs the student that some of her ideas are wrong, so it can be inferred that she has some mistaken ideas about history.

5   **Understanding Attitude Question** | In states that the student has some outdated notions, the professor means that scholars no longer believe the student's explanation is correct.

Lecture 🎧 01-06   p.30

W Professor: In the animal kingdom, the propagation of the species is the utmost goal of every organism. After all, a species that doesn't reproduce—no matter how big or small—will become extinct. Once animals mate and their offspring are born or hatched, whatever the case may be, then something that's known as parental involvement becomes involved. And that's what I'd like to speak about with you today. There are several paths parental involvement can take, so please listen carefully and take good notes because you will be tested on this material.

First, in some cases, there's absolutely no parental involvement in the lives of the offspring. This is common with many species of fish, reptiles, and amphibians. What happens is that a female produces eggs, a male fertilizes them, and then both parents move on while leaving the eggs alone. Later, babies hatch from the eggs and grow up on their own. I'm sure you've all seen documentaries showing turtles that hatch from eggs and then crawl across the beach to try to reach the water. Those turtles are animals with no parental involvement in their lives.

In other cases, the mother remains with her offspring and raises, feeds, and protects them until they mature. However, the father has nothing to do with the offspring. This is known as a uniparental species. There are many species of birds, reptiles, and mammals that engage in this behavior. For example, male deer don't remain with their mates. Instead, the females raise their offspring on their own. Oh, and the third type of parental behavior involves both parents working together to raise and protect their offspring. Wolves and lions are two examples of mammals that act this way.

Why do parents protect their offspring? Some suggest that it could simply be instinctual. Parents feel an urge to protect their progeny until they can take care of themselves. This ensures that the species will continue to live for at least another generation. Of course, there are many dangers to offspring, uh, the biggest of which is predators. Many predators go after the young and the weak since they're easy targets. So, um, parents often have various ways to protect their young. For instance, when a fawn, er, a baby deer, is born, its mother quickly cleans it to prevent the scent of its birth from attracting predators. Then, the mother deer hides the fawn in grass or brush for the first few weeks of its life until it can walk properly. A fawn typically stays with its mother for a year. By that time, it is big enough to feed and protect itself, and it has learned how to avoid predators from its mother.

When both parents look after their young, a common way of doing so is that one parent remains close to the offspring at all times. Many penguin species behave this way. While one parent hunts for food, the other remains close to the chick to guard it. Other bird species—even those with protective nests—do the same thing. Reptiles frequently build protective shelters for their young. Er, I'm referring, of course, to those reptiles that actually take care of their young. Alligators do this. Once their babies hatch, one of them—usually the mother—always remains nearby the young. And believe me when I say that you don't want to get anywhere near a mother alligator that's protecting her young.

Many mammals protect their young by placing them in herds. For some species, all the adults are responsible for protecting the babies in the herd. Musk oxen, for instance, place their young in the center of the herd when they're threatened by predators. And many species of animals place guards around their territory to warn the other members of the herd about predators. These animals act in an altruistic way in that the warning sounds they make attract attention to themselves. Meerkats have often been observed acting this way. Some mammals have adults act as rearguards that protect the rest of the group—especially babies—from predators by fighting to protect the group's retreat. Baboons typically act in this manner. Of course, some predators manage to surprise groups of animals, in which case these animals, if they can't escape, turn and fight to defend themselves and their young.

M Student: Do parents fight to the death to protect their young?

W: As a general rule, no. Animal parents fight and act as members of a group to drive off predators, but the instinct to survive is stronger than the instinct to protect their young. Off the top of my head, I can't think of any documented cases where a parent died to protect its young. I'm sure they exist, but they're rare. [11]No, instead, when predators manage to separate a baby from the herd, the parents rarely make an effort to save it. I will, however, show you a video now of some animals defending their young in herds. This should let you see what I've been talking to you about. **Would someone get the lights, please?**

6 **Gist-Content Question** | The professor mostly lectures about the ways that animals take care of and then protect the offspring that they have.

7 **Detail Question** | The professor explains, "In other cases, the mother remains with her offspring and raises, feeds, and protects them until they mature. However, the father has nothing to do with the offspring. This is known as a uniparental species."

8 **Understanding Organization Question** | The professor notes, "For instance, when a fawn, er, a baby deer, is born, its mother quickly cleans it to prevent the scent of its birth from attracting predators."

9 **Connecting Content Question** | The professor explains to the class how both penguins and alligators protect their offspring from predators.

10 **Making Inferences Question** | The professor says, "Some mammals have adults act as rearguards that

protect the rest of the group—especially babies—from predators by fighting to protect the group's retreat. Baboons typically act in this manner." So the professor implies that baboons might fight other animals that attack their young.

11 **Understanding Attitude Question** | When a person asks another to "get the lights," that person is indicating that the other individual should turn off the lights.

Lecture 🎧 01-07 p.33

M Professor: For the next few minutes, we're going to discuss one of the few female American architects from the nineteenth century. [11]Her name is Harriet Irwin. Does anyone happen to know what she's famous for . . . ? Nobody . . . ? **Oh, there are usually one or two students who are familiar with her.** Anyway, Harriet Irwin is most famous for designing a hexagonal house. She's also unique in that she was a woman who received no formal architectural training. Yet she managed to design and build the house, uh, which she lived in, and she made it as practical as possible with regard to cleaning and maintaining it.

Irwin was born in the state of North Carolina in 1828. She was often sick as a child, so she spent most of her time indoors instead of playing outside. While indoors, Irwin read a lot and wrote some, publishing both magazine articles and books when she was much older. Irwin also developed a fondness for engineering and architecture. She attended a school for young women; however, in those days, women studied subjects such as literature, languages, religion, painting, music, and history, not, um, engineering or architecture. Because of that, Irwin taught those two subjects to herself by reading everything about them that she could get her hands on.

When Irwin was twenty-one, she got married and started a family. She gave birth to nine children and was therefore burdened with many tasks as a housewife. She also still suffered from occasional bouts of illness as she grew older. Additionally, remember that Irwin lived in North Carolina. Well, North Carolina saw some fighting during the Civil War, which ended in 1865, so many areas in the state needed to be rebuilt since they'd been damaged during the war. These factors all inspired Irwin to design a new home for her family. She started doing this in 1869. Her primary objective was to create a home that could easily be taken care of by a woman who was in poor physical condition, much as Irwin herself was for many years.

While considering how to design the house, she hit upon the concept of a hexagonal house. This house had six sides and few corners. The rooms inside it were circular or elongated circles, uh, kind of like . . . hmm . . . kind of like beans I guess. The main issue for her was that she wanted her rooms to have no corners. She did away with them because she had noticed that the corners in square rooms were places where dust and dirt always seemed to collect. I'm sure you've noticed that about your own places, too, huh . . . ? Anyway, Irwin found it hard to clean these corners. In a circular room though, it was much easier to sweep or mop alongside the walls since there were no corners.

Irwin's design also incorporated several other features that made her house easy to manage. For instance, there were no hallways. Instead, each room had a wide set of doors that led to another room. Her house had many windows, which permitted air to circulate easily and let a lot of light into the house as well. These features combined to make the house seem larger than it really was since it appeared to be one big open space. Ah, she also designed the house with a large fireplace in the center. During Irwin's lifetime, most American homes had fireplaces in several rooms since that was the only means to provide heat during winter. Yet her design accomplished the same task by channeling heat from the central fireplace into all of the other rooms. By dramatically reducing the number of fireplaces in the house, Irwin cut down on soot and ash in the house, which therefore reduced the effort required to clean the house.

Irwin submitted her designs to the United States Patent Office and received a patent for the house. However, she wasn't granted exclusive rights over hexagonal houses. She only got a patent for houses that were designed like hers. In fact, Irwin wasn't the first person to design or build a hexagonal house in the U.S. There were actually a few octagonal houses in existence at that time. Nevertheless, Irwin was the first woman to design and receive a patent for a house, which is what makes her stand out amongst nineteenth-century architects. Eventually, the house she designed was built, and she lived in it until her death in 1897.

W Student: It sounds like she was pretty impressive. Did her designs have any influence on later architects?

M: Not really. Only two other hexagonal homes were designed and built by her. Incidentally, one of them is still standing today. In addition, although there are a few hexagonal houses presently in existence, it remains a rather odd shape for a home. Personally, I'd say that the brilliance of Harriet Irwin was her ability to create a living space that, considering her physical limitations, gave her the most freedom of movement while requiring the least amount of maintenance.

12 **Gist-Content Question** | The professor mostly lectures on the house that was designed by Harriet Irwin.

13 **Understanding Organization Question** | The professor mentions that Harriet Irwin was often sick as a child and uses this fact to explain her decision to make a hexagonal house later in her life.

14 **Connecting Content Question** | According to the lecture, one problem was that so many fireplaces created a lot of soot. Lots of dust would also gather in the corners of rooms. As for the solutions that Harriet Irwin came up with, she designed the rooms to be circular, and she put many windows in the house so that more air could circulate.

15 **Making Inferences Question** | When the student asks, "Did her designs have any influence on later architects?" the professor answers, "Not really." So it can be inferred that she was not particularly influential as an architect.

16 **Understanding Attitude Question** | About Harriet Irwin, the professor states, "Personally, I'd say that the brilliance of Harriet Irwin was her ability to create a living space that, considering her physical limitations, gave her the most freedom of movement while requiring the least amount of maintenance."

17 **Understanding Attitude Question** | When the professor comments that he usually has one or two students who are familiar with Harriet Irwin, he is implying that he had expected someone in the class to answer his question about what she was famous for.

Answers

PART 1

1 Ⓑ	2 Ⓑ	3 Ⓒ	4 Ⓐ	5 Ⓒ
6 Ⓑ	7 Fact: ③, ④ Not a Fact: ①, ②		8 Ⓓ	
9 Ⓑ	10 Ⓓ	11 Ⓒ		

PART 2

1 Ⓑ	2 Ⓐ	3 Ⓓ	4 Ⓑ	5 Ⓒ
6 Ⓐ	7 Macronutrients: ②, ③, ④ Micronutrients: ①		8 Ⓒ	
9 Ⓑ	10 Ⓐ	11 Ⓒ		
12 ②, ③	13 Ⓐ	14 Ⓑ	15 Ⓑ	16 Ⓓ
17 Ⓒ				

Scripts & Explanations

PART 1

Conversation 🎧 02-01   p.40

M1 Student: Hello, Professor Perry.

M2 Professor: Good afternoon. May I help you?

M1: Yes, sir. I hope so. I'm a student in your Art History 103 class. I'm here to talk about the paper we are supposed to be writing for your class.

M2: Ah, sure. In that case, why don't you come in and tell me what you've decided to write on? Oh, but, first, can I get your name?

M1: Sure. My name is Eric Daniels. That's D-A-N-I-EL-S.

M2: Let me check your name here on the class list . . . Daniels . . . Craig Daniels?

M1: No, sir. Eric Daniels.

M2: Ah, here you are. That's odd. I don't normally get two students with the same last name in my class. Oh, well, it's no matter. Okay . . . So let's get back to the business at hand—your paper topic.

M1: Yes, sir. Well, um, I was thinking about focusing on the style of Vincent van Gogh. What do you think of that?

M2: Well . . . Personally, I'd rather that you avoid writing about him.

M1: Huh? Why do you say that?

M2: I have two reasons. First, he's a rather famous individual, so there's been a lot written about him. The focus of this paper is to get you to research a less well-known artist. And the second reason is that there aren't any paintings made by Van Gogh on exhibit anywhere in this city. I was hoping that you'd be able to see in person at least one of the works of the artist whom you choose to write on.

M1: Isn't it all right if I just look at a painting in a book and write about that?

M2: Oh, my goodness, no. There is such a huge difference between seeing a painting in a book and seeing it in real life. I mean, you've seen the *Mona Lisa* before in countless images, right . . . ? Sure you have. But when you actually go to the Louvre in Paris and stand face to face with the *Mona Lisa* . . . Well, it's simply another experience.

M1: I had no idea, sir.

M2: That's all right. Anyway, if you don't mind, let me make a suggestion for you concerning your paper topic.

M1: Okay.

M2: How about writing your report on Jean-Francois Millet? He was an artist who lived in the nineteenth century in France. He belonged to the Naturalist and Realist movements, and he also used bright colors, so that sort of makes him similar to Van Gogh. I think that you'll like examining his work. And, as an added bonus, one of the small art galleries in the city is currently exhibiting a few of his paintings, so you'll get a chance to see some of them up close and personal.

M1: Er, all right. I've never heard of that guy, but I guess I can write my paper on him. Oh, what's the name of the art gallery, sir?

M2: Hold on . . . I've got a brochure for it right here . . . Got it . . . That's got a little information about Millet in it, and you can see where the gallery is located. And if you have any more questions, feel free to visit me and ask them.

1 **Gist-Purpose Question** | The student declares, "I'm here to talk about the paper we are supposed to be writing for your class."

2 **Understanding Attitude Question** | The professor says, "I mean, you've seen the *Mona Lisa* before in countless images, right . . . ? Sure you have. But when you actually go to the Louvre in Paris and stand face to face with the *Mona Lisa* . . . Well, it's simply another experience." By saying that seeing it in person is "simply another experience," the professor indicates that the *Mona Lisa* looks better when viewed in person.

3 **Detail Question** | The professor suggests, "How about

writing your report on Jean-Francois Millet?" The student agrees with his suggestion.

4 **Detail Question** | The professor says, "I've got a brochure for it right here," and then he gives it to the student.

5 **Making Inferences Question** | At the end of the conversation, the professor says, "And if you have any more questions, feel free to visit me and ask them." So the professor is indicating that their conversation is over and that the student is going to leave his office.

Lecture 🎧 02-02 p.42

W Professor: Most of the world's cities started out as villages, grew to become towns, and eventually developed into large urban centers. Over the last few centuries, however, a great deal of effort has gone into planning urban areas. Some of the more well-known planned cities in modern times include Washington, D.C., St. Petersburg in Russia, and Canberra, the capital of Australia. Many newer cities have also been carefully planned, and urban developers nowadays are keeping busy by trying to modify older cities to make them more compatible with modern transportation systems and utilities. So, um, what I'd like to go over with you at this moment is some of the factors that are involved in urban planning, whether they're for a new city or an existing one that's being modernized.

Obviously, one of the greatest considerations for modern urban planning is geographical location. The terrain usually determines the type of city that gets built. Countless cities are near freshwater sources such as rivers and lakes while many others are near seas and oceans. Therefore, port facilities are needed in these cities if their citizens intend to engage in waterborne trade. Mountains pose challenges to building a city—as does swampy terrain—so both areas are generally avoided when possible. The type of soil is also important since the stability of buildings and infrastructure such as roads depends on good quality soil. Additionally, many older cities were built in the shadows of volcanoes or in regions prone to earthquakes, hurricanes, or tornadoes. Buildings in these cities must be constructed to withstand shaking and high winds, and other measures must be considered to prevent damage from various natural disasters.

A second consideration is access to transportation links. In the past, traveling by sea and on rivers and lakes was the fastest and most efficient means of transportation. Now, however, most modern cities have access to highway networks, railway systems, and airports. The ease of transportation to and from a city is a major consideration, so connecting a city to these transportation systems is vital. If an airport or railway station is too far from a city, it will inconvenience many of its citizens. Yet most people have little desire to live too close to an airport because of noise and traffic factors, so placing an airport neither too far from nor too near a city is important as well.

What else is there . . . ? Ah, highways. Well, if major highways pass through residential areas, this can result in excessive noise pollution. But within the city, there must be convenient ways to get around. These include roads and also subways and aboveground rail systems, which often take major portions of a modern city's people to and from work. Facilities for these forms of transportation need to be well planned and maintained. But they can't interfere with the roads that carry private forms of transportation such as cars and trucks. I think you're beginning to see how complicated this can be, aren't you?

Another factor that needs to be taken into account when planning or modernizing a city is zoning laws. These are laws that keep the major types of urban areas separate from one another in order to improve the quality of life in a city. What kinds of zones are there . . . ? Well, there are residential zones, where people live in houses and apartments. There are commercial zones, which have offices and shopping areas. Let's see . . . Industrial zones have factories, warehouses, and port facilities, and recreational zones have parks, stadiums, and places where people can enjoy the outdoors. Ah, and areas near cities may be agricultural zones for farming.

M Student: Professor Jackson, what about suburbs? Are they a type of zone?

W: No, Jim, they're not. Suburbs are merely small towns or cities that develop outside the city limits of a larger metropolitan area. Initially, the majority of them were unplanned, but, in the past few decades, many suburbs have been extensively planned prior to being constructed. This has made it easier to construct shopping and educational facilities in more convenient locations.

Now, there's one more consideration that's rather important for urban planning these days. It's the consideration of environmental factors. Pollution is a problem in all urban areas due to their high population densities, large numbers of industries in the cities, and the motor vehicles that people drive in them. [11]In addition, when a city has lots of tall buildings in a small area—like, uh, Manhattan in New York City—well, a great deal of pollution can get trapped in the city due to a lack of air flow. These buildings can cause the temperatures in cities to rise due to something called urban heat island. **But we'll get to that in a bit.** Anyway, urban designers try to mitigate environmental concerns by spacing tall buildings apart, planting trees and rooftop gardens, and studying wind-flow patterns. They're not always successful, but they're getting better at it all the time.

6 **Gist-Content Question** | During her lecture, the professor describes a number of different factors that urban planners have to think about while designing cities.

7 **Detail Question** | According to the professor, many cities are located near water while the soil must be taken into consideration when founding a city. However, many cities are not built in the mountains, and it is false that people do not build cities in regions that get earthquakes.

8 **Making Inferences Question** | The professor states, "If an airport or railway station is too far from a city, it will inconvenience many of its citizens. Yet most people have little desire to live too close to an airport because of noise and traffic factors, so placing an airport neither too far from nor too near a city is important as well." So she implies that airports are not built within the city limits of large urban centers because of the noise and traffic problems they create.

9 **Understanding Organization Question** | During her lecture, the professor goes over the various factors involved in urban planning one by one.

10 **Detail Question** | About suburbs, the professor tells the class, "Initially, the majority of them were unplanned, but, in the past few decades, many suburbs have been extensively planned prior to being constructed."

11 **Understanding Function Question** | When the professor says, "We'll get to that in a bit," when talking about urban heat island, she is implying that she does not want to talk about it now but will discuss it later in the class.

PART 2

Conversation 🎧 02-03   p.46

M Librarian: Good afternoon, Anna. It's nice to finally get a chance to meet you in person.

W Student: I feel the same way, Mr. Geller. And thank you very much for taking some time to talk to me. I'm sure that you must be very busy running the school's library system, so I really appreciate what you're doing now.

M: Well, sure, I'm busy, but I don't mind making time to speak with the president of the school's student body. So, Anna, did my last email clear up all of your questions?

W: Well . . . not exactly.

M: All right. Could you be a little more specific in that case, please?

W: Yes, I can do that . . . First, I'm not quite sure about the plan for the remodeling of the library that has been proposed. I mean, um, the school doesn't have that many funds available, and this remodeling is going to cost a huge amount of money. I believe the figure was one point three million dollars, right? Lots of students that I have spoken with have complained about the cost. They think it's simply too much money. And as their elected representative, it's my job to talk to you about these costs so that I can learn about them and then report back to the students.

M: I'm glad to see you're acting in a responsible manner for the students. Not all student body presidents in the past would have even bothered to meet with me concerning this matter. Anyway, yes, your number is correct. It's one point three million.

W: Okay. So could you tell me, um, tell me exactly what kind of remodeling the library is going to do with all that money?

M: No problem. First, we're going to replace all of the chairs and desks in the entire library. The replacement chairs are going to be much more comfortable for students to sit in. We're also going to get new computers as well as updated audio-visual machinery. Finally, the entire library is going to get a paint job. The interior of the library I mean. We're not doing anything with the exterior.

W: [5]**I definitely understand the need to upgrade the computers and the audio-visual machinery.** But I have no complaints about the chairs and desks. So, er, why are we replacing them?

M: Actually, there have been lots of complaints about them by both students and faculty members. Because of that, we thought we'd make things more comfortable for all of our patrons.

W: Why not take that money and use it for some other purposes?

M: Like what?

W: We could expand the library. I mean, if we really want our school to become a world-class institution, we need a

much larger library. No offense of course.

M: None taken. Believe me when I say that I like your idea. I'd love to expand the library. However, we'd need, oh . . . ten or twenty million dollars to do that. We've only got a little over a million, so we can't even consider enlarging this place.

W: Oh, I wasn't aware it would cost that much.

M: Yeah. Look. Let me show you an itemized list of the prices we're going to pay, and then you can see what I'm talking about.

W: Great. That might give me a better understanding of what exactly the money is being spent on.

---

1 **Gist-Purpose Question** | The student says, "I'm not quite sure about the plan for the remodeling of the library that has been proposed," and, "And as their elected representative, it's my job to talk to you about these costs so that I can learn about them and then report back to the students."

2 **Detail Question** | The student comments, "Lots of students that I have spoken with have complained about the cost. They think it's simply too much money."

3 **Detail Question** | The student tells the librarian, "We could expand the library. I mean, if we really want our school to become a world-class institution, we need a much larger library."

4 **Understanding Attitude Question** | The librarian is polite to the student during the conversation and also treats her with respect.

5 **Understanding Function Question** | When the student says she understands why the computers in the library are getting upgraded, she is implying that they are inadequate and need to be upgraded.

Lecture 🎧 02-04 p.48

M Professor: Plants require three things in order to survive. They are sunlight, water, and good soil. It's the third element—soil—that I want to discuss with you at this moment. There are a couple of important questions that need answering . . . First, what properties of soil are beneficial to plants . . . ? Next, how do plants benefit soil . . . ?

Let's take these questions in the order in which I asked them. There are thirteen varieties of soil nutrients.

They can all be divided into two groups: macronutrients and micronutrients. Macronutrients can be further broken down into primary and secondary macronutrients. There are three primary macronutrients. They are nitrogen, phosphorus, and potassium. All plants require these in order to grow. Unfortunately, when the soil becomes oversaturated with plants that extract nutrients from the soil while putting none back in, these three macronutrients can be rapidly depleted. As for the secondary macronutrients, they are calcium, magnesium, and sulfur. They're not as vital to plant growth and rarely get depleted from the soil. The micronutrients, by the way, are boron, copper, iron, chloride, manganese, molybdenum, and zinc. They're used in small amounts by plants. In fact, they're utilized in such minute quantities that they're virtually never totally removed from the soil.

All nutrients play roles in helping plants grow and remain strong and healthy. Let me tell you about some of them . . . Nitrogen is perhaps the most important nutrient for plant growth. It's an essential part of the green chlorophyll that plants must use in order to undergo photosynthesis. Nitrogen is also essential for speedy plant growth and for increasing the sizes of plants' leaves, fruits, and seeds. Phosphorus contributes to the developing of the roots of plants and the strengthening of plants themselves. Both of these are crucial in that they, uh, they let plants remain anchored to the ground and keep them from collapsing due to their weight. And potassium has a role in photosynthesis while also helping plants fight diseases.

[10]C-c-calcium . . . **Excuse me.** Calcium, meanwhile, is important to the cell wall structures of plants and helps prevent plants from absorbing too much salt and acid. Magnesium is another nutrient needed for photosynthesis and plant growth. Sulfur plays many roles. Let's see . . . [11]It helps plant and seed growth, it increases root strength, it provides protection from cold weather, and it has several other functions. **The micronutrients play essential roles as well. You can take a look at them in your textbooks on page 203.** Okay?

W Student: Professor Reed, where do nutrients come from?

M: Most occur naturally in the soil. They also get replenished in natural ways. For example, nitrogen is replenished through a cycle in which organic matter in the ground is converted to nitrogen that plants need. Many plants in the legume family, which includes soybeans, are able to replace nitrogen in the soil through bacteria that they carry. But in modern high-tech farming, lots of nutrients come from chemical fertilizers. They're effective, but the problem is that they're just chemicals, so they can cause long-term environmental problems when used excessively.

Yet there's often a need for fertilizers. This arises when too many plants take too many nutrients out of the soil without putting anything back. You see, um, if you grow the same plants—say wheat or corn—in the same field year after year, these plants will extract so many nutrients to the point that there will be little or no nutrients left, and then the plants won't grow properly. Historically, farmers learned how to replenish the soil through trial and error. For centuries, they commonly practiced crop rotation. This meant that they left one field out of three fallow . . . uh, that means unplanted . . . so that the field would have time to recuperate. Yet this practice was uneconomical because farmers doing this sort of crop rotation had to leave a third of their fields empty. Over time, farmers learned to grow crops like clover, which replace nutrients, in their fields rather than merely leaving them fallow. Clover could be used as feed for livestock, so growing it benefitted the farmers.

A better method than crop rotation is to grow certain crops together in the same fields. For instance, when the Europeans arrived in the New World, they discovered that the Native Americans had developed a three-crop system utilizing, um, corn, beans, and squash. They grew all three in mixed gardens in such a way that each plant benefitted from the others. The corn had tall stalks that the bean plants could climb and therefore used to get more sunlight. The corn removed nitrogen from the soil, but the bean plants replaced much of the lost nitrogen. The squash had numerous vines that sprawled across the ground, and the shade they created helped keep the soil moist. The European colonists, meanwhile, often grew tobacco in the same fields year after year, which quickly depleted the soil. It took them quite a while to learn that they should avoid doing that.

6 **Gist-Content Question** | The majority of the lecture describes the various nutrients that plants need in order to live.

7 **Connecting Content Question** | According to the lecture, nitrogen, phosphorus, and potassium are three macronutrients. There are also both primary and secondary macronutrients, and they are easily removed from the soil. As for micronutrients, plants only use them in small amounts.

8 **Detail Question** | The professor states, "Nitrogen is also essential for speedy plant growth and for increasing the sizes of plants' leaves, fruits, and seeds."

9 Understanding Organization Question | About crop rotation, the professor notes, "Historically, farmers learned how to replenish the soil through trial and error. For centuries, they commonly practiced crop rotation. This meant that they left one field out of three fallow . . . uh, that means unplanted . . . so that the field would have time to recuperate."

10 Understanding Function Question | Before stating, "Excuse me," the professor stutters while trying to say the word "calcium." By saying, "Excuse me," he is apologizing for stuttering.

11 Making Inferences Question | When the professor tells the students to look at the roles of micronutrients in their books, he is implying that he will not tell the class about their roles during his lecture.

Lecture 🎧 02-05   p.51

M Professor: Something that can often result from the bending and folding of the Earth's crust is what we geologists refer to as a fall line. And, uh, no, I'm not referring to the latest men's and women's fashions for autumn. Instead, um, a fall line refers to a place where one area of hard rock and one of softer rock are separated by a cliff-like boundary. This boundary is the fall line. The hard rock is typically metamorphic or igneous rock while the softer rock is normally some type of sedimentary rock.

The cliff-like boundary is the result of two factors. First, a fault occurs. This is a bending or folding of the ground. As you should remember from our class on earthquakes, faults can occur suddenly, or they can happen over longer periods of time. When a fault occurs, harder rock is pushed up while the softer rock remains at its original level. Once this happens, then the second factor, which increases the difference in the levels of the two types of rocks, comes into play. The second factor is erosion. Erosion wears away the rocks in both areas, but it works more quickly on the softer sedimentary rocks, so this level is lowered even further.

The speed of erosion can be increased by the presence of flowing water, uh, such as a river or stream. This is actually one of the more noticeable aspects of a fall line. In places where the cliff-like boundary exists, there may be many waterfalls if a river or stream cuts across the fall line. Sometimes, um, these waterfalls take on a curved shape as the water slowly erodes the rock back away from the edge of the cliff-like fall line. Now, I keep using the term "cliff-like," but please keep in mind that

the boundary is not always as sharp as the steep drop of a cliff. In fact, it may be much gentler. The boundary may also be relatively short in length, or it can run for hundreds of kilometers.

[16]The eastern part of North America has several prominent fall lines. **These formed as a result of a period of extensive mountain building that happened approximately 400 mil- . . . uh, no . . . 440 million years ago.** During this time, the land was constantly being folded, bent, and pushed up as long mountain ranges formed near the east coast. Most of these mountains are now mere shadows of their former heights since erosion has considerably reduced them in size. But one legacy of this mountain-building period is the creation of numerous fall lines. One obvious example is the fall line that Niagara Falls is located on. That's a dramatic example of the sharp difference between the upper level of hard rock and the lower level of softer rock existing along an escarpment. Other such fall lines are found in Quebec and New England. Yet the most prominent fall line in North America exists along the eastern seaboard of the United States. It runs from New Jersey all the way down to the Carolinas, a distance covering more than 1,400 kilometers. There, the gentle coastal plain meets the Appalachian Mountains on a very sharp fall line.

Look at the map in your books . . . It's on page eighty-two. This will show you where the fall line is located. The higher escarpment is colored in red . . . while the coastal plain is colored in yellow. [17]Now, who can tell me something significant by looking at this map . . . ? Go ahead, Louise.

W Student: A lot of towns and cities seem to be located right on the fall line.

M: Good eye, Louise. You noticed that rather quickly. She's right, class. Take a look at the map . . . We can see Trenton, Newark, Philadelphia, Baltimore, Georgetown, Richmond, and several other cities along the fall line. There's a reason for this. You see, this fall line in the eastern U.S. is crossed by a great number of streams and rivers, including several major ones. Among them are the Raritan and Delaware rivers in New Jersey, the Potomac River on the Maryland-Virginia border, and the Rappahannock River in Virginia. These great rivers—and many smaller ones—create a large number of waterfalls. Why, you may ask, are waterfalls so important . . . ? Well, when colonists began building towns and cities in America in the seventeenth and eighteenth centuries, they had no sources of power other than animals, wind, and water. Falling water therefore became a significant resource. It could power sawmills and mills that ground grain. Later, falling water was used to run early textile factories. So many industries—and also towns and cities—in colonial times developed nearby sources of falling water along fall lines.

Another thing to remember is that ships could travel no further upriver or upstream than the fall line. Consequently, the fall lines became the deepest points of penetration of the American wilderness during colonial times. Eventually, locks that could raise and lower boats were built in some locations so that ships could head further inland. However, for the most part, the fall line was, er, the end of the line for travel by ship in previous centuries.

12 **Detail Question** | The professor states, "The cliff-like boundary is the result of two factors. First, a fault occurs. This is a bending or folding of the ground. As you should remember from our class on earthquakes, faults can occur suddenly, or they can happen over longer periods of time. When a fault occurs, harder rock is pushed up while the softer rock remains at its original level. Once this happens, then the second factor, which increases the difference in the levels of the two types of rocks, comes into play. The second factor is erosion."

13 **Making Inferences Question** | The professor notes, "Now, I keep using the term "cliff-like," but please keep in mind that the boundary is not always as sharp as the steep drop of a cliff. In fact, it may be much gentler." Thus the professor implies that cliff-like fall lines do not all look the same.

14 **Understanding Organization Question** | About Niagara Falls, the professor mentions, "One obvious example is the fall line that Niagara Falls is located on. That's a dramatic example of the sharp difference between the upper level of hard rock and the lower level of softer rock existing along an escarpment."

15 **Gist-Purpose Question** | The professor explains, "Why, you may ask, are waterfalls so important . . . ? Well, when colonists began building towns and cities in America in the seventeenth and eighteenth centuries, they had no sources of power other than animals, wind, and water. Falling water therefore became a significant resource. It could power sawmills and mills that ground grain. Later, falling water was used to run early textile factors. So many industries—and also towns and cities—in colonial times developed nearby sources of falling water along fall lines."

16 **Understanding Function Question** | The professor misspeaks, so he corrects himself by providing the correct number.

17 **Understanding Function Question** | When the professor tells the student that she did a good job and "noticed that rather quickly," he is praising her and therefore giving her a compliment.

Actual Test 03

p.55

Answers

PART 1

1 Ⓑ   2 Ⓐ   3 Ⓓ   4 Ⓐ   5 Ⓐ
6 Ⓐ   7 Ⓒ   8 Ⓑ   9 Primitive Humanoids:
③ Austronesians: ①, ②, ④   10 Ⓒ   11 Ⓐ

PART 2

1 Ⓒ   2 Ⓐ   3 ②, ④   4 Ⓐ   5 Ⓒ
6 Ⓐ   7 Ⓑ   8 Telephone Survey: ④   Mail
Survey: ①   Online Survey: ②, ③   9 Ⓒ   10 Ⓑ
11 Ⓑ   12 Ⓑ   13 Ⓓ   14 Ⓓ   15 Ⓐ
16 Ⓒ   17 Ⓐ

PART 3

1 ①, ④   2 Ⓑ   3 Ⓑ   4 Ⓐ   5 Ⓒ
6 Ⓓ   7 Ⓒ   8 ①, ③   9 Ⓐ   10 Ⓒ
11 Ⓓ

Scripts & Answers

PART 1

Conversation 🎧 03-01

p.58

W Student: [5]Professor Taylor, you're still here. That's good news. I'm, uh, here for our three thirty meeting.

M Professor: Ah, yes, Margaret. **I thought for a moment that you might not show up today.** I was worried you had forgotten.

W: Oh, yeah. Er . . . Sorry about that. I got caught up speaking with Professor Madison after my Greek history class, so that's why I'm just showing up now. I apologize.

M: It's all right. Since you were talking to another professor about your schoolwork, I consider that to be an acceptable excuse.

W: Thank you very much for saying that.

M: All right. Why don't you have a seat now, and we can get started?

W: Okay.

M: Now, I wanted to speak with you today for a specific reason.

W: Yes?

M: It concerns the presentation you just gave in class. I'm curious . . . Where did you get the idea for it? Did you get it from a magazine? Or a website perhaps?

W: Uh, no. To be totally honest, I came up with it myself. Um . . . my presentation was all right, wasn't it?

M: It was perfectly fine. In fact, it got the highest grade in the class . . . By the way, don't tell anyone I said that, please. I won't be giving back grades until next week. But I thought you might like to know how well you did.

W: Definitely. I can't believe I did that well.

M: Well, believe it because it's true. Now, I have another question for you . . . You're not an art history major, are you?

W: No, sir. I'm currently majoring in English literature. My main focus is on writers from the Renaissance, but I also enjoy reading works from different periods. Why do you ask?

M: I'm not sure how good you are at English, but you're outstanding at art history. Have you ever considered changing majors? I mean, the presentation you gave in my class showed that you clearly have an eye for art. Not only that, but you also gave rather sophisticated interpretations of the paintings you spoke about. I thought your interpretations were much better than those of the other students in our class, and some of them are graduate students in the Art History Department.

W: Gee, what a nice thing for you to say. But to answer your question, no, I've never really thought about majoring in art history. Art is something I've always enjoyed though. I like going to galleries and browsing through art books whenever I have time. But majoring in it? No, the thought hadn't ever crossed my mind.

M: Well, it ought to have because I believe you'd make a good art historian. Tell me . . . This isn't your first art history class, right?

W: That's correct. Since my freshman year here, I've taken, um . . . three . . . ? No, four art history classes.

M: And you're a junior, right?

W: That's correct.

M: So I suppose majoring in art history is out of the question. However, you may not be aware of this, but we

offer a minor in art history now. You only need to take five classes to get a minor, and you're almost there. Why don't I give you some information concerning how to minor in the field?

W: Uh, sure. I suppose I can look at it.

1   **Gist-Purpose Question** | As for the reason why he asked to see her, the professor tells the student, "It concerns the presentation you just gave in class."

2   **Detail Question** | About her presentation, the professor comments, "In fact, it got the highest grade in the class."

3   **Making Inferences Question** | The professor states, "I thought your interpretations were much better than those of the other students in our class, and some of them are graduate students in the Art History Department." In saying that, he implies that the student is better than some of the graduate students in his class.

4   **Understanding Attitude Question** | The professor wants the student to think about getting a minor in art history when he tells her, "However, you may not be aware of this, but we offer a minor in art history now. You only need to take five classes to get a minor, and you're almost there. Why don't I give you some information concerning how to minor in the field?"

5   **Understanding Function Question** | When the professor tells the student that he thought she might not show up for their meeting, he is implying that she is late for the meeting.

Lecture 🎧 03-02   p.60

W Professor: What I'd like to cover with you next is Bali, one of the smaller islands in the Indonesian archipelago. Today, it's a major tourist destination in Asia mostly on account of its spectacular scenery and beaches. But that's not what I'm going to talk about. Instead, I'd like to examine the history of the people of the island, and, in order to do that, we have to go back to the distant past.

Anthropologists have determined that a primitive form of one of humanity's ancestors lived on Bali about one million years ago. These humanoids utilized basic stone tools and dwelled in caves on the island. They were most likely related to the Java Man specimen that was found on the nearby large island of Java. As for how these humanoids got to Bali, that's easy. While it's an island today, at various times in the past, Bali was connected to some of the other islands in the region when the sea level was lower. It was during one of these periods that some groups of primitive humanoids simply walked to Bali. Over hundreds of thousands of years, they evolved into more intelligent creatures and became more advanced in both their hunting and food-gathering methods. We know this since some of the artifacts unearthed on Bali include axe-like stone tools, arrow and spear points, and bone tools.

For thousands of years, these humanoids dominated the area around Bali. Then, around forty or fifty thousand years ago, anatomically correct modern humans arrived in the region. Gradually, they outcompeted the remnants of any primitive humanoids that still lived there. Actually, that's what we think happened. But those humanoids may have already been extinct by then. The fossil record isn't very clear about that. Anyway, these anatomically correct modern humans that arrived also went to New Guinea and Australia, where their descendants still live today. Then, around five thousand years ago, a new group of people moved to the Indonesian islands, including Bali. Archaeologists call these people Austronesians. The Austronesians were lighter skinned, had straighter hair, and were more Oriental looking than the first people on Bali, who had darker skin and curlier hair. These Austronesians are thought to have originated in mainland China. Afterward, they moved to Taiwan, then, they went to the Philippines, and, after that, they moved south to Indonesia. From there, they moved to various Pacific islands.

These Austronesians brought knowledge of agriculture, including how to farm rice, with them, and they also brought domesticated pigs and chickens. On every Indonesian island they went to, they outcompeted those anatomically correct modern humans I just mentioned. Those humans were gradually pushed to the east and wound up settling in the islands in the Solomon chain. However, the people on New Guinea had already learned about agriculture, so they were able to prevent a complete takeover of the island by the Austronesians. This is particularly true of the people living in the island's mountainous interior. The Austronesians additionally had limited contact with Australia, so the Aborigines, who had arrived some forty thousand years previously, were able to dominate Australia until the Europeans arrived.

On Bali, these new settlers developed agriculture to a great extent. Bali is a volcanic island, so its soil is quite good for growing crops, which made them be rather productive farmers. These settlers were still using Stone Age tools and weapons when they arrived on Bali. However, they gradually acquired bronze tools and weapons around 600 B.C. I say "acquired" because

bronze is made from tin and copper, but there was no source of either metal on Bali that was known to these people. How did they get these bronze tools and weapons then? Some speculate that the finished items were imported while others claim that the tin and copper were imported and the Balinese then made the bronze works themselves. No one knows for sure. But we have learned that the techniques for making bronze items on Bali were similar to those made in Vietnam, which suggests that there was trade between the Indonesians and Vietnamese.

Starting around 600 B.C., the Balinese people experienced a millennium of relative peace. Over time though, contacts with the outside world began to influence them. The Balinese were mostly influenced by India. They imported religion from India in the guise of both Buddhism and Hinduism, and they imported writing from India, too. Oh, I'm sure many of you know that Indonesia is a Muslim country today. Nevertheless, the influence of Hinduism and Buddhism remains strong on Bali. Many people there still practice a form of Hinduism that's slightly different from the Indian variety. But I believe that's a topic we can cover in detail later when we talk about various religions in Indonesia. [11] Instead of talking about religion, I want to continue discussing the Bronze Age culture that developed in Bali . . . Oh, goodness. I just looked at my watch and realized we've gone over time. **Why don't we wrap things up for today, and we'll continue discussing Bali in Thursday's class?** How does that sound to everyone?

6 **Gist-Content Question** | During her lecture, the professor mostly focuses on the humanoids and humans that once lived on Bali.

7 **Understanding Organization Question** | The professor states, "These humanoids utilized basic stone tools and dwelled in caves on the island. They were most likely related to the Java Man specimen that was found on the nearby large island of Java."

8 **Making Inferences Question** | The professor mentions that the Austronesians arrived in Bali around 5,000 years ago. Then, she says, "These Austronesians brought knowledge of agriculture, including how to farm rice, with them, and they also brought domesticated pigs and chickens." So it can be inferred that agriculture on Bali began around 5,000 years ago.

9 **Connecting Content Question** | According to the lecture, primitive humanoids went to Bali by walking on land bridges when sea levels were low. As for the Austronesians, they brought agriculture to Bali when

they arrived, they used bronze tools and weapons, and they had light skin and straight hair.

10 **Understanding Function Question** | The professor tells the class, "Over time though, contacts with the outside world began to influence them. The Balinese were mostly influenced by India. They imported religion from India in the guise of both Buddhism and Hinduism, and they imported writing from India, too."

11 **Understanding Attitude Question** | When a person says, "Why don't we wrap things up for today?" that individual wants to stop whatever activity is going on. So the professor means that she wants to stop teaching class.

PART 2

Conversation 🎧 03-03   p.64

M Student: Good afternoon, Ms. Chapman. My name is Ray Sanders. I scheduled an appointment with you for this time.

W Guidance Counselor: Ah, yes. Hello, Ray. Please come into my office and have a seat.

M: Thank you very much.

W: It's my pleasure. So, Ray, what exactly would you like to talk to me about today?

M: It's about my future. I'm, uh . . . Okay. Let me give you a little background about myself. I'm a senior majoring in history. I've made the Dean's List for the past four semesters, and I should graduate with honors. I don't particularly want to go to graduate school. Instead, I would prefer to get a job as soon as I graduate. Now, I've heard that there are a couple of job fairs here on campus coming up in the next month . . .

W: Yes, that's correct. Tell me, Ray . . . What kind of job are you looking for?

M: To be honest . . . I-I-I just don't know.

W: Well, may I assume that you're keeping your options open then?

M: So long as the job pays me a regular salary, I'm willing to do just about anything.

W: Okay. It's good that you're open minded about that. Now, you must have some idea as to what sort of work you'd like to do.

M: Hmm . . . Something in finance would be nice. Or a job with a consulting company would be acceptable to me as well.

W: All right. We're narrowing things down now. In that case, you should definitely attend the job fair that is going to be held two weeks from this Saturday. [4]It's the smaller of the two job fairs, but there will be a decent number of companies in the financial industry that are sending representatives there. You can attend the larger one as well, but that's going to be full of companies looking for engineers, computer programmers, and science majors.

M: Er . . . **Perhaps I'll take a pass on that one then.**

W: Okay. That makes sense. Now, you need to do a few things in order to get ready for the job fair. First—and most important—of all, you need to have a résumé.

M: Oh, I made my résumé a while ago. I don't need to worry about that.

W: Did you get it professionally done? Because that's crucial. That's how you're going to be introducing yourself to potential employers, so you want your résumé to be both mistake free and to look as good as possible. Sure, it will cost a bit of money, but if you land a job, it will have been worth the investment.

M: I never considered that. Okay. Thanks for the tip. I'll contact an agency and get that taken care of. Is there anything else I ought to do?

W: Yes, there is. You aren't planning to wear clothes like that to the job fair, are you?

M: What's wrong with a pair of slacks and a button-down shirt?

W: [5]Ray, you absolutely must wear a suit and tie to the job fair. Be as well groomed as possible, too. If you want to make an excellent first impression, you'll dress up as nicely as you can. That's the best advice that I can give you.

M: **I guess I'll have to buy a suit then.** Thanks for the advice. I really appreciate your telling me all of this.

1 **Gist-Purpose Question** | When the guidance counselor asks the student why he is there, he responds by saying, "I would prefer to get a job as soon as I graduate. Now, I've heard that there are a couple of job fairs here on campus coming up in the next month."

2 **Understanding Function Question** | Before the student tells the guidance counselor about himself, he states, "Let me give you a little background about myself."

3 **Detail Question** | The student declares, "Something in finance would be nice. Or a job with a consulting company would be acceptable to me as well."

4 **Understanding Attitude Question** | When a person "takes a pass on" something, it means that the individual

will not do that action. So the student is saying that he will not go to the larger job fair.

5   **Making Inferences Question** | The guidance counselor tells the student to get a suit so that he can look nice for the job fair. When the student responds, "I guess I'll have to buy a suit then," he is implying that he has accepted the guidance counselor's advice.

Lecture 🎧 03-04   p.66

M1 Professor: We need to turn our attention to marketing surveys before we finish up for the day. All right . . . ? Good. A marketing survey is a way to get information about people, which helps a business make better products or sell more products and services. Marketing surveys ask all kinds of questions. Some inquire about personal information such as, um, a person's gender, race, income, marital status, job, and education. [11]Other questions may be concerned with a person's spending habits, the products and services typically used, and the person's willingness to use new products. Naturally, marketing surveys ask questions about specific products and services that companies offer. **There are a number of different types of surveys, so let me go over some of them with you in brief.**

The first is the store survey. It's used to find out if a customer is satisfied with a store's products or services and with certain customer service aspects. An in-store survey may ask a customer to test a product and to give some, uh, feedback on it. This may include doing a taste test of some food or drink and then giving an opinion on it. I think that if any of you shop at large supermarkets with any regularity, you've probably taken part in this kind of survey.

Another common type of marketing survey is the telephone survey. It provides several advantages for the company doing the survey. It's relatively cheap since most phone charges are fairly low these days. Of course, the company has to hire and train people to conduct the surveys, or it must enlist the help of a professional survey company, so that can be a little pricey. Nevertheless, phone surveys allow companies to reach a broad demographic of males and females as well as people of different races and economic backgrounds. They also provide instant feedback. The main problem with them is that people often refuse to respond to them. People frequently simply hang up the phone when marketing surveyors call them. It's a frustrating job. I did it many

years ago when I was a student. A second problem is that some people don't give honest answers. Some people just give whatever answer comes to mind in order to end the survey as quickly as possible. A third disadvantage is that the survey is audio only, so a person cannot test or see any of the products.

Next is the mail survey. People are sent these surveys, uh, which are really just questionnaires, in the mail and are asked to complete them and to mail them back to the senders by using a postage-paid envelope. This type of survey is relatively cheap but involves some amount of effort and lots of paper and envelopes. One major disadvantage is that response times are slow as weeks or even months may pass before all the surveys arrive back at the company. And many people don't bother filling the surveys out but merely throw them away. I must confess that I've done that quite a bit myself. To counter this, companies nowadays provide small free samples of their products in the mail in the hope that people will feel obligated to complete the surveys and return them. Other companies offer rebates or coupons if people fill out and return the surveys.

Online surveys are gaining popularity these days. Most of you probably see them every day while surfing the Internet. A small popup ad appears on your screen and asks you to take some time to answer some questions. The main advantage of this type of survey is that it can reach a broad range of customers. It's also relatively cheap since it only has to be set up, and then a system needs to be made to take the data and to crunch the numbers. People who take online surveys tend to be more honest than those doing phone surveys since they choose to click on the survey popup and therefore opt to answer the questions. These people often take their time and consider their answers, which makes their responses valuable. Additionally, online surveys can be directed toward niche markets by being placed on specific websites. Their major problem is that they don't reach all demographics. People without computers or Internet access, such as many elderly individuals, are always underrepresented on online surveys.

M2 Student: How can marketers reach people without telephones or Internet access and who refuse to do mail surveys?

M1: There's one last chance: the at-home survey. For this, an interviewer goes door to door and asks people to do a survey. The main advantage with this is that the face-to-face contact tends to elicit more honest responses for those surveyed. But it costs a lot since the people conducting the surveys need to be trained and paid. And many people refuse to participate since they don't like opening the door for strangers. Okay. That's all we have time for today. Are there any questions?

6 **Detail Question** | The professor mentions, "An in-store survey may ask a customer to test a product and to give some, uh, feedback on it. This may include doing a taste test of some food or drink and then giving an opinion on it."

7 **Gist-Purpose Question** | The professor talks about telephone surveys to discuss a particular kind of survey.

8 **Connecting Content Question** | According to the lecture, telephone surveys are cheap. As for mail surveys, there are slow response times to them. In addition, online surveys do not represent all demographics, but they have become popular in recent years.

9 **Connecting Content Question** | When talking about telephone and online surveys, the professor mentions the honesty of the people who respond to them.

10 **Making Inferences Question** | The professor says, "That's all we have time for today. Are there any questions?" So he will probably let the class out for the day.

11 **Understanding Function Question** | When the professor says that he will go over some of the different types of surveys, he is implying that he will not discuss every type of survey that people utilize.

Lecture 🎧 03-05   p.69

M Professor: Animals can further be subdivided by both the foods they consume and their overall eating habits. Here are some you should be aware of . . . Some animals only eat plants, some only eat meat, and others eat both. Many animals eat virtually anything while others are pickier and consume only certain types of food. Some animals only hunt and eat at night while others do these activities in the daytime. And many animals eat food wherever they acquire it, but some take it to a different location before eating it. There are benefits and drawbacks to all these types of behavior, and we're going to go over them in detail right now.

So, uh, the easiest and most common way to distinguish animals is by which foods they eat. We can classify them as herbivores, carnivores, and omnivores.

Herbivores only eat plants. Examples of them include a wide variety of mammals, such as horses, cows, sheep, deer, and rabbits. Pure herbivores are rarer among other classes of animals as most fish, reptiles, birds, and amphibians must consume meat to get enough energy. Carnivores, of course, are meat eaters. Examples of them are found in all classes of animals. Some carnivores that often come to most people's minds are lions, tigers, wolves, and sharks, all of which are large predators. Omnivores are animals that eat both plants and meat. They're considered opportunistic eaters since they'll consume practically anything. Rats, pigs, bears, chimpanzees, and many species of birds are omnivores. Humans, as you well know, are also omnivores.

We can further divide animals according to whether they search for food during the daytime or at night. Diurnal animals are those that are active during the day, and nocturnal animals are those that are active at night and therefore hunt and feed then. Owls and snakes are two nocturnal animals many people are familiar with. How can these animals see in the dark? Well, owls—along with many other night creatures—have keen eyesight that enables them to see in the dark. As for snakes, they are able to sense changes in temperatures, so they can home in on living creatures and attack them by sensing their body heat.

Animals also act differently according to where they eat their food. Some animals consume their food right where they acquire it. For instance, a carnivore that makes a kill typically eats its prey on the spot. You've probably all seen documentaries on TV that show lions taking down an animal and then eating right where they killed it. Wolves engage in identical behavior. Yet other species of animals bring back parts of the animals they kill to wherever their groups or family units live so that the members that don't hunt can eat. As for herbivores, most of them eat their food wherever they find it. Grazing animals such as, uh, such as horses, cows, and sheep have little choice since they're unable to carry food anywhere. Yet other herbivores take their food elsewhere. Kangaroo rats do this. They take their food to a secure location where they can eat without having to fear being attacked by predators. Many species of birds gather food for their offspring, so they transport it to their nests. Some birds can even regurgitate food they've eaten so that they can feed their young with it.

A final distinction we can make about animals and food concerns those creatures that consume multiple types of food and those that only eat a single type. Animals that have many food sources can survive in a wide range of environments. They also have greater food security since if one food source runs out, they can consume a different one. Bears, for instance, eat berries and various plants, but they also eat fish and other kinds of meat. So when one food source is in short supply, bears simply look for another. Yet those animals that eat just one type of food can suffer disaster if that food source ever becomes exhausted. Koalas, which only eat eucalyptus leaves, are one such animal. If there are no eucalyptus leaves, the koalas in an area starve to death. In fact, koalas have evolved so that they're totally dependent upon eucalyptus leaves. Unfortunately for them, eucalyptus leaves provide them with little protein and energy, so koalas only move around three to five hours a day, and they do that just to feed. They spend the rest of their time either motionless or asleep.

W Student: Are they sort of, uh, sort of like hibernating animals when they do that?

M: Hmm . . . I suppose you could say they're doing something similar, but they aren't hibernating. You raise a good point though, Claudia. Many hibernating animals, like bears and bats, eat plenty of food and become fat prior to hibernating. Their metabolisms slow down so that their bodies can survive long periods of inactivity when they can't consume any food. Okay. Those are the major differences in the eating habits of animals. Do you have any more questions for me before we move along?

12 **Gist-Content Question** | The professor mostly discusses how different types of animals feed.

13 **Detail Question** | The professor explains, "Pure herbivores are rarer among other classes of animals as most fish, reptiles, birds, and amphibians must consume meat to get enough energy."

14 **Connecting Content Question** | About the two animals, the professor comments, "Owls and snakes are two nocturnal animals many people are familiar with. How can these animals see in the dark? Well, owls—along with many other night creatures—have keen eyesight that enables them to see in the dark. As for snakes, they are able to sense changes in temperatures, so they can home in on living creatures and attack them by sensing their body heat."

15 **Understanding Organization Question** | The professor tells the class, "You've probably all seen documentaries on TV that show lions taking down an animal and then eating right where they killed it."

16 **Making Inferences Question** | The professor explains, "Animals that have many food sources can survive in

a wide range of environments. They also have greater food security since if one food source runs out, they can consume a different one. Bears, for instance, eat berries and various plants, but they also eat fish and other kinds of meat. So when one food source is in short supply, bears simply look for another." So it can be inferred that bears, which eat many kinds of food, can live in a wide range of environments.

17 **Understanding Function Question** | A student asks if the inactivity of koalas is a type of hibernation, so the professor talks about hibernating animals to answer her question.

PART 3

Conversation 🎧 03-06   p.74

M Student: Professor Gregg, I wonder if I could have a few moments of your time. Are you busy now?

W Professor: Not at all, Tim. What's on your mind?

M: I was really fascinated by your discussion on alternative energy in class today. I was particularly interested in what you said about solar power.

W: Thank you. It's always nice knowing that students not only learn in my class but also enjoy what I lecture on.

M: I have a couple of questions though.

W: Sure.

M: First of all, I was under the impression that solar cell technology is not particularly efficient. As far as I'm aware, that's one of the major drawbacks to using solar power.

W: You're right about that being a major disadvantage. But you should know that in recent years, solar cells have increased in efficiency by a large amount. Back in the 1970s and 1980s, they had an efficiency rating of around ten percent. As you know, this means that they were only able to produce ten percent of the possible energy that was available to them.

M: How good are they today?

W: Some solar cells on the market have around twenty-two percent efficiency. In lab tests, a couple of solar cells have achieved more than twenty-five percent. But that was in extremely ideal circumstances. Right now, the objective is to reach twenty-nine percent efficiency.

M: Huh, I wasn't aware that they had improved so much.

W: They sure have. I believe they'll continue to get better as more research is done and better solar cells are developed.

M: Okay, thanks. One more question.

W: Of course.

M: [4]Is it true that people are developing solar roads? They can't possibly be real. **I mean, uh, that sounds like something out of a popular science-fiction novel.**

W: You know, um, many ideas that were first written about in sci-fi stories have become reality in recent times. And, uh, yes, it's actually true that there are solar roads being developed. They'd not only be able to produce energy during the day but would also be able to provide light at night and could melt snow that falls on them by producing heat.

M: Woah, that sounds cool.

W: It is, isn't it? However, right now, the cost of building solar roads is extremely high. We're talking about millions of dollars per kilometer of road. [5]Basically, we need better, stronger materials that can produce energy as well as avoid breaking due to being driven on by vehicles all day and night long.

M: Do you think that solar roads will exist in large numbers in the future?

W: **I'm extremely optimistic about the future.** In fact, I believe that within the next couple of decades, solar power technology will improve to such an extent that it will become much more common. As you should be aware, uh, since I mentioned it in class today, despite the fact that governments around the world are promoting alternative energy sources, they are still used very little in comparison to fossil fuels. However, when the technology gets better and cheaper, you'll see a dramatic move to solar power and a move away from fossil fuels.

M: I sure hope so. That's the kind of future that I'm interested in living in. Thanks so much for your time, Professor Gregg. This chat was really educational.

1   **Gist-Content Question** | The speakers mostly talk about how solar energy can be used and how effective solar cells are.

2   **Gist-Purpose Question** | First, the student says, "I was really fascinated by your discussion on alternative energy in class today. I was particularly interested in what you said about solar power." Then, he asks her a couple of questions about her lecture.

3   **Making Inferences Question** | At the end of the conversation, the student says, "Thanks so much for your time, Professor Gregg. This chat was really educational." Since he indicates that the conversation is over, he will probably leave the professor's office next.

4   **Understanding Attitude Question** | When the student

says that solar roads are like something out of a popular science-fiction novel, he is implying that he does not believe it is possible to make solar roads.

5   **Understanding Function Question** | In stating, "I'm extremely optimistic about the future," in response to the student's question about whether solar roads will exist in large numbers in the future, the professor is giving her opinion about the matter to the student.

Lecture 🎧 03-07   p.76

M Professor: If you're like me, you make a list of the things you need before you go shopping. As a general rule, I write down everything on a list and then try to stick to that list as much as possible. However, when I return home, there are almost always more things in my shopping bags than I had intended to purchase. So the question is this: Why do I buy these extra items? Do I suffer from a faulty memory and forget to add some items to my shopping list? Well, in some cases, that happens. My mind isn't as sharp as it once was. However, most of the extra items I purchase are ones I don't really have a need for. Nevertheless, they end up in my shopping cart, and I pay for them. The main reason I make these extra purchases is something called impulse shopping. It's caused by a number of psychological factors. And here's the worst part: Retail chains know about these factors, and they've found ways to make shoppers succumb to their impulses and buy unnecessary items.

So . . . what's the psychology behind impulse buying? First off, people often buy things to make themselves feel good. They see various items and buy them despite knowing they can't afford these products. Some individuals purchase products to boost their egos . . . Uh, you know, to show other people that they have nice possessions. And some people buy items to help relieve their stress. After all, making a spontaneous purchase acts as a stress reliever for numerous people.

Well, unfortunately for these people, businesses are increasingly taking advantage of certain psychological factors to ensure that more and more shoppers make impulse purchases. Businesses try to make it seem that purchasing something impulsively isn't negative. Instead, they attempt to make shoppers feel good about whatever they buy. There are a number of ways businesses go about doing this. Let me tell you a few of them. After doing so, I believe that, um, the next time you go shopping at your favorite store, you'll notice how what I'm about to tell you has been implemented there.

First and foremost, businesses strive to create in-store environments that make consumers want to purchase items. In these stores, the negative aspects of impulse buying are downplayed while the positive aspects are emphasized. How so . . . ? Let's see . . . Stores employ colorful window displays, ads showing people enjoying themselves while using certain products, and promotional slogans, among others. These play roles in getting people to feel good about making purchases. Stores also become enablers for impulse buyers by increasing their hours of operation, by making it easier for shoppers to obtain credit, and by allowing shoppers to exchange items if they're dissatisfied with the ones they buy. Supermarkets and convenience stores that are open twenty-four hours a day are examples of this. [10]So are slogans such as "100-percent satisfaction guaranteed or your money back." These catchphrases make people feel like they can make a purchase free of any risk to themselves. Think about it . . . **How many times have you heard that particular slogan?** Of course, the people running businesses know that, uh, even if people are unhappy with the products that they buy, most of them won't bother trying to get refunds.

Another important factor is that stores—both physical and online ones—have sales. After all, who can resist a sale . . . ? Sales frequently trigger a desire in people to buy products that they normally wouldn't. Pay attention at the supermarket the next time you go. Look for the offers that announce "buy one; get one free." Many times, people don't even need one of those products, but they wind up buying them because getting two items for the price of one seems like a great deal. Other times, companies offer excessive discounts that cause them to lose money on the sale items. Yet customers who visit these stores typically purchase other unneeded items at their full prices, so the stores profit by selling other products.

A third important way stores trigger impulse buying is through product placement. Have you ever wondered why jewelry and cosmetics are always near the entrances to large department stores? They're sold there because those particular items are frequently impulse purchases. Supermarkets also rely heavily on product placement. Many shoppers go to them for bread, milk, meat, vegetables, and fruit. [11]But tasty items like soda, chips, chocolate, and ice cream are placed near these staples, so customers are more likely to buy them. Yes, Cindy?

W Student: Isn't that what they do at the checkout counters—you know, all those candy bars and other junk food that always seem to be by the cash registers?

M: **I couldn't have said that better myself.** You got it. Those items are placed there to attract people's attention. While waiting to check out, shoppers' eyes are drawn to these items, and they may grab a soda or candy bar at the last moment. I'm sure virtually all of you have fallen prey to this advertising gimmick just like I have.

6 **Gist-Content Question** | During his lecture, the professor mostly focuses on the methods that businesses employ to induce customers to make impulse purchases.

7 **Making Inferences Question** | The professor states, "There are a number of ways businesses go about doing this. Let me tell you a few of them. After doing so, I believe that, um, the next time you go shopping at your favorite store, you'll notice how what I'm about to tell you has been implemented there." He therefore implies that many stores make use of the methods he is explaining.

8 **Detail Question** | The professor tells the class, "Stores also become enablers for impulse buyers by increasing their hours of operation, by making it easier for shoppers to obtain credit, and by allowing shoppers to exchange items if they're dissatisfied with the ones they buy. Supermarkets and convenience stores that are open twenty-four hours a day are examples of this."

9 **Understanding Organization Question** | When talking about produce placement, the professor names many of the items that stores sell by using it. He says, "A third important way stores trigger impulse buying is through product placement. Have you ever wondered why jewelry and cosmetics are always near the entrances to large department stores? They're sold there because those particular items are frequently impulse purchases. Supermarkets also rely heavily on product placement. Many shoppers go to them for bread, milk, meat, vegetables, and fruit. But tasty items like soda, chips, chocolate, and ice cream are placed near these staples, so customers are more likely to buy them."

10 **Understanding Function Question** | When the professor mentions the slogan and then asks, "How many times have you heard that particular slogan?" he is implying that this slogan is used regularly.

11 **Understanding Attitude Question** | When the professor responds to the student by saying, "I couldn't have said that better myself," he is agreeing with her statement.

Answers

PART 1

1 Ⓑ	2 Ⓓ	3 Ⓒ	4 Ⓒ	5 Ⓐ
6 Ⓑ	7 Ⓐ	8 Ⓒ	9 Ⓓ	10 Ⓑ
11 Ⓑ	12 Ⓑ	13 Ⓐ	14 ②, ④	15 Ⓑ
16 Ⓐ	17 Ⓒ			

PART 2

1 Ⓑ	2 Ⓓ	3 Ⓒ	4 Ⓐ	5 Ⓑ
6 Ⓓ	7 Ⓐ	8 Corn: ②, ④ Sugarcane: ①, ③		
9 Ⓒ	10 Ⓐ	11 Ⓒ		

Scripts & Explanations

PART 1

Conversation 🎧 04-01

p.82

W1 Student: Professor Douglas, thank you so much for agreeing to see me on short notice. I know you're not holding office hours today, so I totally appreciate the fact that you cleared up some time in your schedule for this meeting.

W2 Professor: It's really no problem at all, Mandy. I have luncheon for a retiring member of the administration. Is that going to be enough time for you?

W1: Oh, definitely. I just need to chat with you for a couple of minutes about the essay that we're supposed to turn in next week.

W2: Ah, yeah. The essay. What about it?

W1: To be honest, I'm having some problems writing it.

W2: All right. Remind me again what your topic is, please. [5]I know that you turned in your topic and that I approved it, but I can't seem to recall what it is. Sorry about that.

W1: **No problem, ma'am. It is a rather big class.**

W2: Thanks for saying that. Anyway, go on, please.

W1: Sure. Well, I was planning to do my essay on George Washington's life, but, um, I'm having some trouble with that.

W2: Why is that? I mean, surely there's enough information about Washington available in the library for you to look at. You're not having trouble finding any source material, are you?

W1: Oh, goodness. That's not a problem at all. I've got tons of books on Washington. The problem is, um, that I'm worried I won't be able to write anything new about him. After all, people have written hundreds—maybe even thousands—of books about his life, so. . .

W2: Yes?

W1: So, uh, wouldn't it be kind of a boring paper if I just wrote about what Washington did during his life?

W2: Hmm . . . Yes, I see your point. That probably would be a pretty uninspiring paper, and there definitely isn't much about Washington's biography you can write that I haven't read before. In that case, have you considered changing your topic?

W1: Yes. That's actually why I'm here. The only thing is that I've already done a lot of research on Washington, so I don't want to change my topic away from him. Plus, I don't think that I would have sufficient time to do any research on another historical figure from that era. So, um, what do you suggest that I do, Professor Douglas?

W2: How about this . . . ? Don't write about Washington's life in general. Write about a particular incident in his life and give your opinion of it.

W1: Such as what?

W2: Oh, there are many things. I mean, you know that Washington had no children, right? Well, some speculate that he refused to become king after the American Revolution ended—something he could have done easily—because his lack of children meant there would be a problem of succession once he died. You could give your opinion on that. You could write about Washington's management of the war or his handling of foreign diplomacy as president. There are lots of different things you can do.

W1: Wow. I hadn't even considered any of those topics. Okay. Thanks a lot, Professor Douglas. I'll consider what you said and then come up with something new.

W2: Great. Feel free to email me or drop by my office if you have any more problems, Mandy.

1   **Gist-Content Question** | The professor and the student spend most of the conversation talking about what the student is going to write her paper on.

2   **Detail Question** | The student says, "I was planning to do my essay on George Washington's life."

3   **Understanding Attitude Question** | During the conversation, the professor makes some suggestions to help the student with her paper topic, so she is helpful to the student.

4 **Making Inferences Question** | At the beginning of the conversation, the professor tells the student, "I've got about ten minutes before I have to go to a luncheon for a retiring member of the administration."

5 **Understanding Function Question** | When the student gives her response after the professor apologizes for not remembering her topic, the student is accepting the professor's apology.

Lecture 🎧 04-02   p.84

M Professor: Now that I've gone over the syllabus and covered what we're going to do this semester, I want to jump right into our first topic. We may as well start from the beginning—the beginning of everything that is—and discuss the creation of the universe. Let me preface this lecture by stating that, although we have what we think is a fairly good idea about how the universe was created, there are still lots of pieces of the puzzle that we have yet to fill in. Keep that in mind, please. Okay, uh, the prevailing theory on the origin of the universe is the Big Bang Theory. Let me explain it first, and then we can look at a couple of competing theories.

The Big Bang Theory arose from a number of theories and observations about the universe that were made during the 1920s. A Belgian priest, Georges Lemaitre, who also happened to be a scientist working at a prestigious university, proposed that the universe was expanding in 1927. His theory was treated with some skepticism by the leading experts of the day, including Albert Einstein. But then Lemaitre's theory began to gain adherents when some strong evidence was found to support it. Prior to the twentieth century, you see, there were no very large telescopes, so little was known about the universe outside the small section of the Milky Way Galaxy that we occupy.

However, in the 1900s, bigger and better telescopes were made, so astronomers were finally able to get a fairly good look at the cosmos. They discovered that there were many more galaxies aside from our own. In 1929, American astronomer Edwin Hubble discovered that the galaxies in the universe were moving away from Earth as well as away from each other. This had been proposed by people other than Hubble just so you know. However, Hubble managed to prove without a shadow of a doubt that this was actually happening. But this discovery gave rise to a new question: If all of the galaxies were moving away from each other and the universe was expanding, where was the beginning point of the universe? Astronomers realized that, if the universe really was expanding, it must have come from somewhere and must have had a starting point where the entire universe was once together.

A couple of years later, in 1931, Lemaitre proposed a radical new theory. He suggested that at some time in the past, all the matter in the universe was condensed into a single hot, dense point. What it was made of, how it came into existence, and what was there before it are things no one knows. Perhaps we'll never know the answers. However, at some time, this point erupted . . . Again, no one knows how or why this happened. This explosion was dubbed the Big Bang, and the theory concerning it was called, appropriately enough, the Big Bang Theory.

The theory had both supporters and detractors, but, in 1964, it received some support when astronomers discovered that, all throughout the universe, there are remnants of microwave energy that they call cosmic microwave background radiation. Many astronomers believed that this radiation is left over from when the Big Bang occurred. Now, being rather intelligent people, these astronomers were able to measure the radiation and thereby determined how old the universe is. They calculated that the Big Bang took place about thirteen point seven billion years ago.

After the Big Bang, the universe began to expand and cool. The first elements—most likely hydrogen and helium—were then formed. The fact that these two elements are found in enormous amounts all throughout the universe suggests that they have a common origin, which is taken as further proof that the Big Bang took place. Anyway, after the Big Bang, in a process that took billions of years, the first galaxies came into existence, the first stars were born, and then planets formed. Please be aware that I'm simplifying what was a very intricate process. We still aren't quite sure of everything that happened right after the Big Bang, but I still feel that it's the best model we have for the creation of the universe. Yes? You in the front row? You have a question?

W Student: Professor Hudson, what about dark matter? Doesn't this model for the creation of the universe require the presence of dark matter and energy?

M: Ah, yes, you've pointed out the Achilles heel of the Big Bang Theory. Obviously, there are many inconsistencies in the theory. However, some astronomers have stated that two unknown factors—dark matter and dark energy—can explain all of these inconsistencies. Unfortunately, we have yet to prove that dark matter and dark energy, um, actually exist. And because of this problem, some astronomers have put forward other theories on the creation of the universe. Let me tell you about a couple of them right now, and you can see how they compare to the Big Bang Theory.

6 **Making Inferences Question** | At the start of the lecture, the professor says, "Now that I've gone over the syllabus and covered what we're going to do this semester, I want to jump right into our first topic." Since he explains the syllabus and talks about what they are going to do during the semester, it can be inferred that the class is meeting for the first time.

7 **Detail Question** | The professor states, "A Belgian priest, Georges Lemaitre, who also happened to be a scientist working at a prestigious university, proposed that the universe was expanding in 1927."

8 **Gist-Purpose Question** | About Edwin Hubble, the professor states, "However, Hubble managed to prove without a shadow of a doubt that this was actually happening. But this discovery gave rise to a new question: If all of the galaxies were moving away from each other and the universe was expanding, where was the beginning point of the universe? Astronomers realized that, if the universe really was expanding, it must have come from somewhere and must have had a starting point where the entire universe was once together."

9 **Understanding Organization Question** | About cosmic microwave background radiation, the professor notes, "Many astronomers believed that this radiation is left over from when the Big Bang occurred."

10 **Understanding Attitude Question** | About the Big Bang Theory, the professor first remarks, "We still aren't quite sure of everything that happened right after the Big Bang, but I still feel that it's the best model we have for the creation of the universe." Then, he states, "Ah, yes, you've pointed out the Achilles heel of the Big Bang Theory. Obviously, there are many inconsistencies in the theory."

11 **Making Inferences Question** | The professor comments, "However, some astronomers have stated that two unknown factors—dark matter and dark energy—can explain all of these inconsistencies. Unfortunately, we have yet to prove that dark matter and dark energy, um, actually exist." So he implies that if a person proves that dark matter and dark energy actually exist, this will provide support for the Big Bang Theory.

Lecture 🎧 04-03   p.87

W Professor: In the time before photography, painting was the primary method that was used to capture a person's image. As a result, the rich and powerful often commissioned portraits of themselves. These were done on canvas, were large, and were intended to hang on the walls of homes, palaces, and museums. But what about those people who wanted to carry pictures of their family members or, say, the king or queen, around with them? Regular portraits were much too big to be carried around with ease. As a result, a market for small portraits developed in Europe in the sixteenth century, and it would last well into the nineteenth century, when the invention of the camera resulted in the decline of what was known as miniature portrait painting.

As I just noted, the history of miniature portraits began in Europe in the sixteenth century. Some art historians believe that the origin of miniature portrait painting lies with portrait medals. A portrait medal, in case you don't know, was a round medallion upon which the image of a person was etched. However, other art historians suggest that the first miniature pictures were made for books. Whatever the case, the first miniature portraits were not very realistic, but, as time passed, the artists learned better ways to reproduce images of people. Remember, uh, that the Renaissance was still going on during the sixteenth century, so artists then began to utilize rediscovered painting methods from ancient Greece and Rome to make the people in their paintings more anatomically correct. This, naturally, improved the quality of the work they did.

Now, um, the process of making a miniature portrait wasn't easy. It required a skilled hand and a fine eye to duplicate a person's features on such a small scale. Special brushes were needed to apply the paint, and tiny brushstrokes were required as well. Any heavy brushstrokes would ruin the tiny images, so the artists had to be very careful. Throughout the centuries, some artists became experts at painting in miniature and accordingly became highly sought after by people who wanted their portraits done that way.

M Student: Professor Norby, I have a question.

W: Sure. What is it?

M: You said that these artists became highly sought after. By whom? I mean, uh, which people in society wanted their portraits done in miniature?

W: Hmm . . . The portraits were popular with all classes of society in Europe and, years later, in America and other lands. What kinds of people commissioned them? Well, people who traveled or moved away from their homelands often wanted to have images of their loved ones with them at all times. Sailors who made long sea voyages typically carried miniature portraits of their family members. Colonists leaving their home countries for other lands regularly had miniature portraits made of their parents and other relatives so that they wouldn't forget how they looked. Some fathers had miniature portraits made of their daughters so that they could show them to potential suitors who then might get married to them.

These portraits were carried in lockets, brooches, and bracelets, and they were mostly oval shaped. Some were square or rectangular, but ovals were the most popular. Miniature portraits were often incorporated into pieces of jewelry, particularly for husbands and wives who carried pictures of their spouses. [17]By the way, these portraits usually just showed only the head and shoulders of their subjects. The head was often turned slightly to the right or left, which gave a partial profile view.

M: I have another question if it's all right.

W: By all means.

M: Thanks. Were these portraits made with oil paints on canvas like most large portraits then were?

W: No, they weren't. Various other materials were used instead. Most miniatures were done with watercolors although some artists employed oil and enamel. Copper, not canvas, was the material of choice for many miniature artists, but others used vellum and cardboard. By the eighteenth century, watercolors on ivory were being used extensively. Ivory added luminosity to the skin colors and sheen to the hair, which improved the quality of the paintings. Of course, people in different countries had, uh, different preferences. For instance, enamel was common in France and Switzerland, oil on copper was common in the German and Italian states, and watercolors on ivory dominated in England and America. But it mostly depended upon both the individual artists and, of course, the individuals who were commissioning the portraits.

Anyway, by the end of the nineteenth century, the heyday of miniature portraits was coming to an end. Photography was improving in quality, and it provided cheap, realistic images of people. It was also faster and easier to get a picture taken than to have a painting made. Today, many miniature portraits that were done in the past are considered valuable works of art. Fortunately, the school happens to own a few, which I've brought for us to look at today. Now, come up here and take a look at these. But don't touch them. They're fragile. I don't want anything to happen to them.

12 Gist-Content Question | The professor mostly lectures about the history of miniature portrait painting.

13 Making Inferences Question | The professor states, "Some art historians believe that the origin of miniature portrait painting lies with portrait medals. A portrait medal, in case you don't know, was a round medallion upon which the image of a person was etched. However, other art historians suggest that the first miniature pictures were made for books." So the professor implies that art historians disagree about the origins of miniature portrait painting.

14 Detail Question | The professor tells the class, "Sailors who made long sea voyages typically carried miniature portraits of their family members. Colonists leaving their home countries for other lands regularly had miniature portraits made of their parents and other relatives so that they wouldn't forget how they looked."

15 Detail Question | The professor tells the class about many different materials that artists used to make miniature portraits. Then, she comments, "But it mostly depended upon both the individual artists and, of course, the individuals who were commissioning the portraits."

16 Making Inferences Question | At the end of the lecture, the professor says, "Today, many miniature portraits that were done in the past are considered valuable works of art. Fortunately, the school happens to own a few, which I've brought for us to look at today. Now, come up here and take a look at these. But don't touch them. They're fragile. I don't want anything to happen to them."

17 Understanding Attitude Question | When a person asks for permission to do something and another person responds by saying, "By all means," the responder is giving the asker permission to do what that individual requested.

PART 2

Conversation 🎧 04-04   p.92

M Student Activities Office Employee: Good morning. You must be Melissa. Why don't you have a seat right there?

W Student: Thank you, sir. And good morning to you.

M: Is there anything I can get you? Would you like some coffee, water, or something else?

W: That's all right, sir. But thank you for offering.

M: Okay, Melissa. I received your request for a meeting. However, you didn't indicate what you wanted to discuss. How about filling me in, please?

W: Of course. I would like to discuss the mandatory volunteer service which all students have to do in order to graduate from school.

M: Yes? What about it?

W: I, um, I wonder if I'm permitted to change where I'm going to be volunteering.

M: Hmm . . . It has been done on occasion, but I need some more information before I can make a decision. Would you mind providing me with some details?

W: Not at all. Um, a couple of weeks ago, I signed up to do some volunteer teaching at Jefferson Elementary School. I agreed to do some teaching for some first graders there. My friend and current roommate Rebecca Moore also agreed to teach there. You see, uh, the school is about thirty minutes away from campus, but Rebecca has a car, so we were planning to drive there. Well, uh, she was going to drive while I was going to ride with her.

M: Shall I guess that there's some kind of problem involving Rebecca?

W: That's correct, sir. Just last night, Rebecca told me that she's planning to transfer to a university on the other side of the country. That's where she lives. She, uh, she really misses her home, so she applied to a school in her hometown and will be living at home while she goes there.

M: And that means you don't have a way to get there, right?

W: Correct.

M: Is there a bus you can take?

W: I checked. I'd have to transfer twice, and it would take roughly an hour and ten minutes to go from campus to the school. I don't think having a commuting time of nearly two and a half hours three times a week is acceptable.

M: No, that doesn't sound very pleasant. Hmm . . . Do you happen to know if there are any other students who will be doing voluntary teaching there? If there are, perhaps you could get a ride with one of them.

W: Actually, this morning, I called the principal of the school and explained the situation to him. He told me that Rebecca and I were the only students who would be volunteering there next semester. So what you suggested isn't an option.

M: Okay, it sounds like this is a situation entirely outside your control. In that case, I'm authorized to permit you to change the place where you'll be volunteering. Now, uh, do you happen to have any ideas on where you could

volunteer instead?

W: Actually, yes, I do. Apparently, there's an elementary school just down the street from campus. I, uh, I never knew about that until someone in my dorm pointed that out last night.

M: Ah, you're referring to Madison Elementary School. You're in luck because I happen to know the principal there. She's a graduate of this school, and she's always eager to help our students. Would you like me to give Ms. Hanson a call right now?

W: That would be wonderful.

1 **Gist-Purpose Question** | The student asked to meet the man so that she could discuss some volunteer work that she is required to do for the school.

2 **Making Inferences Question** | In response to the student's request, the man states, "It has been done on occasion, but I need some more information before I can make a decision." So he implies that requests like hers are not often approved.

3 **Understanding Function Question** | The student tells the man that her roommate is transferring to another university to explain why she needs to make a change.

4 **Detail Question** | About her roommate, the student says, "Just last night, Rebecca told me that she's planning to transfer to a university on the other side of the country."

5 **Making Inferences Question** | At the end of the conversation, the man asks the student, "Would you like me to give Ms. Hanson a call right now?"

Lecture 🎧 04-05   p.94

W Professor: So, um, how can we reduce harmful emissions from motor vehicles? One possible solution that people have been working on is biofuels. These are fuels made from organic matter such as plants. Virtually any type of vegetation can be converted into biofuels, but corn, sugarcane, and soybeans in particular are ideal choices since they offer the best return on energy from energy used. That means that the fuel created has more energy than the energy used to make it.

Let's first focus on how biofuels are made. We'll take corn as an example. Making biofuel from corn is based on the same principle that people have long used to create homemade whiskey from it. Basically, large distilling plants boil the corn and siphon off the alcohol content from the steam. That's ethanol. Now, ethanol can be used by itself to power cars, but it can also be mixed with gasoline in various combinations. In the United States, most ethanol is combined with gas in a mixture that is eighty-five percent ethanol and fifteen percent gasoline. That, by the way, is called E85. You've heard of it, right . . . ? Okay. Anyway, that mixture gives off twenty-two percent fewer harmful emissions than regular gasoline.

The main problem with using corn as a source of biofuel is that creating corn ethanol requires a significant amount of energy. In fact, ethanol distilleries must use other organic material, natural gas, or coal to heat the corn, and burning these fuels emits lots of harmful emissions. Additionally, the energy produced by corn ethanol is only slightly greater than the energy needed to create it. Another issue is that the price of corn is currently rising since people use it both for food and fuel. This benefits corn farmers as they've been selling their crops for record prices over the past few years, but it doesn't benefit consumers of ethanol at all. Lastly, corn ethanol can in no realistic way replace oil and gas as a major fuel source. If all the corn in the United States were used to create ethanol, it would only provide twelve percent of our fuel requirements. That's just not enough.

A more promising source of biofuel, however, is sugarcane, which has been used in Brazil for several decades to make fuel for automobiles. Sugarcane actually has several distinct advantages over corn as a source of biofuel. To begin with, the wastage from the plant . . . uh, the leaves, stalks, and stems . . . can be used as fuel to run the sugarcane distilleries. This mitigates the need to burn fossil fuels. Second of all, sugarcane ethanol contains eight times the amount of energy used to create it. That's much more than corn if you'll recall. Lastly, a crop of sugarcane can yield twice as much ethanol per acre than a crop of corn. See, uh, an acre of corn can produce between three to four hundred gallons of ethanol whereas an acre of sugarcane can yield six to eight hundred gallons.

[11]In 2005, Brazil produced almost four billion gallons of sugarcane ethanol. **That's a phenomenal amount. And most cars in Brazil have dual-function engines that can operate on gasoline and ethanol.** Another advantage of sugarcane is that sugarcane ethanol produces fifty-six percent less harmful emissions than gasoline. But even sugarcane has its own problems. Most of it is harvested by hand by low-paid workers who spend backbreaking days in the fields. The fields are also often burned first, which makes it easier to harvest the sugarcane. The burning, of course, contributes to the polluting of the environment.

A third choice is biodiesel, which is mostly made in Germany from canola oil and in the United States from soybeans. Biodiesel is extremely environmentally friendly as it releases sixty-eight percent less harmful emissions than regular diesel. Unfortunately, it's quite expensive to make and is also slightly more costly than regular diesel at the pumps. Thus, despite the fact that it's a better choice for the environment, few people are willing to pay the price for it over regular diesel.

As you can see, all three types of biofuels that I've discussed have their good points and their bad points. Interestingly enough, the future of biofuel may not lie with any of them. Instead, the future of biofuel, in my opinion, is algae. Yes, that's right. The green slimy algae found in our ponds, lakes, rivers, and oceans may be the key to reducing harmful emissions. While the science of algae-made biofuel is still relatively young, predictions are that algae-made biofuel will yield up to five thousand gallons per acre. Algae can also be grown virtually anywhere and in artificial conditions that don't require large amounts of land or fertilizer. However, algae-made biofuel is currently only in the research and experimental phases. But I'm fully confident that many people will be operating their motor vehicles on it in the future.

6   **Gist-Content Question** | The professor mostly discusses some different types of biofuels in her lecture.

7   **Making Inferences Question** | The professor declares, "Sugarcane actually has several distinct advantages over corn as a source of biofuels," so she implies that sugarcane is better for making biofuel than is corn.

8   **Connecting Content Question** | According to the lecture, the price of corn has been going up lately, and the ethanol it can make has slightly more energy than the energy used to create it. As for sugarcane, one acre of it can produce around 600 to 800 gallons of ethanol while it has 50% fewer harmful emissions than gasoline.

9   **Detail Question** | The professor mentions, "Unfortunately, it's quite expensive to make and is also slightly more costly than regular diesel at the pumps. Thus, despite the fact that it's a better choice for the environment, few people are willing to pay the price for it over regular diesel."

10 **Understanding Organization Question** | About algae, the professor declares, "Interestingly enough, the future of biofuel may not lie with any of them. Instead, the future of biofuel, in my opinion, is algae."

11 **Understanding Attitude Question** | When something is a "phenomenal amount," it means that there is a large amount of it.

Actual Test 05

p.97

Answers

PART 1

1 ③, ④	2 ⓒ	3 ⓑ	4 ⓐ	5 ⓓ
6 ⓓ	7 ⓑ	8 ②, ③	9 ⓐ	10 ⓐ
11 ⓑ	12 ⓓ	13 ⓐ	14 Fact: ①, ③ Not a	
Fact: ②, ④		15 ⓑ	16 ⓒ	17 ⓒ

PART 2

1 ⓒ	2 ⓑ	3 ⓐ	4 ⓐ	5 ⓒ
6 ⓓ	7 ⓒ	8 ⓑ	9 ⓑ	10 ⓐ
11 ⓐ				

PART 3

1 ⓒ	2 ⓐ	3 ⓓ	4 ①, ③	5 ⓑ
6 ⓑ	7 ⓓ	8 ⓓ	9 ⓑ	10 ⓐ
11 ⓓ				

Scripts & Explanations

PART 1

Conversation 🎧 05-01   p.100

M Student Services Office Employee: Greetings. Is there something I can do for you today?

W Student: I sure hope so. I'm here to find out about some things related to clubs.

M: Do you mean what clubs we have here on campus?

W: Oh, no. Sorry. I guess I was kind of vague there. ⁴I'm the president of the computer design club, but, um, I'm not quite sure about a few things. You see, we just started the club this semester, and, um, I have to be honest with you . . . **I have no clue what I'm doing.**

M: Well, at least you're honest about that. And it's a good sign that you're willing to ask questions. Now, let me tell you about what most clubs do.

W: Sure. That sounds like a good way to start.

M: The majority of clubs here are fairly active. Please note, however, that when I say active, I mean that they have meetings at least once a month.

W: That's active?

M: Er, yeah. You know, lots of students are members of two or more clubs. Plus, students have classes, part-time jobs, and social lives as well. As a result, most of them aren't really interested in meeting more than once or twice a month.

W: Huh. I wasn't aware of that. I was actually planning on having meetings around once a week.

M: Hmm . . . I suppose you could do that. But your membership would probably decline if you met that often. Sure, you'd have a few people who would show up at every meeting. They'd be the really dedicated members. But the more casual members—uh, the ones that are just sort of interested in computer design but aren't devoted to it—would quickly drop their membership in the club.

W: ⁵I see. I hadn't considered that. I think I will just have meetings once every two weeks then.

M: **That's probably a pretty acceptable compromise.** Now, do you have a room to meet in yet?

W: No, I don't. That's one of the things I wanted to ask you about. How do I reserve a room?

M: Well, there are several ways. You can talk to me of course. I can reserve a room for you in one of the buildings on campus. Some clubs choose alternate venues though. For instance, they might meet at the café in the student center. They might meet outside if the weather is nice. Some even meet at, uh, at restaurants and bars in the local area.

W: I think I'll stick to reserving a room here on campus. I'll do that at least until I'm more familiar with what I'm doing.

M: That's definitely the best way to go at first.

W: Thanks. How do I get you to reserve a room?

M: Ah, good question. You can come here and fill out this form . . . here. In general, try to come at least three business days before you want the room. So if you want a room for a Monday, ask me on Wednesday the previous week, not Friday. With three days' advance warning, I can pretty much guarantee you a room somewhere on campus.

W: Excellent. Thanks.

M: Do you have any more questions for me?

W: Yes, one more. I need to know about funding. I mean, what kinds of funds are available to the club, and what can I use them for?

M: Okay. I figured you'd get around to asking about

money. There are quite a few things you can spend money on so long as you get prior approval.

1   **Detail Question** | First, the student and the man talk about the frequency that the club should meet. The student also asks the man, "How do I reserve a room?" and they discuss that topic.

2   **Understanding Attitude Question** | In response to the student's suggestion that the club meet once a week, the man declares, "I suppose you could do that. But your membership would probably decline if you met that often. Sure, you'd have a few people who would show up at every meeting. They'd be the really dedicated members. But the more casual members— uh, the ones that are just sort of interested in computer design but aren't devoted to it—would quickly drop their membership in the club." So he is strongly against having weekly meetings.

3   **Making Inferences Question** | At the end of the conversation, the man is preparing to tell the student about spending money, so the man will probably keep speaking with the student.

4   **Understanding Function Question** | When the student says that she has no clue what she is doing, she is essentially asking for help from the man.

5   **Understanding Attitude Question** | When the man states that the student's idea is "probably a pretty acceptable compromise," he is indicating that he agrees with her decision.

Lecture 🎧 05-02   p.102

M Professor: All around us, moving as fast as the speed of light, is the electromagnetic spectrum. It consists of photons of energy that move as waves across huge distances. This energy is also sometimes called electromagnetic radiation. Objects in space and here on Earth emit electromagnetic radiation. This radiation forms waves, which are oscillating packets of photons moving at the speed of light. This energy is measured by the wavelength and the frequency. Just as a reminder, wavelength is the distance between two crests of oscillating packets of photons while frequency is the number of wavelengths that occur per second. Some waves are longer and less frequent, and others are shorter and occur with greater frequency.

Now, everyone please take a look at the handout that I gave you at the beginning of class. On it, you can see the electromagnetic spectrum scale. On this scale, the different wavelengths and frequencies that I just mentioned are observable by us in various ways. Look in the middle of the scale. That's visible light. It's at a wavelength and frequency that allows us to see colors with our eyes. At the far left of the scale are the shortest and most frequent wavelengths. They are ultraviolet rays, X-rays, and gamma rays. They all contain a great deal of energy and are harmful to living organisms that are exposed to these rays for too long. On the right-hand side of the scale are the longer wavelengths, which have lower frequencies and less energy. They are, moving from left to right, infrared light, microwaves, and radio waves.

W Student: [11] How is the electromagnetic spectrum produced in the first place?

M: Hmm . . . **Well, I guess that now is as good a time as any to explain that.** To answer your question, the electromagnetic spectrum is produced in two ways: by thermal emissions and by non-thermal emissions. Thermal emissions consist of blackbody radiation and spectral line emissions. Non-thermal emissions consist of synchrotron emissions, pulsars, and masers. Since most electromagnetic radiation is produced by blackbody radiation, let's look at that as an example. Blackbody radiation is the simplest form of radiation. All objects that have temperatures above absolute zero have molecules inside them that are moving. As they move, they bump into one another, which causes some particles to accelerate. Anytime a particle accelerates, it emits electromagnetic radiation. That's blackbody radiation. When the temperature is higher and there's more movement, then higher amounts of electromagnetic radiation are produced. All of the objects in the universe emit electromagnetic radiation in this way. All of the stars, the planets, and even the objects in this classroom, uh, they all have some form of energy that they're emitting.

Next, uh, I want to discuss each aspect of the electromagnetic spectrum in turn. We'll start with radio waves. Radio waves are the longest and least frequent parts of the electromagnetic spectrum. They also have the least amount of energy. As a result, they're the least harmful part of the electromagnetic spectrum. They're also quite useful to us, um, as we've been using radio waves for communication purposes since the early twentieth century. Of course, to hear radio waves, we must use an instrument that can turn the waves into sounds our ears can hear. The frequencies of radio waves are measured in bands that consist of different wavelengths. We measure these wavelengths in hertz, which are expressed as the number of wavelengths per second. We also have the terms kilohertz, megahertz, and gigahertz to express wavelengths with very high frequencies. As for radio waves, they range from three hertz to 300 gigahertz. Each radio band is placed somewhere in this range, and each is used for different communication purposes. Again, let me direct your attention to the handout so that you can see a list of the different bands.

At the lowest end are extremely low and super-low frequencies ranging from three to 300 hertz. The sole purpose of these frequencies is communication with submarines. Since submarines operate underwater and radio waves can't penetrate water well, only frequencies this low can do the job well enough to enable communication. Next are the ultralow frequencies ranging from 300 to 3,000 hertz. This band is used for communicating in mines, where layers of rock and dirt must be penetrated. After that are very low frequency and low frequency bands, which are used for navigational signals, radio broadcasting, and amateur radio communications. These bands are between three and 300 kilohertz. Above that is medium frequency, which is mostly used for AM radio broadcasting. This band ranges between 300 and 3,000 kilohertz.

Above this level are the three most commonly used frequencies in communications: high frequency, very high frequency, and ultra-high frequency. These three bands range between three and 300 megahertz. Most TV broadcasting is in this range as are citizen band radios, Bluetooth systems, cell phone transmissions, GPS systems, and FM radio broadcasting. Even higher frequencies, uh, in the range of three to 300 gigahertz, are used for radar systems, satellite transmissions, and microwave transmission devices.

6 **Gist-Content Question** | The professor mostly talks about the different types of waves that are found on the electromagnetic spectrum while discussing it.

7 **Understanding Organization Question** | During his lecture, the professor constantly has the students refer to the handout that he gave the students.

8 **Detail Question** | The professor says, "On the right-hand side of the scale are the longer wavelengths, which have lower frequencies and less energy."

9 **Detail Question** | The professor notes, "We measure these wavelengths in hertz, which are expressed as the number of wavelengths per second."

10 **Making Inferences Question** | The professor mentions, "At the lowest end are extremely low and super-low frequencies ranging from three to 300 hertz. The sole purpose of these frequencies is communication with submarines. Since submarines operate underwater and radio waves can't penetrate water well, only frequencies this low can do the job well enough to enable communication. Next are the ultra-low frequencies ranging from 300 to 3,000 hertz. This band is used for communicating in mines, where layers of rock and dirt must be penetrated." Thus it can be inferred that radio waves penetrate rock more easily than water.

11 **Understanding Function Question** | After the student asks her question, the professor responds by saying, "Well, I guess that now is as good a time as any to explain that." It can therefore be inferred that he was not going to discuss that topic until later but he changed his mind when the student asked him the question.

Lecture 🎧 05-03 p.105

M1 Professor: I'd like to move on to talk about ancient Greek music. Unfortunately for us, very few fragments of Greek music have survived in note form. This has allowed modern musicians to interpret some of it. Some have even attempted to recreate ancient Greek music, but we'll never really know how close their interpretations are to the way it originally sounded. Anyway, what I'm going to concentrate on is what the ancient Greeks used music for, which instruments they used, and how Greek music styles changed.

Music in ancient Greece, just like modern-day music, had a variety of purposes. It was used during various ceremonies, such as the Olympics. It was used during stage performances. It had a role in rites, such as funerals. It was also a part of many people's everyday lives. The Greeks frequently associated music with their myths, and, in many of their ancient stories, music played important roles. As you can see, music was rather important to the ancient Greeks.

Now, um, I said that we don't know what Greek music sounded like. That's true. But we do know that it was monophonic. The Greeks therefore played one set of melodies at a time. There is some evidence that the Greeks made a few exceptions to this; however, for the most part, you should think of ancient Greek music as being monophonic. The reason for this was connected to the Greeks' philosophy on music, which is something I will get into in just a moment.

The ancient Greeks played three basic types of instruments. These were wind instruments, stringed instruments, and percussion instruments. If you look up here at the screen, you can see some pictures of these instruments. First, we have a picture of the Pan pipes. This instrument was called the *syrinx* by the Greeks. That's S-Y-R-I-N-X. It was played by blowing across an opening in it, not by blowing into it. Notice the tubes are of varying lengths . . . This was done so that the Pan pipes could produce different tones. The ancient Greeks also used a trumpet made from brass and which had a bone mouthpiece. This trumpet was curved and is often depicted in Greek pottery art as wrapping around the body of the musician playing it. Here's a shot of it . . . Rather interesting, isn't it? Another wind instrument was the *aulos*, which was similar to the modern-day flute. It came in two versions. One had a single pipe leading from the mouthpiece. This is what it looks like . . . And the other version had two pipes. Here's a two-pipe *aulos* for you to see . . .

[17]As for stringed instruments, the lyre was by far the most common of those. Take a look up here . . . Note that it had seven strings . . . Each was tuned differently so as to produce different sounds. **The lyre was ubiquitous in ancient Greece and was often played in music groups, played as a solo instrument, and even used to accompany poetry recitals.** The *kithara* . . . uh, spell it just like it sounds . . . was another stringed instrument that had a wooden box that helped produce the sounds the musician wanted.

M2 Student: Wait a second. That instrument looks sort of like a guitar.

M1: Er, yes, it did rely upon the same principles as the modern guitar, which was developed in Spain. As for whether or not there's a connection between the *kithara* and the guitar . . . Well, I'm not sure about that, but it wouldn't surprise me if the *kithara* influenced the first guitar makers.

So, um, what about the music that the Greeks played? Here's something you might find interesting: Early Greek music was based on mathematics and is believed to have been developed somewhat by the ancient Greek mathematician Pythagoras. He was the person who developed the concepts of harmonies and overtones and showed how they related to each other in a mathematical way. Pythagoras's discoveries led to the creation of some standard musical forms. But people in various Greek city-states also developed their own unique styles based upon these concepts. That's something you should remember.

Ancient Greek music was quite varied. Thus we can talk about the Dorian style, the Athenian style, and so on.

The Greek philosopher Plato often mentioned music in his writings. In some dialogues, he indicated that Greek music was originally rather staid and that audiences were expected to listen to it merely for enjoyment and weren't expected to clap or to make any sounds regarding the music's quality. Plato's writings make it sound as if Greek music was rigorously controlled and that a musician who made any changes or innovations to what was expected from the audience would be met with displeasure. However, right around 400 B.C. or so, which was during Plato's lifetime, ancient Greek music began to undergo a few changes. Fortunately for us, we know what these changes were. Here's what happened.

12 **Gist-Content Question** | The professor mostly describes what ancient Greek musical instruments looked like when he talks about them.

13 **Understanding Organization Question** | While talking about ancient Greek musical instruments, the professor shows the students slides on a screen and talks about them while they look at the pictures.

14 **Detail Question** | According to the lecture, ancient Greek music utilized three basic kinds of instruments. It was also played for many different reasons. However, the music was almost always monophonic, and it cannot be replicated by modern musicians.

15 **Understanding Organization Question** | About Pythagoras, the professor states, "Early Greek music was based on mathematics and is believed to have been developed somewhat by the ancient Greek mathematician Pythagoras. He was the person who developed the concepts of harmonies and overtones and showed how they related to each other in a mathematical way."

16 **Making Inferences Question** | About Plato, the professor remarks, "The Greek philosopher Plato often mentioned music in his writings. In some dialogues, he indicated that Greek music was originally rather staid and that audiences were expected to listen to it merely for enjoyment and weren't expected to clap or to make any sounds regarding the music's quality. Plato's writings make it sound as if Greek music was rigorously controlled and that a musician who made any changes or innovations to what was expected from the audience would be met with displeasure." It can therefore be inferred that Plato's writing is an important source of information about ancient Greek music.

17 Understanding Function Question | The professor notes that the lyre was used all over Greece and mentions some occasions during which it was played. In doing this, the professor stresses how important the lyre was in ancient Greece.

Conversation 🎧 05-04   p.110

W Student: Pardon me, but would you happen to be Mr. Clemons?

M Theater Manager: Yes, I am. Is there something that I can do for you?

W: Er, yes, I hope so. You're the theater manager here, right?

M: I sure am. I take it that you're in one of the acting troupes that is getting ready for a play?

W: Yes, I am. I'm in the troupe that is going to put on a performance of *Hamlet* in about a month from now.

M: Okay. I see. What can I do for you today? Do you need to reschedule your rehearsal times or something like that?

W: No, not at all. All of us are actually very pleased with the arrangements that you made for us.

M: That's good to hear.

W: But there's one thing that we aren't sure about. You see, we've got a bunch of props for the performance, but we don't have anywhere to put them.

M: Are you saying that you didn't sign up to reserve a storage room?

W: Uh . . .

M: Okay. I'll take that as a no. Shall I assume that nobody in your group knows that it's possible to reserve storage rooms for props, outfits, and that sort of thing?

W: I guess not. ⁴Um, this is the first play for most of us in the group, so, uh, I guess that we still haven't learned the ropes yet. Nobody told us anything about storage rooms being available.

M: Well, whichever professor is serving as your group's advisor should have let you know about them. **If you tell me your professor's name, I can do something about that oversight.** Anyway, what are you doing with all of your props now?

W: Well, we're storing them in various performers' dorm rooms for the time being.

M: You're kidding me . . . ? Okay, um, maybe you're not.

W: Sorry. We thought that was normal, but some of our

props are really big, you know. ⁵It's hard for the students to drag their props halfway across campus from their dorms to this building just for rehearsal. Then, of course, they have to take them back home again. Plus, some people's dorm rooms are getting really cramped these days.

M: **I can imagine.**

W: So, um, are there any storage rooms available right now? That would be so awesome if we could get access to one.

M: Technically, no. They're all already reserved by other groups.

W: Oh . . .

M: However, my personal storage room is only about half full right now. And since it seems like your professor isn't doing much to help you, here's what I'm going to do. I'm going to let you store your stuff in my storage room, but you won't get a key to it. I've got some of my own personal stuff in there. That's why. You'll have to arrange with me to open the room to get your props out and to put them back in. But at least you'll have a place to put everything. Sound good?

W: It sounds perfect. Thank you. That is so incredibly kind of you.

M: Ah, don't mention it. It's the least I can do for you. Anyway, let me show you where the room is so that you and your group will know where to go. Come on and follow me.

1　**Gist-Purpose Question** | The student talks with the theater manager because she needs to know where the members of her acting group can put their props, so she is trying to solve a problem.

2　**Detail Question** | The theater manager says, "I'm going to let you store your stuff in my storage room."

3　**Making Inferences Question** | At the end of the conversation, the theater manager tells the student, "Anyway, let me show you where the room is so that you and your group will know where to go. Come on and follow me."

4　**Making Inferences Question** | The theater manager indicates that the group's advisor should have let the members know about the storage room. When he asks for the professor's name and states, "I can do something about that oversight," he is implying that he will contact the group's advisor.

5　**Understanding Attitude Question** | When a person

responds by saying, "I can imagine," that individual is agreeing with what the other person stated.

Lecture 🎧 05-05   p.112

W Professor: Do animals form memories like people do? That's the question we're going to try to answer in today's class. The idea that animals form memories has sparked a great amount of debate mostly because of the problems we have communicating with them. Since we can't talk to animals, how can they tell us if they remember something or not? To solve this problem, scientists have conducted experiments that can show whether or not animals have the ability to remember. The conclusion most have reached is that some species of animals have both short-term and long-term memories.

First, let me clarify what scientists mean by short-term and long-term memories. Short-term memories refer to those memories that are retained for a few seconds. Most scientists consider twenty seconds to be the limit. Long-term memories are any memories which last longer than that. Now, that may seem like a, er, a ridiculously short time for us to call it a long-term memory, but we need to understand that we humans retain memories of minor events for short periods of time yet recall more significant events for long periods, sometimes even our entire lives. Think about it like this . . . You've probably already forgotten what you did ten minutes before class started because it was so trivial. However, you can most likely easily recall your first date, your high school graduation, and the death of a loved one because they're much more important memories.

M Student: So you're saying that animals can remember significant events just like people can?

W: Er . . . No, not exactly. What I mean is that when I say animals can form long-term memories, we shouldn't think of years or decades like we would for humans' long-term memories. Instead, we should think more about minutes or days. It's mostly perspective. Dogs and cats, for instance, live much shorter lives than humans. What's long to them isn't necessarily so for us.

Now, returning to my main point . . . What animals were tested, and what experiments were conducted to test their memories? Well, the first animal I want to discuss is the western scrub-jay. It's a small bird that gathers food and then hides it in various places. The first conclusion that animal behaviorists reached was that by storing food, the jays were planning future meals. They had extra food, so they buried it to utilize it in the future. The scientists also noted that the birds seemed to remember where they had hidden the food and knew that it could spoil, so they managed to retrieve the food and eat it before it went bad. This behavior suggested that they retained some long-term memories of when and where they had hidden the food.

The behaviorists devised an experiment with scrub-jays involving worms and nuts. The nuts were less perishable while the worms would go bad quickly. The behaviorists wanted to see if the scrub-jays could tell the difference. The birds were allowed to choose between the nuts and the worms. At first, they often chose the worms, which they seemed to enjoy eating more. But they also stored some of the worms they had chosen. After some time passed though, the scrub-jays began ignoring the worms and started choosing only the nuts. The scientists concluded that the worms went bad when the birds stored them to consume later. As a result, the birds selected the nuts, which could last for much longer. This, the scientists believed, was proof of memory.

Another aspect of scrub-jays that you should know is that they are, well, thieves. In the wild, they readily spy on other scrub-jays, note where those birds hide their food, and then steal the other birds' food and hide it elsewhere to eat later. But if one scrub-jay notices another observing it while it's hiding food, the bird will transfer the food to a new location. Why does it do this? The conclusion the behaviorists reached was that the scrub-jays remember their thieving behavior and realize that other scrub-jays may act similarly.

What can be deduced from these experiments and observations of scrub-jays? The most significant conclusion is that the birds are able to recall specific past events. They know where they hid their food, and they know when to retrieve it. They know that they have stolen food in the past, and they can project this behavior onto other scrub-jays. This is often termed episodic memory. This is something that can only happen if a species can mentally travel back in time to recall a specific event.

As you can no doubt imagine, this research has come under a lot of criticism. Some experts claim that the scrub-jays' behavior is instinctive and that they form no memories whatsoever. Others argue that all animals are stuck in time. They cannot conceive of the past, present, or future, so they don't make memories. I happen to disagree with these people and firmly believe that animals can make memories. Let me give you some examples of research on memory in primates that I feel should persuade you.

6 Gist-Content Question | The professor discusses the

possibility that animals have memories in her lecture.

7 **Detail Question** | Concerning memories, the professor remarks, "What I mean is that when I say animals can form long-term memories, we shouldn't think of years or decades like we would for humans' long-term memories. Instead, we should think more about minutes or days. It's mostly perspective. Dogs and cats, for instance, live much shorter lives than humans. What's long to them isn't necessarily so for us."

8 **Detail Question** | The professor mentions, "After some time passed though, the scrub-jays began ignoring the worms and started choosing only the nuts."

9 **Understanding Organization Question** | The professor declares, "The conclusion the behaviorists reached was that the scrub-jays remember their thieving behavior and realize that other scrub-jays may act similarly."

10 **Understanding Attitude Question** | The professor tells the class, "I happen to disagree with these people and firmly believe that animals can make memories."

11 **Making Inferences Question** | At the end of the lecture, the professor states, "Let me give you some examples of research on memory in primates that I feel should persuade you."

PART 3

Conversation 🎧 05-06   p.116

M Professor: Alice, I need a quick word with you.

W Student: Sure, Professor Watson. What is it?

M: You haven't submitted any lab reports yet. We've done two labs so far, and we'll be doing a third this week, but I haven't received anything from you. What's going on?

W: Oh, I didn't think it was important to write them, so I didn't bother. Is that a problem?

M: It's a huge problem.

W: Really? But why? I mean, uh, you already know the results of the lab experiments that we're doing.

M: Um . . . Yes, that's true, but you're supposed to do the lab reports so that I know that you did the work and that you understood everything involved in the process. Plus, uh, you get graded on the lab reports you submit, and right now, you've gotten two zeros. That's not going to help your final grade.

W: Oh . . .

M: So are you going to submit a lab report this time?

W: Yes, sir. I will. Can I submit lab reports for the two previous experiments?

M: No, you can't. The deadline has already passed, and it wouldn't be fair to the other students in the class to give you extra time when they didn't get any.

W: Okay. I understand. But, um, I still don't get it. Why do we write lab reports in the first place? What's so special about them?

M: Didn't you ever write any lab reports for experiments that you did in high school chemistry?

W: Er . . . I never took chemistry in high school. It wasn't offered at my school.

M: Okay, I guess that sort of explains things. Let me think . . . Do you know why we do experiments?

W: Uh, to see what happens when we mix chemicals together?

M: That's part of it. Basically, what we do in the lab is that we take the information we learned in the lecture, and then we apply it to the laboratory. By conducting experiments, we can better understand the information covered in the lecture. Now, uh, before you conduct an experiment, you're expected to create a hypothesis. That's a theory on what you believe is going to happen in the experiment. Then, you conduct the experiment and determine whether or not your hypothesis was right by analyzing the results.

W: And that's what I should write about?

M: Yes, that's correct. You need to include all of that information in your lab report. Write down every single step that you take and make notes on the results of the experiment. This allows me to determine whether or not you did the experiment correctly. If you did, then anyone should be able to replicate your results by following the steps you write about exactly.

W: Okay, I can do that.

M: There's one more thing about lab reports. Essentially, writing them will help you improve several other skills. You'll learn to write better. You'll also learn to organize your thoughts well. You'll learn to pay close attention to detail and to create a hypothesis and to test it.

W: That makes a lot of sense, sir. Thanks so much for having this chat with me. I'll be sure to write a report on the remainder of the experiments we conduct this semester.

1 **Gist-Content Question** | The professor remarks, "You haven't submitted any lab reports yet. We've done two labs so far, and we'll be doing a third this week, but I haven't received anything from you."

2 **Understanding Attitude Question** | About lab reports,

the student first says, "Oh, I didn't think it was important to write them, so I didn't bother," and then says, "I mean, uh, you already know the results of the lab experiments that we're doing."

3   **Detail Question** | When the student asks if she can submit her missing lab reports, the professor responds, "No, you can't. The deadline has already passed, and it wouldn't be fair to the other students in the class to give you extra time when they didn't get any."

4   **Detail Question** | The professor notes, "Essentially, writing them will help you improve several other skills. You'll learn to write better. You'll also learn to organize your thoughts well."

5   **Making Inferences Question** | During the conversation, the professor talks about how important lab reports are, so it can be inferred that he tries to change the student's mind on lab reports.

Lecture 🎧 05-07

p.118

W1 Professor: The next aspect of pre-Columbian art in the Americas that we should discuss is that of the Mayan Empire. Surviving examples of Mayan art consist mostly of sculptures and ceramics, but there are some paintings as well. Mayan art was made of various materials, um, mostly certain types of stone, such as sandstone, marble, jade, and obsidian. But the Mayans used clay for pottery and made carvings from wood and trinkets out of metal. Please note, however, that they seldom made pieces from metal since the Mayans had little knowledge of metallurgy and possessed few metal resources. Ah, the Mayans also used a form of paper to make paintings and applied plaster to walls to create both stucco and terra cotta artwork. The vast majority of their art was commissioned by the rulers of their numerous city-states, and it was typically done with the intention of showing off the rulers' accomplishments and glorifying their reigns.

First, I'd like to talk about Mayan sculpture in more detail. The most common form of sculpture they made was the stela. Spell that S-T-E-L-A by the way. You can see some examples of them on the screen here . . . and here . . . and look at this one here, too . . . Stelae are carvings done on the surface of enormous slabs of rocks and which are then placed upright in vertical positions. Most of the stelae the Mayans created were several meters wide and high. They were transported great distances from the places where they were created to the Mayan palaces and

temples where they were displayed. The stelae typically depicted Mayan gods or rulers, and many had writing chiseled into them. Some other types of Mayan sculptures included obsidian figurines like this one . . . jade figurines . . . and wood carvings . . . Beautiful, aren't they? Ah, you should realize that Mayan sculptures were not uniform in nature. They had different characteristics depending on the types of sculptures they were, the time periods in which they were created, and the parts of the empire in which they were made. But as a general rule, Mayan sculptors carved realistic representations of humans in their works. This is especially true for the ones depicting rulers, so they allow us to have a good idea as to, uh, as to what some of them actually looked like.

The Mayans used stucco in many of their buildings. They created it by mixing an organic compound found in certain trees with burned limestone and a few other minerals. The organic compound they used gave the stucco an adhesiveness that allowed the mixture to stick to the stone walls. The Mayans then applied wet stucco to the walls, carved it into the patterns they desired, and left it to harden. See here . . . and here . . .

What about Mayan paintings? Unfortunately, very few Mayan paintings have survived to the present day. The damp, humid climate of Central America just isn't suitable for paintings to survive. In fact, the few that have survived were mostly done on stone as murals inside buildings and caves. See here . . . Pay attention to the vibrant colors in this painting . . . It's such a shame there are so few of them considering how wonderful the extant ones look. Teresa, you have a question?

W2 Student: Yes, ma'am. I'm curious about the paint the Mayans used. What did they make it from?

W1: Ah, good question. The paint the Mayans used came from both vegetable and mineral sources. They mixed the ingredients together to produce paints of various hues. One of the most beautiful is something we call Maya Blue. See it up here on the screen . . . Fabulous, isn't it? Maya Blue is a shade of turquoise. Only the Mayans knew how to make it. It's found in all kinds of artwork, including murals, sculptures, and pottery. The secret to making it was lost in the sixteenth century, but, fortunately for us, the process was recently rediscovered. What's remarkable about Maya Blue is that it's highly resistant to weathering and lasts a long time.

The next form of art to explore is ceramics. This includes ceramic figures . . . pottery . . . vases . . . and common household dishes . . . The Mayans also used ceramics to make burial urns for the ashes of their dead. Like most ceramics, they were made from fired clay that was shaped and painted. The Mayans mixed volcanic ash with the clay. Studies of pottery shards and other ceramic figures show that about twenty percent of the clay mixture was volcanic ash. That's just an interesting bit of trivia for you there. Mayan artists frequently developed their own highly individualistic styles of ceramics and usually put their names on their pieces just like modern artists do. The best ceramic makers were highly sought after by the nobility. [11]Since ceramics were often used as a medium of exchange and for gift giving, getting the best ceramics was important to Mayan nobles. **When it came to painting ceramics, Mayan artists let their imaginations run wild . . .** They painted scenes of gods and rulers but also painted everyday scenes from the lives of commoners. Let me show you a few of my favorites now.

6 **Detail Question** | The professor explains, "The most common form of sculpture they made was the stela."

7 **Making Inferences Question** | The professor states, "Ah, please note that Mayan sculptures were not uniform in nature. They had different characteristics depending on the types of sculptures they were, the time periods in which they were created, and the parts of the empire in which they were made." In saying this, she implies that sculptures made during the same time period could have had different characteristics.

8 **Understanding Attitude Question** | The professor declares, "What about Mayan paintings? Unfortunately, very few Mayan paintings have survived to the present day."

9 **Detail Question** | The professor comments, "The paint the Mayans used came from both vegetable and mineral sources. They mixed the ingredients together to produce paints of various hues. One of the most beautiful is something we call Maya Blue."

10 **Understanding Organization Question** | During her lecture, the professor focuses on some different types of Mayan art.

11 **Understanding Function Question** | When artists "let their imaginations run wild," they are acting in creative manners.

Answers

PART 1

1 Ⓓ 2 Ⓑ 3 Ⓐ 4 Ⓒ 5 Ⓑ
6 Ⓐ 7 Ⓒ 8 Ⓒ 9 Trichromatic Theory:
[1], [2] Opponent Process Theory: [3], [4] 10 Ⓑ
11 Ⓑ

PART 2

1 Ⓐ 2 Ⓒ 3 [1], [4] 4 Ⓑ 5 Ⓑ
6 Ⓒ 7 Ⓓ 8 Ⓐ 9 Sir Isaac Newton:
[1], [2] Gottfried Leibniz: [3], [4] 10 Ⓑ 11 Ⓐ
12 Ⓒ 13 Ⓑ 14 Ⓓ 15 Ⓐ 16 [1], [2]
17 Ⓓ

Scripts & Explanations

PART 1

Conversation 🎧 06-01   p.124

M Student: If you don't mind, ma'am, there's one more thing that I'd like to chat with you about before I leave. Do you have a few more moments to spare for me, or do you have another class to go to now?

W Professor: I have plenty of time for you, Matt. What else do you need to discuss?

M: [1]I remember that you made a comment in one of our classes a couple of weeks ago about doing extra work— uh, for bonus points. Exactly what kind of extra work would I need to do in order to get some bonus points?

W: **Matt, do you really believe that you need to get some bonus points in my class?**

M: It couldn't hurt to get some.

W: Remind me again what your grade on the midterm exam was.

M: It was a 97, but, uh, you never know. I could mess up on the final exam, or-or-or something else bad could happen. I just want to be sure about my grade.

W: All right. I see your point. And the answer to your question is that, yes, there are a large number of projects you can do to get some bonus points in my class.

M: Cool. What do I need to do?

W: You need to visit the library to find out about the

projects. Go to the reserve desk and ask to see the file for the class. Inside the file—um, it's actually a three-ring binder—anyway, inside the file, you will find a section labeled "Bonus Projects for Engineering 72." Each student in the class is permitted to do one bonus project per semester. [5]But you don't just get bonus points for trying to do a project. You have to complete the project you choose in a manner that I find satisfactory.

M: That sounds fair. What kinds of projects are there in the file?

W: **That's for you to find out, Matt.** But let me tell you a couple of things before you check out the file: The projects in that file are not easy. You'll have to use the information that we're learning in this class to solve them, but they also require knowledge you should have acquired in other classes. In short, it is possible to do them successfully, but they'll require a lot of time and effort. In addition, you can work by yourself on this project, or you can work together with up to two more students. You just need to let me know what project you're going to try and who you're going to be doing it with before you start. Is that okay?

M: It sounds perfect to me. Oh, one more question.

W: Go ahead.

M: Why don't you tell the class about these projects?

W: Hmm . . . Mostly, it's about taking initiative. Students like you—and a few others—take the initiative to come here and ask me about bonus projects. When they do that, I tell them about the opportunities that are available to them. But as for students who don't care enough to ask . . . Well, I don't see the need to enlighten them. Remember that these are bonus points. Students with initiative will try to get them while those who have none won't.

M: I see what you're saying. That makes sense to me. Okay. I think I'll check out that file now.

1   **Gist-Content Question** | The student asks the professor about an extra project he can do for bonus points, so that is what they mostly talk about.

2   **Understanding Attitude Question** | The professor states, "Mostly, it's about taking initiative. Students like you—and a few others—take the initiative to come here and ask me about bonus projects." So it can be inferred that the student is showing initiative by speaking with the professor about the extra project.

3   **Making Inferences Question** | At the end of the conversation, the student states, "I think I'll check out that file now." Since the file is in the library, the student will probably go there next.

4   **Making Inferences Question** | When the professor asks the student if he thinks that he really needs bonus points in her class, she is implying that he has a high grade and does not need any bonus points.

5   **Understanding Function Question** | When the professor declares, "That's for you to find out, Matt," in response to his question about what kinds of projects are in the file, she is letting him know that he needs to find out for himself and that she will not answer his question.

Lecture 🎧 06-02 p.126

M Professor: How can the human eye see different colors? First, before I explain, I think I should talk about what color is. Color comes from light. Most of the time, we can't see this light since it's what we call white light. White light, you see, is comprised of all the colors of the spectrum. Sir Isaac Newton recognized this when he passed white light through a prism and noticed that it divided into the colors of the rainbow. However, Newton believed these colors were particles and that each color was composed of different colored particles. Obviously, Newton was wrong about that. Color isn't made of particles; instead, each color has its own wavelength on the electromagnetic spectrum. It's these wavelengths that we perceive as colors.

Now that we know more about color, I can ask my question again: How does the human eye recognize different colors? When white light hits an object, most of the colors of the spectrum are absorbed by that object. However, some aren't. Instead, they're reflected. For example, look at this pencil I'm holding. As you can see, it's yellow. This means that every color of the spectrum except for yellow is absorbed by the pencil.

W Student: Professor Venters, what about white and black objects?

M: White objects absorb all the colors of the spectrum, so they have no color at all. Black objects, on the other hand, absorb no colors yet also reflect no colors, so they're neither white nor colorful. Some people claim that this means black isn't a color but is actually an absence of color.

As we discussed earlier, the retina in the eye contains many cones and rods. These cones and rods help us see light. The rods perceive light in low-light conditions.

This is scotopic vision. The cones perceive color in very bright light. This is photopic vision. We use the rods in dim light, so they're quite sensitive and can pick up weak wavelengths of light. Yet they have no role in color perception. The cones, however, play a major role in our perception of color.

There are two main theories concerning how the cones perceive color. The first is the trichromatic theory. It states that the eye perceives color based on the cones, of which there are three different types: long, medium, and short. Each type of cone is attuned to a different wavelength of color for the three primary wavelengths: red, blue, and green. This theory was first proposed during the 1800s and has been widely accepted ever since then. The other major theory is the opponent process theory. It states that the three types of cones seek differences in colors. They do this because the cone receptors have some overlap in the three main colors they can see. Therefore, the cones set up three pairs of opponent colors when they're processing color information. These three pairs are blue-yellow, red-green, and black-white.

For decades, it was believed that these two rival theories on color perception were isolated and had absolutely no connection to one another. However, the prevailing mindset among scientists nowadays is that the theories are essentially part of the same process. What many now think is that the three types of cones first detect the color wavelengths by using the trichromatic process. After that, the cones interpret the various colors by using the opponent process. Scientists also believe that different parts of the cones are responsible for each process. The opponent process is thought to be interpreted by the retinal ganglion cells, which are neurons found in the retina. There are a little more than one million retinal ganglion cells in each retina, and they're connected to the more than one hundred million cone receptors found in each retina. Thus each retinal ganglion cell is connected to approximately one hundred cone receptors.

After the color wavelength signals reach the retinal ganglion cells, they're sent to the brain by the optic nerve, which is connected to the eye. How does the brain interpret these signals? What happens is that the signals end up in the primary visual cortex center of the brain. This is located near the back of the brain in the occipital lobe. There, the visual signals are interpreted by the brain in an extremely complex process. I'd like to explain how that happens, but we don't have time to do that today. However, what I'd like you to do is go to the class website and look under the heading "Visual Cortex." Be sure to read the information there and check out the diagrams. Then it will be much easier for you to understand the

next lecture. Okay, I think it's time to call a halt to today's lesson. Please remember that we're having our midterm exam a week from today, so we've got two more lessons to go until test time. I'll be in my office until four in case any of you need to visit me.

6 **Gist-Content Question** | The professor mostly lectures on how humans can perceive colors.

7 **Understanding Organization Question** | About Sir Isaac Newton, the professor notes, "Sir Isaac Newton recognized this when he passed white light through a prism and noticed that it divided into the colors of the rainbow."

8 **Detail Question** | The professor states, "The rods perceive light in low-light conditions. This is scotopic vision."

9 **Connecting Content Question** | According to the lecture, the trichromatic theory was created in the 1800s and claims that each cone is attuned to a different wavelength of color. As for the opponent process theory, it says that the cones overlap in terms of which colors they perceive, and it also is interpreted by retinal ganglion cells.

10 **Understanding Function Question** | When the professor says, "However, what I'd like you to do is go to the class website and look under the heading 'Visual Cortex.' Be sure to read the information there and check out the diagrams," he is assigning the students some homework to do.

11 **Making Inferences Question** | At the end of the lecture, the professor dismisses the class and tells them, "I'll be in my office until four in case any of you need to visit me." So he will probably return to his office next.

PART 2

Conversation 🎧 06-03   p.130

M1 **Cafeteria Manager:** Nick, you've finished your shift for the day, haven't you? If you're not doing anything, would you mind coming over here for a bit?

M2 **Student:** Sure thing, Mr. Carter. I just got off work right now. What do you need to chat with me about?

M1: It's about your schedule for next semester.

M2: You're already making the schedule for the spring semester? Isn't it kind of early to be doing that?

M1: Not really, Nick. I mean, we're already in the middle

of December, and I need to make sure we have enough students working here at the cafeteria as soon as winter break comes to an end in mid-January.

M2: Yeah, I guess that makes sense. I suppose you wouldn't want to be shorthanded for the first week or two of the semester.

M1: Precisely. So, first question . . . Are you planning on working here next semester?

M2: Totally. I love working here in the cafeteria. The hours are great, the pay is really good, and I like all of the people I work with.

M1: That's good to hear, Nick, because I've decided to make you a student manager as of next semester. You're getting a promotion.

M2: A manager? Me?

M1: Yes, you. Congratulations. You're the hardest-working student employee that I've got, Nick, and I believe you'd make a fine manager. However, there are a couple of things you need to know about the job . . . First, you'll have to work twenty hours a week. Well, you have to work anywhere between twenty and thirty hours that is. Is that acceptable to you?

M2: Twenty hours? Hmm . . . I'm doing eighteen a week at the moment, so I expect that increasing my workload by another two hours wouldn't be too strenuous. Can I choose the hours I'm going to work?

M1: To some extent, yes. But I'd like for you to work at least four days a week in the evening. Uh, you know, the dinner shift. I think you'll be needed more then than during the lunch shift.

M2: Evenings are no problem at all. I was actually planning to ask you to let me work then instead of doing the lunch shift since I've got a few classes scheduled for right around noon next semester.

M1: Oh, okay. Then there won't be any problems with scheduling. Now, here's the good part . . . As you can probably imagine, being promoted to manager comes with a pay raise. [5]You'll get an extra two dollars an hour for being manager. And since you'll be working the evening shift, you will receive another increase of one dollar per hour for any work that you do after five o'clock. **It looks like you're going to be making the big bucks next semester, Nick.**

M2: That's awesome. Thanks so much, Mr. Carter. I'm glad you have faith in me like that.

M1: The pleasure is all mine. Ah, one more thing . . . Are you planning on staying around here during winter break? The cafeteria will be open, so I need a few employees to work at that time.

M2: Oh, sorry. I'm flying home to see my family during the break, so I can't help you with that. But I know Karen Cooke is going to be here. You might try asking her.

M1: I wasn't aware of that. Thanks for the tip.

1 **Gist-Content Question** | At the beginning of the conversation, the student asks the manager what he wants to talk about, and the response is, "It's about your schedule for next semester."

2 **Making Inferences Question** | The student comments, "You're already making the schedule for the spring semester? Isn't it kind of early to be doing that?" The manager responds that he needs to make sure he has enough students working when the semester begins. So it can be inferred that the manager likes to plan ahead for the future.

3 **Detail Question** | The manager tells the student, "But I'd like for you to work at least four days a week in the evening." He also states, "First, you'll have to work twenty hours a week. Well, you have to work anywhere between twenty and thirty hours that is."

4 **Understanding Function Question** | The manager says, "Are you planning on staying around here during winter break? The cafeteria will be open, so I need a few employees to work at that time."

5 **Understanding Attitude Question** | When a person makes "the big bucks," it means that the person earns a lot of money.

Lecture 🎧 06-04   p.132

W Professor: Sir Isaac Newton had one of the greatest scientific minds in history. His work on gravity, the laws of motion, optics, and color has served as a cornerstone in the scientific world ever since the seventeenth century. However, in one aspect of his work, there remains a major controversy. It concerns the development of calculus. Namely, who developed it first? Newton and his supporters claimed he was the first to theorize and develop calculus while others claimed—and continue to do so—that Gottfried Leibniz of Germany was the first. A thorough examination of the evidence has led me to the conclusion that both men worked on the same ideas independently and arrived at the same conclusions.

Now, I have no interest in getting into a big discussion about calculus or the theories behind it. Instead, I merely want to examine the controversy surrounding these two men. Firstly, you need to be aware that neither man entirely developed calculus. After all, some of the ideas it's based on have been around since ancient times. Let me see . . . The Egyptians, the Greeks, and the Chinese all did work related to calculus. But what Newton and Leibniz both did was, uh, well, they took the sum of these ideas and put them together to form a unifying theory. Newton claimed to have begun working on calculus in 1666 yet didn't publish his ideas until 1693. Leibniz, meanwhile, began working on his theories in 1674 and made his initial publication in 1684. It was on a visit to London in 1676 that Leibniz saw one of Newton's unpublished manuscripts on calculus. He and Newton also corresponded, which perhaps gave Leibniz some clues as to what Newton was working on. These events have provided ammunition for the Newton faction, which has steadfastly claimed that Leibniz was a plagiarist. Yet Leibniz's supporters declare that Newton had access to Leibniz's work, which was published first.

It was, um, 1699 when Leibniz was first accused of plagiarism, yet the matter didn't become full blown until 1711. When word of the accusations reached Leibniz's ears, he demanded a retraction and an investigation into the matter by the Royal Society of London. The Royal Society, if you don't know, was the most august scientific body of its day. It conducted an investigation, and, um, it is said—though this hasn't been proven—that the results were written by one of its members. That individual was none other than Newton himself. I'm sure you can imagine what the results were, right? This biased report found in favor of Newton and claimed that his calculus was the original. Leibniz's case wasn't even presented, nor was he permitted to submit any evidence on his behalf.

The German scientist, who at that time was aged and worn out by the controversy, had little time to spend away from his work. Nor was he able to recall events that had occurred forty years prior, so he wouldn't have been able to provide much of a defense anyway. Well, at that time, reputation mattered more than the truth. And Newton had a reputation for being a man of the highest moral character. He was additionally considered the preeminent scientist of his day not only in England but also in most of Europe. [11]He had been knighted by Queen Anne for his work in reforming the mint, which put an end to the counterfeiting that had plagued England. **Leibniz was also a scientific star of the day, yet he wasn't in Newton's league.** Leibniz was employed by various nobles in the German states, where he worked as a lawyer, diplomat, and historian. He actually conducted most of his scientific studies in his leisure time. This

controversy dealt a severe blow to his reputation, and his death in 1716 failed to put an end to the matter.

A careful examination of the facts reveals that both men were working on the same thing simultaneously. Interestingly, Newton's case is harder to prove than Leibniz's. See, uh, Leibniz left many notes on how he developed his theory of calculus, so from them, mathematical and historical experts can rather easily trace the path of development. It's clear from his notes that most of his ideas were developed independently of Newton's methods. The problem is that we don't know much about Newton's methods. There's little evidence showing how he reached his conclusions, and it's only in his published works on calculus that his ideas are revealed. This seems to provide support for Leibniz, but there's no evidence at all that Newton made use of any of Leibniz's ideas.

Newtonian calculus was considered the, uh, true calculus during much of the eighteenth century, especially in England. Subsequent investigations into the controversy have revealed that both men did the work independently and arrived at similar conclusions. While this matter may seem unimportant, I want you to think about how a scientist's reputation can have a strong bearing on whether his theories are accepted or not. Let me give you an example of what I mean when I say that.

6 **Gist-Content Question** | The professor spends the majority of the lecture describing the controversy between Newton and Leibniz concerning which of them developed calculus.

7 **Understanding Organization Question** | The professor covers the events in the controversy in the order in which they happened, so she discusses them chronologically.

8 **Making Inferences Question** | The professor says, "Firstly, you need to be aware that neither man entirely developed calculus. After all, some of the ideas it's based on have been around since ancient times. Let me see . . . The Egyptians, the Greeks, and the Chinese all did work related to calculus. But what Newton and Leibniz both did was, uh, well, they took the sum of these ideas and put them together to form a unifying theory." So she implies that many people helped develop calculus.

9 **Connecting Content Question** | According to the lecture, Sir Isaac Newton was credited with inventing calculus by the Royal Society, and he was also considered the greatest scientist in Europe. As for Gottfried Leibniz, he published his work on calculus

before Newton did, and he was also accused of being a plagiarist in 1699.

10 **Detail Question** | The professor states, "The problem is that we don't know much about Newton's methods. There's little evidence showing how he reached his conclusions, and it's only in his published works on calculus that his ideas are revealed."

11 **Understanding Attitude Question** | When the professor says that Leibniz "wasn't in Newton's league," he means that Leibniz was not as good a scientist as Newton.

Lecture 🎧 06-05 p.135

W Professor: One of the most commonly used metals since antiquity is copper. The ancients mined copper and used it to make a large number of metal tools and weapons. They utilized it in particular to make bronze, an alloy formed by a combination of copper and tin. In the past, most copper was mined from deposits located near the surface. That still holds true today as most copper comes from open-pit mines. However, it's sometimes mined from places deep underground. The type of mine used to extract copper ore depends upon where the ore is located. When the ore is relatively close to the surface, an open-pit mine is used. On the other hand, if the ore is located deep underground, then tunnels must be dug to extract it. As a general rule, open-pit mining is the more preferred method since it's cheaper and easier to remove the ore. Oh, uh, it's also a lot safer for the miners, who don't have to risk their lives in underground tunnels.

Let me talk about open-pit copper mining for a bit. In an open-pit copper mine, the soil and the rock that cover the copper ore are collectively called the overburden. The overburden needs to be blasted with dynamite or scraped away by earth-moving machines so that miners can get to the ore. Sometimes, if the overburden rock is of good quality, it may be sold to be used for construction and other purposes. This earns the mining company a small profit. In many cases, veins of ore start from near the surface and run deep underground. In these instances, the miners continue blasting and digging. As they descend further into the ground, they expand the open-pit mine.

The miners make the open-pit mine much larger to enable them to extract the ore in as safe a manner as possible. This results in some mines of, well, of enormous size. Take a look at your books. I believe there's a picture of an open-pit mine on page ninety-five . . . Everyone see it . . . ? Okay, good. You can clearly see the different levels, right? Each level is called a bench. As the benches descend deeper, they appear to be flat areas with steep—yet not quite vertical—drops to the next bench. [17] The steep inclines between benches are known as batters. In case you're curious, the reason that the batters aren't totally vertical is that this lessens the danger from falling rocks. **Anyway, notice how the mine looks like a set of stairs or, uh, terraces.**

Another important aspect of an open-pit mine is the network of roads that run from the bottom to the top. These roads are built on some of the benches and often follow a circuitous route as they ascend. These roads are used to take the ore out of the mine in massive trucks. They're also used to transport machinery and supplies to the bottom of the mine. When a mine is operating at full capacity, these trucks go up and down all day and night long without interruption. So, uh, once the trucks reach the surface with their loads of ore, the ore is either processed in a place nearby the mine or shipped to a processing plant by truck or rail. It's during the processing when the rock surrounding the copper is removed and the copper is made viable for commercial use.

M Student: What happens when all of the copper is extracted from the ground?

W: When the ore is all gone or when operating the mine becomes uneconomical, the mine gets shut down. What remains is a big open pit. So let me guess your next question: What happens to the pit? Many times, the company leases the land to the local government, which uses the pit as a landfill. Okay, um, I know many of you are probably wondering about the environmental effects of open-pit mines. While it's true that mining companies in the past cared little about any damage they caused to the environment, that's definitely not the case nowadays. Before mines are ever opened, extensive environmental studies are carried out. Studies of the water table in particular are emphasized so that the groundwater doesn't get contaminated by the mine.

What's really the main problem with open-pit mining nowadays is that it leaves a huge ugly scar on the landscape. Some locals insist that companies fill in the mine and plant trees on the land when they're done mining. This at least helps restore the land somewhat. Another big problem has to do with the overburden and other unused materials. As the overburden is removed, if it's not sold, it typically gets piled up near the pit. This becomes something of an eyesore. Mines also have to deal with tailings. Ah, tailings are waste materials created from the processing of copper ore. Tailings are often contaminated with chemicals, so they can, if they're not stored properly, poison the local water system. That actually happened at the Pebble Mine in Alaska. And that's what we need to explore next. There were a lot of problems that this mine caused.

12 **Gist-Content Question** | The professor mostly talks about open-pit copper mines in her lecture.

13 **Detail Question** | The professor explains, "In an open-pit copper mine, the soil and the rock that cover the copper ore are collectively called the overburden."

14 **Making Inferences Question** | The professor mentions, "When a mine is operating at full capacity, these trucks go up and down all day and night long without interruption." So it can be inferred that some mines operate twenty-four hours a day.

15 **Understanding Attitude Question** | The professor declares, "While it's true that mining companies in the past cared little about any damage they caused to the environment, that's definitely not the case nowadays."

16 **Detail Question** | Concerning the problems with open-pit copper mining at the present, the professor notes, "What's really the main problem with open-pit mining nowadays is that it leaves a huge ugly scar on the landscape. Some locals insist that companies fill in the mine and plant trees on the land when they're done mining. This at least helps restore the land somewhat. Another big problem has to do with the overburden and other unused materials. As the overburden is removed, if it's not sold, it typically gets piled up near the pit. This becomes something of an eyesore."

17 **Understanding Function Question** | When the professor makes that statement, she is making a comparison.

Answers

PART 1

1 Ⓒ	2 Ⓑ	3 Ⓒ	4 Ⓒ	5 Ⓐ
6 Ⓐ	7 Ⓒ	8 ②, ④	9 Ⓒ	10 Ⓓ
11 Ⓓ				

PART 2

1 Ⓓ	2 Ⓐ	3 Ⓑ	4 ①, ③	5 Ⓒ
6 Ⓑ	7 Ⓒ	8 Cause: ①, ②, ④ Effect: ③		
9 Ⓒ	10 Ⓐ	11 Ⓓ		

PART 3

1 Ⓑ	2 Ⓒ	3 ①, ④	4 Ⓐ	5 Ⓑ
6 Ⓑ	7 Ⓐ	8 Ⓑ	9 Ⓓ	10 Ⓐ
11 Ⓒ	12 Ⓓ	13 Ⓒ	14 Ⓐ	15 Ⓒ
16 Ceres: ②, ③ Vesta: ①, ④		17 Ⓒ		

Scripts & Explanations

PART 1

Conversation 🎧 07-01   p.142

W Professor: Thanks for dropping by my office this afternoon, Jeff. I assume you know why I asked you here.

M Student: Um, actually, Professor Kimble, I'm not really sure about that. I mean, uh, my midterm exam grade was good, I've turned in all of my assignments, and I've been to every class this semester. Have I done something bad?

W: Hmm . . . I wouldn't say you've done anything bad, but you're definitely wrong about having done all of your assignments. There's still one you haven't submitted yet.

M: There is? B-b-b-but I've done all the homework. I remember turning everything in with the other students.

W: No, Jeff, it's not your homework. I've gotten all of those papers you turned in. I'm referring to your final paper.

M: But that's not due for, uh, three more weeks, right?

W: That's correct. However, you were supposed to turn in your proposal for the paper by the end of last week. I've gotten proposals from every student in the class except you. By any chance, uh, do you happen to have your proposal with you?

M: We were supposed to turn that in?

W: Yes. Yes, you were.

M: Oh . . . I'm sorry. I totally misunderstood. I thought that only students who weren't sure about what they were going to write on had to turn them in. Since I already know what topic I'm going to do, I didn't think I needed to give you my proposal.

W: **⁴You know, with most other students, I wouldn't believe them, but I actually believe you, Jeff.** It sounds like this was all just a misunderstanding.

M: Yes, ma'am. So shall I write up my proposal and get it to you tomorrow? Er, actually, I've already written half of my paper. I hope you don't find anything wrong with what I'm going to do.

W: Jeff, this is a little unorthodox, but I've got an idea. Why don't you just tell me about your idea right now? Then, I can let you know if you're doing the right thing or not. And it will keep you from having to write up a proposal as well.

M: Okay. That's fine.

W: Go ahead then.

M: Well, I've decided to look at the history of the city of Aspen for my project.

W: Aspen? You mean the ritzy ski resort?

M: That's right. See, um, it didn't start out that way. It was originally a mining town. It was sort of a boomtown I suppose. Then, for various reasons, the economy crashed, and it became a virtual ghost town.

W: Okay. So what angle are you thinking of taking with it?

M: As you know, Aspen is a town where the rich and famous gather nowadays. What I want to do is look at how the town managed to, um . . . to change its identity I suppose I should say. I want to explore how it saved itself from completing emptying out and having no one living there.

W: All right. I like the sound of that. You might want to compare the decisions the city managers there made to those made in cities that never experienced the revival that Aspen did.

M: Ah, that's a good idea. Thanks for the tip. I'll be sure to do some research on that.

W: ⁵Great. Okay. **I'd say that this matter is settled, wouldn't you?**

M: I sure would. Thanks a lot, Professor Kimble.

1 **Gist-Purpose Question** | The professor tells the student, "However, you were supposed to turn in your proposal for the paper by the end of last week. I've gotten proposals from every student in the class except for you."

2 **Making Inferences Question** | When the student says, "I mean, uh, my midterm exam grade was good, I've turned in all of my assignments, and I've been to every class this semester," he implies that he believes that his grade in the class is good.

3 **Gist-Purpose Question** | Before the student tells the professor about the history of Aspen, the professor suggests, "Why don't you just tell me about your idea right now? Then, I can let you know if you're doing the right thing or not. And it will keep you from having to write up a proposal as well."

4 **Understanding Attitude Question** | When the professor indicates that she believes the student whereas she would not believe other students, she is indicating that she knows the student and the work that he does.

5 **Understanding Function Question** | When a professor states that she believes the "matter is settled," she is indicating that there is nothing more to talk about, so the student is free to leave her office.

Lecture 🎧 07-02 p.144

M Professor: Trains are a means of transportation that I doubt many of you have ever taken. Or, if you have, you've likely only ridden on a train once or twice. However, in the United States, trains were an incredibly important form of transportation in the past. This was especially true during the 1800s. I'm going to show you a short film on the history of railroads in the United States, but prior to doing that, I want to go over a few facts about them with you first. So bear with me for a couple of minutes while I, uh, while I cover a few highlights of railroads in the 1800s.

Some primitive forms of railroads actually existed in Europe back in the sixteenth century. However, they were nothing at all like the railroads that developed after the Industrial Revolution began. Instead, these primitive railroads were mostly used around mines and were pulled along wooden tracks by men or horses. When the steam engine was perfected in the 1700s though, it was inevitable that someone would attach one to a railroad and create a train. It took a while for this to happen, but in the early 1800s, railroads were introduced to the U.S.

It was in 1815 that Colonel John Stevens was granted the first railroad charter in North America. Colonel Stevens was rather slow off the mark though, so it took him until 1832 to complete his railroad line. In the meantime, other people got involved in the railroad industry as well. The Baltimore and Ohio Railroad, which was established in 1827, is typically credited with being the real beginning of the American railroad industry. It was the first American railroad to be chartered as a common carrier of freight and passengers.

The Baltimore and Ohio Railroad wasn't the only railroad in the country though. In actuality, numerous railroads suddenly started being built everywhere. One of the more famous ones was the South Carolina Canal and Railroad Company, which began carrying passengers on Christmas Day in 1830. At that time, it had a mere six miles of track, yet this made it the longest operating railroad line in the country.

In the 1830s, there was a veritable boom in the construction of railroad lines. Think about it. The United States is a big country. A lot of people fail to realize that, but the country is huge. And by the 1830s, people were spreading out across the continent and were moving west past the Mississippi River. Given the choices of walking, riding on horseback, taking a stagecoach, or riding on a train, the best option was obvious. People also recognized that trains could carry much larger loads than anything else on land. This is why, by 1840, a mere thirteen years after the first American railroad was established, there were more than 2,800 miles of train track in the country east of the Mississippi. By 1850, that number had increased to more than 9,000 miles of track. But please be aware that much of it was concentrated in the Northeast with the remainder being in the Southeast and Midwest.

What this huge increase in the amount of track did was help bring the country together. People could travel rapidly by train throughout much of the eastern United States as far west as the Mississippi River. Additionally, railroads enabled the expansion of the agricultural industry, particularly in the Midwest. Chicago, Illinois, became a major transportation hub as farmers from Wisconsin, Minnesota, and other areas brought crops and animals there to be transported to markets further east.

I should also mention that the 1860s was a crucial decade in the history of railroads for two important reasons. First, as I'm sure you're aware, the American Civil War was fought from 1861 to 1865. This was the first war in which railroads played a major role. The Union had many more miles of track than the Confederacy, which made moving troops and equipment much easier for the Union. This was a major factor that contributed to the Union's victory. The other crucial event in the 1860s was

that work on a transcontinental railroad connecting the Atlantic Ocean with the Pacific Ocean started in 1862. The railroad wasn't finished until May 10, 1869, when the last spike was hammered in at Promontory Point, Utah. Nevertheless, the country was finally united, and it was railroads that did that.

[11]Railroads continued expanding throughout the rest of the century. By 1900, there were around 193,000 miles of railroad track throughout the country as well as five transcontinental railroad lines. **Also of importance was that railroad operators had reached agreements on the width of standard track, which let them connect their railroads to one another.** The 1800s was truly the golden age for railroads in the country. All right. I think that's enough of me talking. Let's sit back and watch this film on the history of railroads in the U.S. And before anyone asks, yes, I expect you to know this information, so please take notes while you're watching.

6 **Gist-Content Question** | The professor mostly lectures about the history of railroads in the United States in the nineteenth century.

7 **Gist-Purpose Question** | The professor explains, "In the 1830s, there was a veritable boom in the construction of railroad lines. Think about it. The United States is a big country. A lot of people fail to realize that, but the country is huge. And, by the 1830s, people were spreading out across the continent and were moving west past the Mississippi River. Given the choices of walking, riding on horseback, taking a stagecoach, or riding on a train, the best option was obvious."

8 **Detail Question** | The professor first states, "I should also mention that the 1860s was a crucial decade in the history of railroads for two important reasons. First, as I'm sure you're aware, the American Civil War was fought from 1861 to 1865. This was the first war in which railroads played a major role." Then, he mentions, "The other crucial event in the 1860s was that work on a transcontinental railroad connecting the Atlantic Ocean with the Pacific Ocean started in 1862."

9 **Understanding Attitude Question** | The professor says, "The 1800s was truly the golden age for railroads in the country."

10 **Understanding Organization Question** | The professor's talk on the history of railroads in the United States covers the events that happened in chronological order.

11 **Making Inferences Question** | The professor mentions

that the usage of standard track "let them connect their railroads to one another." This implies that, prior to standardization, trains were unable to operate on some tracks because the sizes of the rails were different.

Conversation 🎧 07-03   p.148

W Student: Mr. Jessie, Stewart said that you wanted to talk to me for a minute.

M Orchestra Conductor: Yes, Kelly, that's right.

W: Um, okay. Is there something I can help you with? I've got to get to a study group that's meeting at the library in about fifteen minutes.

M: Don't worry, Kelly. I don't think this is going to take up too much of your time. You're not going to be late for the study group. Anyway, Kelly, I noticed that you've seemed a little distracted during practice the last few days. I'm sorry to say this, but your performance lately hasn't really been up to par. Is there something going on with you that I need to know about?

W: Er . . . Actually, yes. You see, uh, I've been, um . . . Well, I've been giving some thought to quitting the orchestra.

M: Quitting? You can't possibly be serious, can you? What on earth would make you want to do that?

W: My grades. You see, um, I've been having a lot of trouble keeping my grades up this semester. In my first two years, I got at least a 3.50 GPA every semester, so I always made the Dean's List. But my grades on my midterm exams weren't nearly as good this semester. And I'm starting to fall way behind in a lot of my class work. Everyone says that chemical engineering gets really tough your junior year, and, well, it seems like those people are all right. And if my grades go down, it's going to be difficult for me to land a decent job when I'm a senior next year.

M: So you're thinking of quitting the orchestra in order to concentrate on your studies?

W: Yes, sir. I mean, we practice for two hours every single weekday, and I just don't have that much time to dedicate to the orchestra. I'm really sorry, but I've got to focus on my studies.

M: How about if we come up with something like a compromise?

W: How so?

M: Let's do this . . . Go ahead and take the rest of this week off. That will give you four days away from here, so you can use that time to catch up with your studies, do your homework, and get your grades higher.

W: Okay. But then what happens next week? Do I need to attend practice every day?

M: No, I don't think so. Why don't you try coming to practice three or four days a week instead of coming every day? I think practicing for three or four days each week will be sufficient to make sure you're prepared for the winter concert we're going to perform next month. What do you think of that idea?

W: Hmm . . . It might just work. I think I'll go ahead and give it a try.

M: That's great. But be sure to do one thing for me, Kelly.

W: What's that?

M: Take care of your own needs first. If being in the orchestra is too much for you to handle, I totally understand if you drop out to focus on your studies. I'll miss having you here, but your grades absolutely must come first.

W: Thanks for saying that. It's nice to hear that from you, sir. I admire a person who puts the welfare of others over himself.

1   **Gist-Purpose Question** | The conductor asks the student, "Anyway, Kelly, I noticed that you've seemed a little distracted during practice the last few days. I'm sorry to say this, but your performance lately hasn't really been up to par. Is there something going on with you that I need to know about?"

2   **Detail Question** | When the conductor says that the student's recent performance "hasn't really been up to par," he is indicating that her performance has been below average for a while.

3   **Making Inferences Question** | The student states, "I've been having a lot of trouble keeping my grades up this semester. In my first two years, I got at least a 3.50 GPA every semester, so I always made the Dean's List. But my grades on my midterm exams weren't nearly as good this semester." The student therefore implies that her current grades are below the level that is necessary to make the Dean's List.

4   **Detail Question** | First, the conductor tells the student, "Go ahead and take the rest of this week off." Then, he says, "Why don't you try coming to practice three or four days a week instead of coming every day? I think practicing for three or four days each week will be sufficient to make sure you're prepared for the winter concert we're going to perform next month."

Understanding Attitude Question | At the end of the conversation, the student tells the conductor, "I admire a person who puts the welfare of others over himself." So she respects how he is treating her.

Lecture 🎧 07-04   p.150

M Professor: You know, as summer approaches, the weather starts to get pretty hot around here. When the temperature rises, I enjoy getting out of the city here and escaping to the countryside. One reason I do this is that the temperature tends to be a few degrees cooler in rural areas than it is in urban centers. [11] I wonder if any of you have ever noticed that. Heather?

W Student: My family lives on a farm a couple of hours away from here. I've definitely noticed that there's a difference in temperature between rural and urban areas. **It can be so much cooler on the farm than it is here on campus.**

M: That's exactly what I'm talking about, class. We have a name for this phenomenon. We call it urban heat island. There are a number of factors that can cause the temperatures in cities to be higher than they are in rural settings. In fact, some rural areas can be between five to nine degrees Celsius cooler than any nearby urban areas. That's quite a dramatic difference, isn't it? Well, let me tell you why this happens.

Consider rural areas. These places are primarily fields and forests and have few buildings, roads, sidewalks, and other manmade structures. During the day, the sun shines on rural areas. Any solar energy that's absorbed near the ground causes water in both vegetation and soil to evaporate. When this water evaporates, it creates a cooling effect. In addition, when the wind blows in rural areas, there aren't many structures to obstruct it. Thus the wind blows uninterrupted. Why is this important? Well, when the wind blows, it makes the air circulate. This causes both hot air and cold—or cool—air to mix with one another. As a result, the hot air cools off, which lowers the temperature. As you can see, the lack of manmade structures, the presence of large amounts of vegetation, and the fact that the wind circulates combine to lower temperatures in rural areas.

However, what about urban areas . . . ? First, in urban areas, there's much less vegetation than there is in rural areas. Sure, a city may have a park or two, but, as a general rule, there simply aren't that many trees and bushes in cities. So there's little evaporation of water in cities to help cool them off. In addition, consider this:

When rain falls in rural areas, it gets absorbed into the soil. Later, this moisture can be evaporated by the sun's rays. However, what happens to rain that falls in a city? It doesn't get absorbed into the ground. After all, the ground is usually paved, right? Instead, the rainwater gets taken away by the city's drainage system, which thereby precludes it from providing an evaporative cooling effect later in the future.

Cities have very little vegetation. But what do they have lots of . . . ? Um, buildings, for one. There are many roads, sidewalks, parking lots, and other manmade structures, too. When the sun shines, all of them absorb the sun's heat. You should remember that these structures are made from brick, concrete, tar, and asphalt, among other materials. Unfortunately for people living in cities, these materials are excellent conductors of heat. This means that during the day, they absorb and retain lots of heat. Just touch a concrete surface on a hot day, and you'll see what I mean. Since these structures retain heat, they remain warm even during the night. This helps increase the temperatures in cities.

You should also think about the numerous motor vehicles in operation in urban centers. There are cars, trucks, buses, trains, subways, and other types of motorized conveyances operating throughout them. These objects generate heat, much of which enters the atmosphere. So they contribute to higher temperatures in urban areas. Finally, remember what I said about the wind blowing unobstructed in rural areas . . . ? Okay, think about our neighborhood. We're surrounded by tall buildings. The wind doesn't blow as much here, which means that the air circulates much less. As a result, hot air remains in cities since the wind can't blow any cool air in to disperse it.

Urban heat island isn't just a summer phenomenon either. It happens all year round and during both day and night. The temperature difference between a city and its outlying rural area is usually the greatest on calm, clear evenings. The reason is that rural areas cool off much faster at night than urban areas. So around three to five hours after sunset, a period known as maximum heat island effect takes place. During this time, the temperature difference between the two regions is at its greatest.

Urban heat island can have some seriously adverse effects on an area and its residents. People can suffer from heatstroke, and some, particularly the elderly, die because of the extremely hot conditions in summer. People use more energy in summer to run their air conditioners as well. And the lack of air circulation leads to increased air pollution. Fortunately, it's possible to reduce the effects of urban heat island. Let me tell you some ways to do this.

6　**Gist-Content Question** | About urban heat island, the professor mostly lectures on its causes.

7　**Understanding Organization Question** | The professor compares rural and urban areas to let the class see how urban heat islands get formed.

8　**Connecting Content Question** | According to the lecture, manmade structures blocking the wind from blowing is one cause of urban heat island. So are rainwater getting washed into drainage systems and buildings retaining lots of heat from the sun. As for an effect of urban heat island, temperatures are higher in urban areas than they are in rural areas.

9　**Detail Question** | The professor notes, "So around three to five hours after sunset, a period known as maximum heat island effect takes place. During this time, the temperature difference between the two regions is at its greatest."

10　**Detail Question** | The professor states, "People can suffer from heatstroke, and some, particularly the elderly, die because of the extremely hot conditions in summer."

11　**Making Inferences Question** | When the student declares that there is a temperature different between rural and urban areas and then says, "It can be so much cooler on the farm than it is here on campus," she is implying that the campus is in an urban area.

PART 3

Conversation 🎧 07-05　　　　　　　　p.154

W Student: Good afternoon, Dean Chambers. Thank you for setting aside some time to meet with me.

M Dean of Students: It's my pleasure, Janet. Why don't you make yourself comfortable, and then you can tell me about your big plans for campus?

W: Thank you, sir . . . Let me get to the point. I believe the campus could be improved in its appearance in many ways, and I'd like to organize a volunteer group to assist in doing so.

M: That's rather ambitious.

W: Well, I love the school and the campus, but there's room for improvement. And I'd like to help.

M: What exactly do you think needs to be improved?

W: Several things. First of all, there's too much litter around the campus. I mean, almost everywhere you go, you can see trash on the ground somewhere.

M: Okay, now, uh, that's something that the Maintenance Department is in charge of. It may be possible that some custodians aren't working as hard as they could, but if you have a bunch of students picking up trash for free, I don't think the members of that department are going to be too pleased.

W: Really? Why is that?

M: They'd be out of jobs if there's no trash to clean up.

W: Ah . . . I see.

M: You have some other ideas though?

W: Yes, sir. I do. I think that there are several places around campus that could be beautified.

M: Beautified?

W: Yes. For instance, the area around the student center is pretty dull and boring. It's just full of concrete. I wonder if we could, hmm . . . let students display some artwork there or perhaps allow some talented art students to paint murals on the concrete walls. I think that would really help beautify the campus.

M: Hmm . . . That's a possibility. I'll make a note about that and will contact Terry Sommers. He'll let me know if something like that is feasible.

W: Thank you so much.

M: Is there anything else?

W: One more thing for now. The area around Granite Lake at the eastern end of campus is pretty boring. There's nothing by the shore there. There should be picnic tables for people to eat at, and the grass should be cut more often. So many students would enjoy going there if only it were slightly more presentable.

M: Hmm . . . You may have a point there. I was just at the lake the other day and had a couple of similar thoughts. All right, uh, here's what I'm going to do. I personally can't authorize any of the projects that you're contemplating, but I like your ideas. So I'm going to set up a meeting for you with Janet Anderson. She's one of the vice presidents here. You need to talk to her about your ideas. But let me give you a word of advice.

W: Yes, sir?

M: Be better prepared when you talk to her. You need to have a couple of handouts listing your ideas and how you propose to solve what you perceive as problems. Ms. Anderson is very busy, so you'll only get around ten minutes to sell her on your ideas. If she thinks you're wasting her time, she'll cut you off immediately. Okay?

W: I totally understand. Thank you.

M: Great. I'll contact you when the meeting is all set up.

1 **Gist-Purpose Question** | The student asked to see the dean of students in order to tell him about her plans for a volunteer group.

2 **Understanding Function Question** | The dean of students first says, "Okay, now, uh, that's something that the Maintenance Department is in charge of. It may be possible that some custodians aren't working as hard as they could, but if you have a bunch of students picking up trash for free, I don't think the members of that department are going to be too pleased," and then he adds, "They'd be out of jobs if there's no trash to clean up."

3 **Detail Question** | The student wants to improve the area around the lake as well as the student center.

4 **Detail Question** | The dean of students tells the student, "So I'm going to set up a meeting for you with Janet Anderson. She's one of the vice presidents here. You need to talk to her about your ideas."

5 **Making Inferences Question** | The dean of students remarks, "Be better prepared when you talk to her. You need to have a couple of handouts listing your ideas and how you propose to solve what you perceive as problems. Ms. Anderson is very busy, so you'll only get around ten minutes to sell her on your ideas. If she thinks you're wasting her time, she'll cut you off immediately. Okay?" It can therefore be inferred that he does not believe the student was prepared for their meeting.

Lecture 🎧 07-06   p.156

W Professor: One of the most common musical instruments is the violin, which has several forms and is used in a plethora of genres of music. Of course, it serves as a primary instrument in most orchestras. But it's also used in various types of folk music and is often a part of American country and western bands, where it's known as a fiddle. Today, to begin with, we're going to talk about the history of the violin, its various parts, and some famous makers of violins.

The exact origins of the violin are unknown, but it more than likely was developed to be an improvement over stringed instruments from the past, uh, namely the lute and lira. In fact, makers of stringed instruments such as violins are called luthiers, so it's likely there's a connection between the two. Now, the use of a bow to play a stringed instrument is believed to come from Central Asia since

there are quite a few stringed musical instruments that need bows to make music that originated in this region. Over time, these instruments spread westward to the Middle East and Eastern Europe. In the Byzantine Empire, which was mostly in the land that is modern-day Greece and Turkey, the lira was a stringed instrument that was extremely popular in the ninth century. It had a hollow body and an oval shape and was played with a bow that moved across strings while the musician held it upright, much in the same manner that a cello is played. Here's a picture of a lira on the screen . . . Notice the unmistakable similarities to the modern violin.

Yet the violin as we know it doesn't come from the Byzantine Empire. It instead originated in northern Italy around the port cities of Venice and Genoa during the middle of the sixteenth century. Venice and Genoa were two of the richest and most powerful city-states in Italy at that time. They had extensive trading connections with the Middle East and the Ottoman Empire, which supplanted the Byzantine Empire in the middle of the 1400s. It's likely that the violin arrived in the West this way and that it was an improvement on the lira as well. The oldest known violin, by the way, has been dated at 1560. Anyway, by the end of the 1500s, the violin was well known throughout Western Europe. Over time, improvements have been made to it, but the basic shape and style of the violin have remained essentially the same since the 1500s.

Okay, uh, let's look at a schematic of a violin and examine its parts. Look up here at the screen, please . . . The violin has two main parts: the body . . . and the neck. The main part of the neck is the fingerboard, which is where the violinist presses his or her fingers to change the pitch of the four strings. At the end of the neck here . . . is the decorative scroll-shaped piece. In addition, the peg box is there. Here you can see four pegs, which can adjust the tension on the strings and change their pitch. Note that the body has an hourglass shape. The upper part is called the upper bout. That's spelled B-O-U-T by the way. The lower part, uh, as you can guess, is the lower bout. The narrow section in the middle here . . . is the waist. The body of the violin is hollow and contains two S-shaped narrowing openings, which are called F holes. One of the crucial parts of the body is the bridge. See it . . . ? It's where the strings form an arch over the body. The strings are attached to the body by the tailpiece, um, this black section at the end. Next to the tailpiece is the chinrest, which is where the violinist places his or her chin. Now, violins are made of . . . Yes?

M Student: Um, sorry for the interruption, but what about the bow?

W: Ah, yes. My bad. I nearly forgot about a crucial piece. The bow is about seventy-five centimeters long and is very light. It's made of wood and horsehair fibers. At the end of it is a nut called a, er, a frog, which adjusts the tension on the horsehair. You can see the frog right here . . .

As for their composition, violins are made of wood. The type of wood determines the quality of their sound. Other factors, such as the thickness of the wood and the quality of the varnish used on it, can affect the sound as well. The age of the violin is yet another factor as its sound quality improves with age. Naturally, the oldest violins are considered the best. Originally, all violins were made in northern Italy, and the best ones come from this region. [11]Perhaps the most famous luthier was Antonio Stradivari. He lived and worked in the late seventeenth and early eighteenth centuries. His violins are prized for their craftsmanship and enduring quality, and they sell for millions of dollars today. **Wouldn't you love to get your hands on one of those?**

6   **Gist-Content Question** | The professor mostly describes the origin and the structure of the violin in her lecture.

7   **Making Inferences Question** | The professor states, "The exact origins of the violin are unknown, but it more than likely was developed to be an improvement over stringed instruments from the past, uh, namely the lute and lira." Thus it can be inferred that the lira was invented before the violin was.

8   **Detail Question** | The professor notes, "Yet the violin as we know it doesn't come from the Byzantine Empire. It instead originated in northern Italy around the port cities of Venice and Genoa during the middle of the sixteenth century."

9   **Understanding Organization Question** | While talking about the schematic of the violin, the professor shows the students pictures of the violin and points out the various parts as she lectures.

10 **Detail Question** | About the bridge, the professor states, "One of the crucial parts of the body is the bridge. See it . . . ? It's where the strings form an arch over the body."

11 **Understanding Function Question** | The professor states that violins made by Stradivari "sell for millions of dollars today," and then she asks, "Wouldn't you love to get your hands on one of those?" In asking that, she is emphasizing how valuable the violins that he made are.

M Professor: All right. [17]Have you all handed in your homework assignments to me . . . ? Yes . . . ? Good. I'll try to get them back to you by Monday of next week. **I really hope they're better than the work many of you submitted the previous time.** Now, we need to get started on today's class. We're going to begin with a little bit of history. On January 1, 1801, the astronomer Giuseppe Piazzi discovered Ceres. It was found in an area between Mars and Jupiter, which was right where most people had expected there to be a planet. Because of this, Ceres was initially catalogued as a planet. However, over the next six years, three more celestial bodies similar to Ceres were found in roughly the same region. This included Vesta, which was discovered in 1807 by Heinrich Wilhelm Olbers, a German astronomer.

As you may guess, this sparked a large amount of controversy since most astronomers realized that these bodies didn't fit the conventional notion of a planet. The reason was that they were so small that they couldn't be seen by the naked eye; they could only be observed with a telescope. In 1802, following the discovery of the second body, Pallas, William Herschel coined the word "asteroid." Nevertheless, many astronomers persisted in calling these bodies planets, so, by the 1820s, eleven, er, planets had been identified in the solar system. By 1851, there were a total of fifteen heavenly bodies that had been found orbiting the sun between Mars and Jupiter. Finally, astronomers then realized that these bodies represented a new class of objects and started referring to them as asteroids. They, uh, obviously accepted the name that Herschel had proposed half a century earlier. Today, this region of space is collectively known as the asteroid belt. Around 100,000 asteroids as large as six miles in diameter have been discovered. Of them, Ceres, with a diameter of around 590 miles, is the largest, and Vesta, with a diameter of 330 miles, is the third largest.

W Student: Professor Martinez, I thought that Ceres was a dwarf planet. Or am I mistaken?

M: You're not mistaken at all, Paula. Thanks for bringing that up. I should point out that, in 2006, the International Astronomical Union created a new term for celestial bodies: dwarf planet. This was when Pluto was demoted from being a planet to being a dwarf planet, and I suppose we could say that Ceres was promoted to dwarf planet status. Ceres is, by the way, the smallest of the few dwarf planets in our solar system.

Now, both Ceres and Vesta are intriguing to

astronomers for a few reasons. In fact, they're so interesting that the NASA satellite *Dawn* was sent to explore them up close. *Dawn* began orbiting Vesta in the summer of 2011. It remained there for approximately a year and then left for Ceres, where it arrived around 2015. One of the reasons for the *Dawn* mission was to determine the composition of these two heavenly bodies. See, uh, studies from the Earth have shown that Ceres and Vesta have compositions that may provide clues to the conditions and processes involved in the formation of planets.

Ceres appears to have an outer coating of dust that's lying atop a thick layer of ice. This ice may be as much as sixty miles deep, and it's believed to be wrapped around a ball of rock. Interestingly enough, Ceres most likely lacks an iron core. Another intriguing aspect of Ceres is that of all the large, icy bodies in the solar system that might have interior heat that could provide enough warmth for subsurface water to exist, it's the closest to the sun. Why is that important? Well, as we consider sending manned missions to places beyond the moon, we will require access to resources throughout the solar system. It's highly likely that Ceres contains more water than we could ever hope to use. Given its location in the solar system, Ceres would be an ideal stopping point for manned missions heading to the outer solar system, which includes Jupiter, Saturn, Uranus, and Neptune. Oh, and, if it has liquid water, there's always the possibility— no matter how remote—that Ceres could harbor life. It might be extremely primitive life forms, but it would be, uh, a pivotal event in history if we were to discover that life exists elsewhere.

Now, what about Vesta? Well, it's rather different from Ceres. While Ceres is relatively round on account of its large size and the effect gravity has had on it, Vesta has an irregular shape. And Vesta is bone dry, which makes it quite different from Ceres. Vesta also has an inner core made of iron. One of the reasons *Dawn* was sent there was to determine why Vesta and Ceres are so different. Also of interest is that astronomers estimate that approximately one in every twenty meteorites that have been found on the Earth originated from Vesta. I have no clue why that has happened. That was a mystery that people were hoping the *Dawn* mission would clear up as well.

12 **Understanding Organization Question** | The professor describes how some asteroids were discovered by talking about the events in chronological order.

13 **Detail Question** | The professor states, "By 1851, there were a total of fifteen heavenly bodies that had been

found orbiting the sun between Mars and Jupiter. Finally, astronomers then realized that these bodies represented a new class of objects and started referring to them as asteroids. They, uh, obviously accepted the name that Herschel had proposed half a century earlier. Today, this region of space is collectively known as the asteroid belt."

14 **Gist-Purpose Question** | A student asks the professor about the status of Ceres, so he explains to the class why Ceres is now considered a dwarf planet and not an asteroid.

15 **Understanding Attitude Question** | The professor declares, "Oh, and, if it has liquid water, there's always the possibility—no matter how remote—that Ceres could harbor life." By noting that the possibility of life existing is remote, the professor indicates that it is unlikely any kind of life lives on Ceres.

16 **Connecting Content Question** | According to the lecture, Ceres may have water underneath its surface, and it was discovered before Vesta was. As for Vesta, its inner core is made of iron, and a lot of the meteorites found on the Earth come from it.

17 **Understanding Function Question** | When the professor says that he hopes that the students' work is better than what they previously submitted, he is letting the students know that he is not pleased with the work that some of them did.

TOEFL® MAP

ACTUAL TEST

New TOEFL® Edition

Michael A. Putlack
Stephen Poirier
Angela Maas
Maximilian Tolochko

Listening **2**

Translations

DARAKWON

TOEFL MAP ACTUAL TEST

New TOEFL Edition

Listening 2

Translations

DARAKWON

Actual Test 01

PART 1

Conversation
p.16

서점 매니저: 실례지만 구입한 책을 반품하는 것에 대해 학생이 제 직원과 이야기하는 것을 들었어요. 대화를 엿들었다고 해서 학생이 불쾌해 하지는 않았으면 좋겠군요. 하지만 제가 이곳 관리자이니 제게 문제를 설명해 주는 것이 어떨까요? 아마도 제가 처리해서 학생에게 도움을 줄 수 있을 거예요.

학생: 오, 그래요. 그렇게 할게요. 음, 저는 철학 수업 교재로 이 책을 샀는데, 오늘 그 수업의 수강 신청을 취소해서 더 이상 이 책이 필요 없게 되었어요.

서점 매니저: 이해가 가는군요. 계속해 보세요.

학생: 저는 이번 학기에 책을 사느라 막대한 돈을 썼어요. 교재를 전부 구입하는데 총 300달러 이상 쓴 것 같아요. 아시겠지만 제가 여기에 온 이후로 책 가격이 계속해서 크게 오르고 있죠. 그 점에 대해서는 선생님께서 정말로 무슨 조치를 취하셔야 할 거예요.

서점 매니저: 학생의 심정은 이해가 가지만 저는 이곳의 매니저일 뿐이에요. 도서 가격이 바뀌기를 바란다면 저보다는 책을 만들어 내는 출판사에 불만을 토로하는 편이 훨씬 나을 거예요. 그건 그렇고, 철학 교재를 구입하는데 얼마를 쓰셨나요?

학생: 비용이… 흠, 잠시만요… 65달러요. 가장 비싼 책이었죠.

서점 매니저: 그러면 환불을 원하는 것이죠, 맞나요?

학생: 네, 그래요. 하지만 방금 전에 이야기를 나누던 직원분께서는 환불을 받을 수 있는 기간이 이미 끝났다고 하시더군요. 이 책을 구입한지 3일밖에 되지 않았기 때문에 그렇다고 한다면 정말 억울할 것 같아요. 거의 펴 보지도 않았거든요.

서점 매니저: 좋아요. 두 가지를 말씀드릴게요.

학생: 네.

서점 매니저: 원칙적으로 책의 환불 기간은 지났어요. 어제였죠.

학생: 오, 이런.

서점 매니저: 잠시만요. 아직 안 끝났어요. 학생이 제 말을 듣는다면 학생에게 좋은 소식이 될 수도 있는 이야기를 말해 줄게요.

학생: 그 점에 대해서는 죄송해요.

서점 매니저: 자, 학생은 이 책을 3일 전에 구입했다고 했어요. 맞나요?

학생: 네, 맞아요. 아시겠지만 4일 전에 수강 신청을 했죠. 첫 수업을 들은 후 수업이 끝나자 마자 바로 여기로 와서 책을 구입했고요.

서점 매니저: 4일 전에 수강 신청을 했는데 벌써 수강 신청을 철회한다고요?

학생: 어, 예. 그러니까 강의 계획서를 보다 자세히 살펴보니 교수님께서 너무 많은 것을 시키려고 하시는 것 같았어요. 제 말은, 그 수업이 선택 과목이거든요. 보고서를 세 편 쓰고 시험을 두 번 볼 시간은 제게 없어요. 수강 신청을 취소하는 이유가 그것 때문이죠.

서점 매니저: 그래요. 어쨌거나 제가 상관할 바는 아니군요. 그러니 학생이

영수증을 갖고 있고 이 책을 3일 전에 구입했다고 하면, 어, 그래요, 전액을 환불받을 수 있어요.

학생: 잘 되었군요. 정말 감사합니다. 오, 어, 질문이 하나 더 있는데요… 책이 비닐로 싸여 있었는데, 보시다시피, 어, 제가 뜯어버렸어요. 그래도 이 책을 받아 주실 거죠, 그렇죠?

서점 매니저: 책에 손상이 없는 한 전액을 환불해 드릴게요.

학생: 정말로 듣고 싶었던 말이군요. 이제 어떻게 하면 환불을 받을 수 있나요?

WORD REMINDER

listen in 엿듣다, 도청하다   deadline 최종 기한, 마감 시간   depressing 침울하게 만드는   barely 겨우, 거의 ~ 않는   syllabus (강의의) 요강, 교수 요목   way 훨씬, 너무   elective 선택 과목   that's music to my ears 듣던 중 반가운 말이다

Lecture • Biology
p.18

교수: 오늘날 인간이 섭취하는 칼로리의 약 50%는 옥수수, 쌀, 귀리, 보리, 그리고 밀과 같은 곡물에서 비롯됩니다. 이번 시간에는 이러한 각각의 곡물에 대해 살펴보고, 인간이 이들을 변화시켜서, 어, 오랜 시간에 걸쳐 실제로 품질을 향상시킨 방법에 대해 알려 드리고자 합니다. 밀에 대한 이야기로 시작해 보죠.

오늘날 재배되는 밀은 약 10,000년 전 '비옥한 초승달 지대'에 있던 일부 야생종에 그 기원을 두고 있습니다. 비옥한 초승달 지대는 현재의 이스라엘, 레바논, 시리아, 요르단, 그리고 이라크를 포함한 지역입니다. 그 이후로 밀은 보다 많은 낟알을 갖도록, 그리고 다양한 조건에서 살아남을 수 있도록 개량되었습니다. 이러한 개량은 지속적인 시행착오를 겪으면서 수천 년에 걸쳐 이루어졌죠. 하지만 현대에도 밀은 집중적인 실험의 대상이었습니다. 과학자들은 서로 다른 종의 밀을 대상으로 선택적 교배를 실시함으로써 그 특성을 크게 개선시키는 방법을 알아냈습니다.

사람들이 개량된 밀… 혹은 어떤 개량된 품종도 마찬가지로 이를 만드는 두 가지 주된 목적은… 식물당 생산되는 식량의 양을 증가시키는 것과 질병에 대한 식물의 저항력을 증대시키는 것입니다. 오랜 농업의 역사를 통해 농부들은 이러한 일을 해 오고 있습니다. 하지만 이러한 과정이 과학의 수준까지 이르게 된 것은 비교적 최근의 일입니다. 교배와 관련된 수천 번의 과학 실험을 통해 농학자들은 현재 다양한 기후에서 살아남을 수 있고, 다양한 질병에 견딜 수 있으며, 보다 큰 과실이나 낟알을 생산해 냄으로써 수확량을 증대시킬 수 있는 식물을 만들고 있습니다. 밀 역시 일정한 변화를 겪어왔기 때문에 예외가 아닙니다. 하지만 1900년대 중반까지 밀 생산량은 과거의 생산량과 비슷했고, 밀은 여전히 질병으로 큰 피해를 입고 있었습니다.

이러한 사실은 1950년대 한 사람의 노력으로 바뀌게 되었습니다. 바로 노먼 볼로그입니다. 솔직히 말씀드리면, 그와 그의 업적에 대해서는 아무리 칭찬을 해도 부족할 것이라고 생각합니다. 자, 어, 그가 어떤 일을 했는지 말씀을 드리죠. 볼로그는 미국인 과학자로, 식물 유전학의 전문가였습니다. 그는 멕시코에서 12년 이상 진행해 온 연구를 통해 두 가지 주요한 혁신적인 결과를 이끌어 냈습니다. 첫째, 그는 교배를 통해 주요 질병인 녹병을 견딜 수 있는 품종의 밀을 개발했습니다. 녹병은 멕시코 및 기타 지역에서 작물의 손상을 일으키는 주된 원인이었어요. 둘째, 볼로그는 보다 크고 무거운 낟알을 생산하는 밀의 품종을 만들어 냈습니다. 낟알이 커진다는 것은 하나의 밀 줄기에서 보다 많은 식량이 나온다는 점과 경작지당 식량 생산량이 증가된다는 점을 의미했습니다.

하지만 사소한 문제가 하나 있었습니다. 줄기가 너무 가늘었기 때문에 밀이 자라 낟알이 무거워지면 줄기가 꺾였습니다. 밀 줄기는 진화론적인 특성을 지니고 있는데, 이들은 주위의 다른 밀 줄기보다 더 많은 햇빛을 받기 위해 가능한 높이 자람으로써 다른 줄기들과 경쟁을 합니다. 볼로그는, 운이 좋게도, 이러한 문제에 대한 해결책을 가지고 있었습니다. 그는 일본으로부터 난쟁이 밀을 수입했습니다. 이 난쟁이 밀의 줄기는 키가 작고 튼튼했습니다. 이들과 낟알이 큰 밀을 교배시킴으로써 그는 줄기가 튼튼하고 짧으면서 보다 크고 무거운 알곡을 생산해 내는 밀 품종을 만들 수 있었습니다.

볼로그 실험의 최종 결과가 현재 '녹색 혁명'이라고 불리는 것입니다. 실제로 멕시코의 밀 생산량은 두 배가 되었습니다. 볼로그는 이후 파키스탄과 인도에서 연구를 했고, 이들 나라에서 그가 개발한 품종의 밀은 폭발적으로 증가하던 그곳 인구에 많은 양의 식량을 제공해 주었습니다. 많은 전문가들은 볼로그의 육종 밀이 없었다면 그러한 국가에서 수많은 사람들이 굶어 죽었을 것이라고 생각합니다. 주로 볼로그의 노력 덕분에 전 세계 밀 생산량은 지난 50년에 걸쳐 3배로 증가했습니다. 그의 노력 때문에 볼로그는 노벨상 및 기타 다수의 상을 수상했고, 그는 현대 식량 혁명의 아버지로 여겨지고 있습니다.

학생: 그가 유전자 조작 식품을 만들지 않았나요? 인간에게 해로운 것이라고 들은 적이 있습니다.

교수: 직접적인 유전자 조작을 통해 개량한 작물을 이야기하고 있는 것 같군요. 우리가 차후에 살펴볼 주제입니다. 그리고 볼로그가 결코 하지 않았던 일이기도 하죠. 그의 연구는 단지 다양한 품종의 밀을 교배시키는 것과 관련된 것이었습니다. 그가 한 일에 결코 해로운 것은 없었습니다. 실제로 1950년대 이후로 전 세계 수십만 명의 사람들이 — 아마도 수십억 명의 사람들이 — 그의 밀로 만들어진 음식을 먹어 왔기 때문에 그에 대한 증거는 명백합니다. 일부 비판가들이 교배는 자연적이지 못한 것이라고 주장하는 것은 사실이나, 수천 년 동안 농부들은 작물을 교배해 오고 있다는 점을 기억해 둡시다. 실제로, 어, 여러분이 드시고 있는 모든 곡물들은 본래 다양한 야생종으로부터 비롯된 것입니다. 그리고 그의 도움을 받았던 사람들의 입장에서 볼로그의 업적을 생각해 봅시다. 볼로그 덕분에 현재 수많은 사람들이 꾸준히 식량을 공급받고 있습니다. 육종 밀이 인류에게 혜택을 주었다는 점은 우리 모두가 동의할 수 있는 부분이라고 생각합니다.

볼로그는 자신의 연구가 환경에도 도움이 된다고 생각했습니다. 그는 단위 면적당 더 많은 식량을 생산하게 됨으로써 농지를 얻기 위해 숲을 개간하는 경우도 줄어들고 토양에 더해지는 화학 비료의 양도 적어질 것이라고 말했습니다. 분명 고려해야 할 문제입니다. 좋아요, 밀에 대해서는 충분히 다룬 것 같군요. 그 다음으로 쌀에 대해 알아봅시다.

WORD REMINDER

oats 귀리   barley 보리   account for 설명하다; 차지하다   strain 종류, 종   trial-and-error 시행 착오의   enhance 향상시키다 selective 선택적인   crossbreeding 교배   resistant to ~에 대한 저항력이 있는   devastate 황폐화시키다   genetics 유전학   rust 녹병 starve to death 굶어 죽다   manipulation 조작   gene 유전자

PART 2

Conversation

p.22

학생: Marrone 선생님, 선생님의 메시지를 받자마자 왔어요. 제가 너무 늦었나요?

재정 지원 사무실 직원: 어… 미안하지만, 학생이 누구인지 잘 모르겠군요.

학생: 오, 예. 그렇군요. 제 이름은 Katie Alderson입니다. 선생님께서 오후 2시쯤 제 음성 사서함에 메시지를 남기셨어요. 그때는 수업 중이라서 전화기가 꺼져 있었죠. 약 5분 전에 메시지를 확인하고 캠퍼스를 가로질러 여기까지 뛰어왔어요.

재정 지원 사무실 직원: 아, Katie. 알겠어요. 이제 기억이 나는군요. 안타깝게도 너무나 많은 학생들을 상대하고 있기 때문에 모든 사람들을 기억하는 일은 쉽지가 않아요. 하지만 학생의 경우는 기억하고 있죠.

학생: 잘 되었네요. 그러면, 음, 얼마나 곤란한 문제인가요?

재정 지원 사무실 직원: "문제"라는 단어를 사용해야 할지 잘 모르겠네요.

학생: 음, 음성 사서함 메시지에서 서류 작업이 제대로 되어 있지 않아서 제가 다음 학기에 장학금을 타지 못할 수도 있다고 말씀하셨어요. 꽤 큰 금액의 장학금이기 때문에 장학금을 타지 못하면 큰 문제가 될 것이라고 말씀드려야 할 것 같아요.

재정 지원 사무실 직원: 네, 좋은 지적일 수도 있겠군요. 좋아요. 어떤 일이 있는지 알려 줄 테니 상황을 알게 될 거예요.

학생: 네.

재정 지원 사무실 직원: 먼저 장학금을 계속 받기 위해서는 학기마다 약간의 서류 작업을 해야 해요. 지난 3학기 동안은 실수 없이 이루어졌지만 이번 학기에는 학생의 서류 작업에 두어 가지의 문제가 있었어요. 잠시만요… 여기 제 책상 위에 학생의 파일이 있어요. 무엇이 잘못되었는지 알려 줄게요.

학생: 잘못되었다고요? 흠… 제 생각엔 틀림없이 지시 사항이 너무 복잡했던 것 같아요.

재정 지원 사무실 직원: 음, 첫 번째 실수는 복잡한 것이 아니었어요. 여기를 보면… 3페이지 문서에 서명을 하는 것을 잊었어요.

학생: 오, 이런. 믿을 수가 없네요. 펜이 있나요…?

재정 지원 사무실 직원: 여기 있어요.

학생: 좋아요… 문제가 해결되었군요. 다음 문제는 무엇이죠?

재정 지원 사무실 직원: 성적 장학금이기 때문에 학생은 학기마다 성적표 사본을 제출해야 해요. 그렇게 해야 학생의 평점이 장학금 규정에서 요구되는 최소한의 학점이 되는지 저희가 확인할 수 있죠. 하지만, 음, 이번에는 학생의 성적표 사본을 받지 못했어요.

학생: 받지 못하셨다고요? 하지만 제가 학부에 가서, 어… 2주나 3주 전이었는데 사본을 보내 달라고 요청했어요. 잠시만요… 제 지갑에 영수증이 있어요… 보세요… 그러한 요청을 이미 해 두었죠. 하지만 선생님과의 이야기가 끝나는 대로 다시 그쪽으로 가서 그곳에 있는 사람에게 무슨 일이 있었는지 물어볼게요.

재정 지원 사무실 직원: 좋아요. 영수증으로 얼마 전에 학생이 성적표를 요청했다는 점이 드러났으니 학생 탓은 아니군요. 그에 대한 잘못은 분명 학적과에서 나온 것이죠.

학생: 혹시, 어, 다른 문제도 있나요?

재정 지원 사무실 직원: 신청과 관련된 주요한 두 가지 문제는 그것이 다예요. 모두 해결되었기 때문에 학생이 걱정할 것은 없어요. 하지만 서류상 지금 바로 살펴봐야 할 문제가 두어 개 더 있어요. 그것들을 처리하면 전혀 문제될 것이 없을 거예요.

학생: 정확히 제가 듣고 싶었던 말이네요.

재정 지원 사무실 직원: 좋아요. 여기 5페이지를 보세요. 밑에서 세 번째 줄을 보면…

Lecture • Architecture p.24

교수: 로마의 토목 기술 중 또 다른 중요한 측면은 로마인들이 건설한 경이로운 수도교에 있었습니다. 먼저 그것이 무엇인지에 대해 설명해야 할 것 같군요. 수도교는 한 곳에서 다른 곳으로 물이 흐를 수 있도록 해 주는 구조물입니다. 전형적으로는 먼 곳으로부터 물을 끌어 와서, 예컨대 도시와 같이 많은 사람들이 사는 곳으로 물을 보냅니다. 중력을 통해 수도관이 그러한 일을 하는 것이죠. 물이 아래로 흐르는 원리와 같습니다. 지상 혹은 지하의 파이프나 수로 시스템을 통해 중력이 물을 옮겨다 줍니다. 보다 현대적인 시스템에서는 펌프를 이용해 물을 수송하지만, 로마 시대 당시에는 중력에 의해 모든 일이 이루어졌습니다.

여러분들도 짐작할 수 있듯이 어려운 점은 시공하는 과정에서 수도교의 경사도, 즉 각도를 올바르게 설정하는 일이었습니다. 너무 가파르면 물이 너무 빨리 흘러서 수도교가 끝나는 곳에 피해가 발생하거나, 혹은 물이 넘칠 수 있었습니다. 반면에 경사도가 충분히 가파르지 않은 경우, 물이 너무나, 음, 느리게 흐르거나, 심지어 전혀 흐르지 않을 수도 있었습니다. 로마인들은 이러한 토목 기술 상의 난제들을 해결해서 로마 제국 전역에 수도교를 건설했습니다. 그리고 여러분이 궁금하실 할 것 같아 미리 말씀을 드리면, "수도교"라는 단어는 두 개의 라틴어 단어에서 비롯된 것입니다: "물"을 의미하는 *aqua*라는 단어와 "수로"를 의미하는 *ductus*라는 단어가 그것이죠.

수도교의 목적은 이중적인 것이었습니다. 첫째, 수도교는 마시고, 요리에 사용하고, 그리고 목욕에 사용할 수 있는 깨끗한 물을 마을과 도시로 가져다 주었습니다. 둘째, 물은 한 지역의 하수 시스템 내에 있는 오물을 제거하는데도 사용되었습니다. 이로써 로마인들은, 사람들로 붐비는 도시 중심부의 사람들에게 영향을 끼쳤던 질병의 수를 감소시킬 수 있었습니다. 실제로 수도교 시스템은 너무나 효과적이어서 로마의 마을 및 도시에서는, 로마 제국의 몰락 후 유럽에서 매우 일반적이었던 질병들이 집단적으로 발생하는 경우가 거의 없었습니다.

자, 수도교는 튼튼하게 지어져야 했고 잘 보호되어야 했습니다. 대부분은 벽돌, 석재, 그리고 로마인들이 화산 분출물로 만들었던 특별한 종류의 시멘트로 건설되었습니다. 물을 흘려 보냈던 수로들은 돌, 진흙, 그리고 납관으로 만들어졌습니다. 대부분의 공사는 노예, 임금을 받는 노동자, 그리고 제국의 변방에서 임무를 수행하던 로마 군인들에 의해 이루어졌습니다. 당연하게도 노동자들은 수도교 건설에 능숙한 기술자들의 감독을 받았습니다. 또한 먼지, 동물의 사체, 그리고 적들의 침입으로부터 물을 보호하기 위해 수도교는 주로 지하에 건설되었습니다.

학생: 지하요? 하지만 유럽의 일부 지역에서 아직도 존재하고 있는 아치로 된 거대한 수도교는요?

교수: 음, 그래요, 때때로 지상에도 지어졌습니다. 하지만 그러한 수도교들은 거대한 시스템의 작은 부분일 뿐이었어요. 실제로 로마인들은 높고 아치 형태의 수도교를 좋아하지 않는데, 물의 흐름이 방해받지 않도록 수도교의 경사도를 일정하게 유지시키면서 계곡을 가로질러야 하는 경우에만 주로 그러한 형태가 세워졌습니다. 로마인들이 이를 좋아하지 않았던 이유는 아치 형태의 부분이 풍화 작용뿐만 아니라 적들의 침입에도 취약하기 때문인데, 그 결과 이들은 종종 수리를 받아야 했고 항상 순찰의 대상이 되어야 했습니다. 반면에 지하 수로들은 보호하기가 더 쉬웠고 쉽게 손상되지도 않았죠.

그래서, 음, 물이 도시나 마을에 도달하면 거대한 수조로 들어가게 되었고, 이로써 지속적인 물 공급이 이루어질 수 있었습니다. 그 다음에는 보다 많은 파이프들로 — 이는 주로 납으로 만들어진 것이었는데 — 이루어진 시스템을 통해 목욕탕, 거대한 저택, 그리고 사람들이 식수를 얻을 수 있는 공공 장소 등으로 물이 수송되었습니다. 하지만 이러한 물은 공짜가 아니었습니다. 로마에서는, 예컨대 물을 공급받기 위해 집에 수도관을 연결하려면 비용을 지불해야 했습니다. 이렇게 모아진 돈은 종종 수도교를 건설하고 유지하는데 사용되었습니다.

전체 시스템이 얼마나 광범위한 것인지 생각해 볼 수 있도록 로마 제국의 가장 큰 도시를 살펴보도록 합시다. 약 500년이라는 기간 동안 로마인들은 각기 다른 11개의 수도교를 건설하여 수도로 물을 공급했습니다. 첫 번째 수로는 기원전 312년에 완공되었고 아피아의 루트를 따랐습니다. 아마 여러분들은 '아피아가도'로 알고 있을 것 같군요. 마지막 수도교는 기원후 226년에 완공되었습니다. 로마에 이르는 가장 긴 수도교는 그 길이가 거의 100킬로미터에 이르렀습니다. 음, 전성기 때는 로마의 수로 시스템으로 하루에 최대 백만 명의 사람들이 최소한 1평방 미터의 물을 공급받았을 것으로 추측되고 있습니다.

안타깝게도 수도교 시스템은 지속되지 못했고 로마 제국이 붕괴하자 허물어졌습니다. 이탈리아를 침공했던 게르만 부족들이 로마의 수도 공급을 차단하기 위해 로마로 이어져 있던 대부분의 수도교들을 파손시켰습니다. 오직 하나의 수도교만이, 이는 지하로만 연결되어 있던 것이었는데, 맹공을 피해 살아남을 수 있었습니다. 로마 제국의 다른 지역에서도 수도교들은 손상을 입거나 완전히 파괴되었습니다. 하지만 일부는 로마 제국이 멸망한 후 수 세기 동안 사용되기도 했습니다. 그러나 몇몇 지역의 인구가 감소함에 따라 깨끗한 물에 대한 필요성도 줄어들었고, 그 결과, 음, 여러 수도교들이 황폐화되었습니다. 로마 제국이 붕괴된 후 거의 천 년이 지난 르네상스 시대에 이르러서야 유럽의 도시들은 다시금 상하수 시설에 대한 진지한 계획을 세우기 시작했습니다.

PART 3

Conversation p.28

교수: Janet, 제가 퇴근하기 전에 여기에 들르겠다고 해 줘서 고마워요. 좋은 하루를 보내고 있기를 바라요.

학생: 실제로 그래요, 교수님. 교수님 이메일을 받고 최대한 빨리 도착한 거예요. 저 때문에, 어, 저 때문에 나가지 못한 것은 아니시죠, 그런가요?

교수: 전혀 그렇지 않아요. 보통 이 시간에 나가기는 하지만, 학생과 이야기를 나눌 수 있는 시간은 항상 낼 수 있어요.

학생: 고맙습니다, 교수님. 그러면, 음… 무엇 때문에 저와 이야기를 나누어야 하시나요?

교수: 이번 주 월요일에 학생이 제출한 기말 보고서의 개요에 대해 이야기하고 싶어요. 살펴보던 중이었는데, 학생의 것이 눈에 띄어서 학생에게 연락하는 것이 중요하다고 생각했어요.

학생: 음… 좋은 건지 나쁜 건지 모르겠네요.

교수: 음, 한번 보죠.

학생: 좋아요.

교수: 알다시피, 어… 학생이 사용한 용어는 적절하지가 않아요.

학생: 어떤 용어요?

교수: 구체적으로 중세 시대를 암흑기라고 부르는 것을 언급하는 거예요. 자, 어, 왜 암흑기라는 용어를 사용했는지 얘기해 볼래요?

학생: 그럴게요. 어, 저는 암흑기가 유럽에서 로마가 붕괴된 후, 어, 르네상스 이전까지의 기간이라고 배웠어요. 기본적으로 로마 제국 때보다 크게 퇴보했기 때문에 사람들이 이 시기를 암흑기라고 불렀어요. 암흑기 동안 로마의 지식들이 유실되었고, 사회와 기술이 발전하지 않았으며, 그리고 유럽의 전반적인 문화가 쇠퇴했다는 의미에서요.

교수: 음… 그건 당시 일어났던 일에 대한 다소 구시대적인 생각이에요.

학생: 정말인가요?

교수: 네, 정말이에요. 수십 년 전 일부 역사가들이 그렇게 생각했던 것은 사실이지만, 연구에 따르면 이 시기는 매우 역동적이었어요. 자, 어, 학생이 암흑기라고 부르는 기간은 주로 로마 제국이 붕괴한 기원후 476년에 시작하는 것으로 말해지고 있어요. 오늘날 역사가들은 이 기간을 중세 시대라고 부르죠. 또한 중세 시대는 초기, 중기, 그리고 후기로 구분할 수 있어요. 대체적으로 중세 초기는, 말했듯이, 샤를마뉴가 신성 로마 제국의 황제가 된 800년에 끝이 나죠. 암흑기라는 용어를 사용하는 대부분의 사람들은 암흑기가 476년에서 800년까지 지속된 것으로 생각해요.

학생: 좋아요, 하지만 그러면 왜 사람들이 그때를 암흑기라고 불렀나요?

교수: 로마가 붕괴했을 때 유럽 대부분의 지역에는 더 이상 중앙 권력이 존재하지 않았어요. 또한 많은 지식이 유실되었기 때문에 쇠퇴한 점도 있었죠. 하지만 초기 중세 시대는 퇴보한 것이 아니었어요.

학생: 어째서죠?

교수: 이 시기에는 가톨릭교가 가장 큰 권력을 가지게 되었어요. 수도원들이 세워졌고 이들이 중요한 교육 중심지가 되었죠. 이곳에서 고대 그리스 및 로마의 많은 지식들이 보존되었고요. 기본적으로 그곳들이 서구 문명을 구했다고 말할 수도 있을 거예요.

학생: 그 밖에는요?

교수: 기술에서도 발전이 이루어져서 농업에서 이득을 보았어요. 또한 뛰어난 학자들과 신학자들이 그 당시에 살기도 했고요. 그래서, 어, 제 생각에 학생이 개요를 다시 작성하는 것이 좋을 것 같아요. 암흑기에 대한 오해들에 초점을 맞추는 것이 어떨까요? 어떻게 들리나요?

학생: 그렇게 할 수 있어요. 지금부터 이틀 후의 수업이 끝난 다음에 개요를 다시 제출해도 될까요?

교수: 좋아요.

WORD REMINDER

outline 개요; 윤곽   terminology 전문 용어   term 용어   outdated 시대에 뒤떨어진   notion 관념, 생각   crown 왕관; 왕관을 씌우다   authority 권위   monastery 수도원   theologian 신학자

Lecture • Zoology   p.30

교수: 동물계에서 종의 번식은 모든 생명체들의 최우선적인 목표입니다. 어찌되었던 번식을 하지 못하는 종은 — 크기가 아무리 크거나 작건 간에 — 멸종하게 될 것입니다. 동물들이 짝짓기를 해서 새끼가 태어나거나 부화를 하면, 어떤 경우이던 부모 개입이라고 알려진 것이 시작됩니다. 그리고 바로 그것이 오늘 여러분들께 말씀드리고자 하는 것입니다. 부모 개입이 이루어지는 경로는 몇 가지가 있는데, 이러한 내용에 관한 시험이 있을 예정이므로 주의 깊게 들어 주시고 필기를 잘 해 두시길 바랍니다.

우선, 새끼들의 삶에 있어서 부모 개입이 전혀 이루어지지 않는 경우가 있습니다. 이러한 경우는 어류, 파충류, 그리고 양서류 종에서 일반적입니다. 암컷이 알을 낳고 수컷이 수정을 시킨 후 부모 모두는 알을 남겨 두고 떠납니다. 이후 새끼들은 알에서 부화를 하고 스스로 성장하게 되죠. 알에서 부화한 후 물가에 닿기 위해 해변을 기어가는 거북이에 관한 다큐멘터리를 틀림없이 모두를 보셨을 것이라고 확신합니다. 그러한 거북이들은 평생 동안 부모 개입을 경험하지 못하는 동물입니다.

어미가 새끼와 함께 남아서 새끼가 성숙할 때까지 이들을 기르고, 먹이고, 보호하는 경우도 있습니다. 하지만 아비는 새끼와 아무런 관련이 없습니다. 이는 단위 생식을 하는 종으로 알려져 있습니다. 많은 종의 조류, 파충류, 그리고 포유류들이 이러한 행태와 관련되어 있습니다. 예를 들어 수컷 사슴은 자신의 짝짓기 상대와 함께 남아 있지 않습니다. 대신 암컷들이 단독으로 새끼를 기르죠. 오, 그리고 세 번째 유형의 부모 행동은 부모가 함께 자식을 기르고 보호하는 것과 관련이 있습니다. 포유류 중 늑대와 사자들이 이러한 방식으로 행동하는 예입니다.

부모들은 왜 새끼를 보호할까요? 몇몇 사람들은 단지 본능 때문이라고 주장합니다. 부모는 자식들이 스스로를 보호할 수 있을 때까지 자식을 보호하려는 충동을 느낍니다. 이는 종이 최소한 한 세대를 더 살아갈 수 있도록 해 주죠. 물론 새끼에게는 많은 위험이 존재하며, 어, 그 중 가장 위험한 것은 포식자들입니다. 많은 포식자들이 어리고 약한 대상을 쫓는데, 그 이유는 그들이 손쉬운 목표가 되기 때문입니다. 그래서, 음, 종종 부모들은 다양한 방법으로 새끼를 보호합니다. 예를 들면 새끼 사슴이, 어, 사슴의 새끼죠, 태어날 때 어미는 태어났을 때의 냄새가 포식자들을 유인하지 않도록 재빨리 새끼의 몸을 깨끗하게 만듭니다. 그런 다음 어미 사슴은, 새끼 사슴이 제대로 걸을 수 있을 때까지, 새끼 사슴이 태어난 후 몇 주 동안 이들을 풀밭이나 수풀 속에 숨깁니다. 새끼 사슴은 통상 1년 동안 어미와 함께 지냅니다. 그러는 동안 새끼는 스스로 먹이를 먹고 스스로를 보호할 수 있을 정도로 몸집이 커지고, 어미로부터 포식자로부터 달아날 수 있는 방법을 배우게 됩니다.

부모 모두가 새끼를 돌보는 경우, 그렇게 하는 일반적인 방법 중 하나는 부모 중 하나가 항상 자식 곁에서 지내는 것입니다. 여러 종의 펭귄들이 이러한 방식의 행동을 보입니다. 부모 중 하나가 음식을 구하는 동안 다른 부모는 새끼 곁에 남아 새끼를 보호합니다. 기타 조류 종들도 — 보호를 해 주는 둥지를 가지고 있는 종들 조차 — 같은 행동을 합니다. 파충류들은 종종 새끼를 보호하기 위한 거처를 만들기도 합니다. 어, 물론, 실제로 새끼를 돌보는 파충류들에 대해 말씀드리고 있는 것입니다. 악어가 그렇습니다. 새끼들이 부화하면 부모 중 하나가 — 보통 어미가 — 항상 새끼들 곁을 지킵니다. 분명 여러분들은 새끼를 보호하고 있는 어미 악어 가까이에 가고 싶지 않을 것입니다.

많은 포유류들이 새끼를 무리 속에 넣음으로써 새끼들을 보호합니다. 몇몇 종의 경우, 성숙한 모든 동물들이 무리의 새끼들을 보호하는 책임을 집니다. 예컨대 사향소들은 포식자들에게 위협을 받는 경우 새끼들을 무리의 중앙에 둡니다. 그리고 많은 종의 동물들은 무리의 나머지 구성원들에게 포식자에 관한 경고를 하기 위해 영역 주변을 경계하기도 합니다. 이들이 내는 경고음으로 인해 무리들이 주의를 기울이게 된다는 점에서 이러한 동물들은 이타적인 행동을 하는 것이죠. 미어캣이 이러한 행동을 보이는 경우가 종종 관찰됩니다. 일부 포유류들의 성체는 무리의 퇴각을 돕기 위한 싸움을 함으

로써 포식자들로부터 무리의 나머지들을 — 특히 새끼들을 — 보호합니다. 전형적으로 비비가 이러한 방식으로 행동을 합니다. 물론 일부 포식자들은 동물 무리에게 기습을 가할 수도 있는데, 이때 동물들은, 달아날 수 없는 경우라면, 몸을 돌려 싸움을 함으로써 스스로와 새끼들을 보호하기도 합니다.

학생: 새끼들을 보호하기 위해 부모들이 죽을 때까지 싸우나요?

교수: 일반적으로는 그렇지 않습니다. 부모 동물들은 포식자들을 쫓아내기 위해 무리의 일원으로서 싸우고 행동하지만, 살아남고자 하는 본능이 새끼를 보호하려는 본능보다 더 강합니다. 당장은 기억이 잘 나지 않는데, 부모가 새끼를 보호하기 위해 죽는 경우가 보고된 적이 있는지 잘 모르겠군요. 그럴 수 있으리라 확신하지만 드문 경우일 것입니다. 아니, 그 대신, 포식자가 새끼 한 마리를 무리로부터 떼어내는 경우, 부모가 이를 구하기 위해 노력하는 경우는 거의 없습니다. 하지만 무리의 새끼들을 보호하는 몇몇 동물에 관한 비디오를 보여 드리도록 하겠습니다. 그러면 제가 여러분께 말씀드리는 바를 알 수 있을 것입니다. 누가 불 좀 꺼 줄래요?

WORD REMINDER

propagation 번식 utmost 최대한도의, 극도의 extinct 멸종한 fertilize 기름지게 하다; 수정시키다 crawl 기다, 기어가다 have nothing to do with ~와 관련이 없다 uniparental 단위 생식의 on one's own 혼자서, 단독으로 instinctual 본능적인 urge 충동, 욕구 progeny 자손 fawn 새끼 사슴 scent 냄새 muskox 사향소 altruistic 이타적인 meerkat 몽구스류, 미어캣 rearguard 후위(부대) retreat 퇴각 baboon 비비, 개코원숭이 drive off 몰아내다, 쫓아내다 separate A from B A를 B에서 분리시키다

Lecture · Architecture
p.33

교수: 다음 몇 분 동안은 19세기의 몇 안 되는 미국인 여성 건축가 중 한 명에 대해 논의하도록 하겠습니다. 그녀의 이름은 해리엇 어윈입니다. 그녀가 무엇으로 유명한지 아는 사람이 있나요…? 없나요…? 오, 보통 그녀를 아는 학생이 한두 명 정도는 있는데요. 어쨌든, 해리엇 어윈은 6각형 주택을 설계한 것으로 가장 잘 알려져 있습니다. 또한 그녀가 정식으로 건축 교육을 받지 않은 여성이었다는 점도 특이합니다. 하지만 그녀는 주택을 설계하고 건축했으며, 어, 그곳에서 살기도 했고, 집을 청소하고 관리하는 측면에서 최대한 실용적인 주택을 만들었습니다.

어윈은 1828년 노스캐롤라이나 주에서 태어났습니다. 어렸을 때 자주 아팠기 때문에 대부분의 시간을 야외에서 노는 대신 실내에서 보냈습니다. 실내에서 어윈은 많은 책을 읽고 글을 쓰기도 했는데, 이러한 글은 그녀가 나이가 들었을 때 잡지 기사와 책으로 출간되었습니다. 어윈은 또한 공학 및 건축에 흥미를 갖게 되었습니다. 그녀는 여학교를 다녔습니다. 하지만 당시 여성들은 문학, 언어, 종교, 회화, 음악, 그리고 역사와 같은 과목을 공부했지, 음, 공학이나 건축은 공부하지 않았습니다. 그러한 점 때문에 어윈은 그 두 과목에 관해 구할 수 있는 책은 모두 읽음으로써 이들을 독학했습니다.

어윈은 21세 때 결혼을 해서 가정을 꾸렸습니다. 9명의 아이를 낳았는데, 이로써 가정 주부로서 많은 일을 떠맡게 되었죠. 또한 나이가 들수록 이따금씩 병치레로 고생했습니다. 또한 어윈은 노스캐롤라이나에서 살았다는 점을 기억해 주세요. 음, 미 독립 전쟁 중 노스캐롤라이나에서는 몇 차례의 전투가 벌어졌는데, 1865년 전쟁이 끝나자 그 주에서 전쟁으로 피해를 입은 많은 지역들이 재건되어야 했습니다. 이러한 요인들 모두가 어윈으로 하여금 가족을 위한 새로운 집을 설계하도록 만들었습니다. 그녀는 1869년에 이러한 일을 시작했습니다. 그녀의 주된 목표는, 여러 해 동안의 자기 자신과 같이, 건강이 좋지 못한 여성에 의해서도 쉽게 관리될 수 있는 집을 만드는 것이었습니다.

집을 어떻게 설계할까 고민하다가 그녀는 6각형 주택이라는 개념을 생각해 냈습니다. 이 집은 6개의 면을 가지고 있었고 모서리는 거의 없었습니다. 내부의 방들은 원형이거나 길쭉한 형태의 타원형이었는데, 어, 마치… 흠… 일종의 콩과 같은 형태라고 생각됩니다. 그녀에게 있어서 주요한 이슈는 그녀가 방에 방구석이 없기를 바랐다는 점이었습니다. 사각형 방의 방구석이 항상 먼지 및 흙이 모이는 장소라는 점을 알고 있었기 때문에 방구석을 없앤 것이었죠. 여러분의 집을 통해서도 그러한 사실을 알고 있으리라고 확신합니다. 그렇죠…? 어쨌든, 어윈은 이러한 방구석을 청소하기가 어렵다고 생각했습니다. 하지만 원형인 방에서는, 방구석이 없기 때문에 벽을 따라 쓸고 닦는 일이 훨씬 더 쉬웠습니다.

또한 어윈의 설계에는 집을 관리하는 일을 쉽게 만드는 몇 가지 다른 특징들도 포함되어 있었습니다. 예를 들면, 복도가 없었습니다. 대신 각각의 방을 다른 방과 연결시켜 주는 넓은 문이 있었습니다. 그녀의 집에는 창문이 많았는데, 이로써 공기가 쉽게 순환되고 또한 많은 빛이 집 내부로 들어올 수 있었습니다. 이러한 특징들이 합쳐져 집은 실제보다 더 크게 보였는데, 이는 집이 하나의 커다란, 막힘이 없는 공간처럼 보이기 때문이었습니다. 아, 그녀는 또한 중앙에 커다란 벽난로가 있는 집을 설계했습니다. 어윈이 살던 당시 벽난로는 겨울철에 온기를 제공해 주는 유일한 수단이었기 때문에 대부분의 미국 가정에는 여러 개의 방에 벽난로가 있었습니다. 하지만 그녀의 설계에서는 온기가 중앙 벽난로로부터 다른 방으로 전달됨으로써 그와 동일한 효과가 발생했습니다. 주택 내 벽난로의 수를 크게 줄임으로써 어윈은 집 내부에 생기는 그을음과 재를 감소시킬 수 있었고, 그 결과 집을 청소하는데 필요한 노력이 줄어들 수 있었습니다.

어윈은 자신의 설계도를 미 특허청에 제출했고 그러한 주택에 대한 특허를 얻었습니다. 하지만 6각형 주택에 대한 독점적인 권리를 인정받지는 못했습니다. 그녀의 집과 같이 설계된 주택에 대해서만 특허를 얻었을 뿐이었죠. 사실 미국에서 6각형 주택을 설계하거나 지은 것은 어윈이 처음은 아니었습니다. 실제로 당시 8각형 주택이 몇 채 존재하고 있었습니다. 그럼에도 불구하고 어윈은 주택을 설계하고 그에 대한 특허를 받은 최초의 여성이었으며, 이러한 점 때문에 그녀는 19세기 건축가 중 돋보이는 인물이 되었습니다. 마침내 그녀가 설계한 집이 지어졌고, 1897년 사망할 때까지 그녀는 그곳에서 살았습니다.

학생: 그녀가 꽤 인상적인 사람이었던 것처럼 들리는군요. 그녀의 설계가 이후 건축가들에게도 영향을 끼쳤나요?

교수: 그렇지는 않습니다. 그녀에 의해 두 개의 6각형 주택만이 더 설계되고 지어졌을 뿐이었죠. 여담이지만 그 중 한 채는 오늘날에도 여전히 존재하고 있습니다. 또한 현재 6각형 주택은 몇 채 되지 않지만, 주택으로서는 특이한 형태로 남아 있습니다. 개인적으로, 해리엇 어윈의 뛰어난 점은 자신의 신체적 한계를 감안해서 최소한의 관리만이 필요하고 동시에 움직임을 가장 자유롭게 만들어 주는 주거 공간을 창조한 그녀의 능력에 있다고 말씀드리고 싶습니다.

WORD REMINDER

hexagonal 6각형의 unique 독특한, 특이한 with regard to ~에 관해서 fondness 좋아함, 기호, 취미 teach ~ to oneself ~을 독학으로 배우다 give birth to ~을 낳다 bout of illness 병치레 inspire 영감을 주다, 고무시키다 objective 목적, 목표 hit upon 갑자기 ~을 생각해 내다 elongate 늘이다 mop 걸레질하다 alongside ~ 옆에, 나란히 incorporate 합치다; 포함하다 circulate 순환하다 fireplace 벽난로 channel 나르다, 보내다 dramatically 극적으로 soot 숯, 그을음 patent 특허 exclusive 배타적인, 독점적인 octagonal 8각형의 incidentally 그건 그렇고; 우연히 brilliance 광명; 뛰어난 능력

Actual Test 02

PART 1

Conversation
p.40

학생: 안녕하세요, Perry 교수님.

교수: 좋은 오후예요. 제가 도울 일이 있나요?

학생: 네, 교수님. 도와 주시면 좋겠어요. 저는 교수님의 미술사 103 수업을 듣고 있는 학생이에요. 교수님 수업 시간에 작성하기로 되어 있는 보고서에 관해 말씀을 드리려고 왔어요.

교수: 아, 그래요. 그런 경우라면 안으로 들어와서 무엇을 쓰기로 결정했는지 얘기해 주지 않을래요? 오, 하지만 먼저 학생의 이름을 알 수 있을까요?

학생: 물론이죠. 제 이름은 Eric Daniels입니다. D-A-N-I-E-L-S죠.

교수: 여기 출석부에서 이름을 확인해 볼게요… Daniels… Crag Daniels인가요?

학생: 아니오, 교수님. Eric Daniels입니다.

교수: 아, 여기에 있군요. 이상하네요. 수업에서 이름이 같은 학생이 있는 경우는 흔치가 않거든요. 오, 음, 상관없죠. 좋아요… 그러면 당면한 문제로 돌아가도록 하죠 — 보고서 주제로요.

학생: 네, 교수님. 저, 음, 저는 빈센트 반 고흐의 스타일에 초점을 맞추려고 생각하고 있었어요. 이에 대해 어떻게 생각하시나요?

교수: 음… 개인적으로 그에 대해 글을 쓰는 것은 피하라고 하고 싶군요.

학생: 네? 왜 그런 말씀을 하시는 거죠?

교수: 두 가지 이유가 있어요. 첫째, 그는 매우 유명한 사람이기 때문에 그에 관한 글은 많이 있어요. 이번 보고서의 초점은 잘 알려져 있지 않은 화가에 대해 학생들이 조사를 하도록 만드는 것이죠. 그리고 두 번째 이유는 우리 도시의 어떤 전시관에서도 반 고흐의 그림은 없어요. 글쓰기 주제로 선택한 화가의 작품 중 최소한 한 점이라도 학생들이 직접 볼 수 있기를 바라고 있었거든요.

학생: 책에서 그림을 보고 그에 대해 글을 쓰면 괜찮지 않을까요?

교수: 오, 이런, 안 돼요. 책으로 그림을 보는 것과 실제 그림을 보는 것 사이에는 엄청난 차이가 있어요. 제 말은, 수많은 사진으로 *모나리자*를 본 적이 있을 거예요, 그렇죠…? 반드시 그랬을 거예요. 하지만 실제로 파리의 루브르 박물관에 가서 바로 앞에서 *모나리자*를 보면… 음, 전혀 다른 경험이죠.

학생: 몰랐어요, 교수님.

교수: 괜찮아요. 어쨌든 학생이 괜찮다면 학생의 보고서 주제에 대해 제가 한 가지 제안을 하도록 할게요.

학생: 좋습니다.

교수: 장 프랑수아 밀레에 대해 보고서를 작성하는 것이 어떨까요? 그는 19세기에 프랑스에서 살았던 화가예요. 자연주의와 사실주의 사조에 속해 있었고 또한 밝은 색을 썼기 때문에 반 고흐와 비슷하다고 할 수 있죠. 그의 작품을 조사하는 것을 좋아하게 될 것이라고 생각해요. 그리고 한 가지 더 추가하자면, 시내 작은 미술관 중 한 곳에서 현재 그의 작품들이 전시되고 있기 때문에 몇몇 작품들을 가까이에서, 그리고 직접 볼 수 있는 기회를 갖게 될 거예요.

학생: 어, 좋아요. 그런 사람은 들어본 적이 없지만 그에 관한 보고서는 쓸 수 있을 것 같아요. 오, 그 미술관 이름이 무엇인가요, 교수님?

교수: 잠시만요… 그에 대한 소책자가 여기에 있어요… 찾았군요… 밀레에 관한 약간의 정보가 들어있고, 미술관이 어디에 위치해 있는지도 알 수 있을 거예요. 그리고 다른 질문이 있으면 부담 갖지 말고 제게 와서 물어보도록 해요.

WORD REMINDER

odd 이상한, 기묘한   at hand 수중의; 당면한   in person 몸소, 직접
in real life 실제의   face to face 얼굴을 맞대고   currently 현재

Lecture · Urban Development
p.42

교수: 전 세계 대부분의 도시들은 마을로 시작해서 작은 도시로 성장한 후 결국 거대한 도시지로 발전했습니다. 하지만 지난 몇 세기 동안에는 도시를 계획하는데 막대한 노력이 투입되었습니다. 현대의 계획 도시 중 보다 잘 알려져 있는 것으로 워싱턴 D.C., 러시아의 상트페테르부르크, 그리고 호주의 수도인 캔버라를 들 수 있습니다. 또한 보다 더 새로운 많은 도시들이 세심하게 계획되고 있으며, 현재 도시 개발업체들은 오래된 도시를 변화시켜 이들을 현대적인 교통 시스템 및 시설에 보다 적합한 곳으로 만들기 위해 분주히 활동하고 있습니다. 그래서, 음, 제가 이번 시간에 여러분과 함께 검토하고자 하는 것은, 그것이 신도시를 위한 것이던 혹은 현대화되고 있는 기존 도시를 위한 것이던, 도시 계획과 관련된 몇 가지 사항들입니다.

분명 현대의 도시 계획에서 가장 중요하게 생각해야 할 사항 중 하나는 지리적 위치입니다. 통상 지형에 따라 지어질 도시의 유형이 결정됩니다. 수많은 도시들이 강이나 호수와 같은 담수 근처에 위치해 있고, 바다나 대양 주변에 위치한 도시들도 많습니다. 따라서 이곳 시민들이 해상 무역에 종사하고자 한다면 이러한 도시에는 항구 시설이 필요합니다. 산악 지대는 — 습지대와 마찬가지로 — 도시를 건설하는데 문제가 되기 때문에 일반적으로 이 두 지역은 가능하면 제외됩니다. 토양의 종류 또한 중요한데, 그 이유는 건물의 안정성 및 도로와 같은 기반 시설의 안전성이 토질에 달려 있기 때문입니다. 덧붙여 말하면, 오래된 다수의 도시들은 화산 지대 근처나 지진, 허리케인, 혹은 토네이도에 취약한 지역에 세워졌습니다. 이러한 도시의 건물들은 흔들림과 강한 바람에 견딜 수 있도록 지어져야 하며, 다양한 자연 재해로부터 비롯될 수 있는 피해를 예방하기 위한 기타의 수단들이 강구되어야 합니다.

두 번째로 고려해야 할 사항은 교통망과의 연결성입니다. 과거에는 바다 및 강, 그리고 호수로 이동하는 것이 가장 빠르고, 가장 효율적인 교통 수단이었습니다. 하지만 현재 대부분의 현대 도시들은 고속 도로, 철도, 그리고 공항과 연결되어 있습니다. 도시로 들어가고 도시에서 나오는 교통의 용이함이 중요한 고려 사항이기 때문에 이러한 교통 시스템과 도시를 연결시키는 것은 필수적입니다. 공항이나 기차역이 도시에서 너무 멀리 떨어져 있으면 많은 시민들이 불편해할 것입니다. 하지만 대다수의 사람들은 소음과 교통 문제로 인하여 공항과 너무 가까운 곳에 살고 싶어하지는 않기 때문에, 도시에서 너무 멀리 떨어져 있지 않으면서도 도시와 너무 붙어있지 않는 곳에 공항을 건설하는 것이 중요합니다.

그 밖에 또 무엇이 있을까요…? 음, 주요 고속 도로가 주거 지역을 통과한다면 그러한 결과로서 과도한 소음 공해가 발생할 것입니다. 하지만 도시 내에는, 돌아다닐 수 있는 편리한 방법들이 있어야 합니다. 여기에는 도로, 지하철, 그리고 지상 철도 시스템이 포함되는데, 이들은 종종 현대 도시인들의 출퇴근을 상당 부분 책임지고 있습니다. 이러한 형태의 교통 시설들은 잘 계획되고 운영되어야 합니다. 하지만 이들이 자동차나 트럭과 같이 사적인 형

태의 교통 수단들이 이용하는 도로를 방해해서는 안 됩니다. 이러한 일이 얼마나 복잡한 것인지는 여러분들도 알게 될 것이라고 생각합니다, 그렇지 않을까요?

도시를 계획하거나 현대화할 때 고려해야 할 또 다른 사항은 토지사용제한법입니다. 이는 도시에서의 삶의 질을 향상시키기 위해 주요 유형의 도시 지역을 서로 분리시키는 법입니다. 어떤 종류의 지역들이 있을까요…? 음, 주거 지역이 있는데, 여기에서는 사람들이 주택과 아파트에서 거주합니다. 사무실과 쇼핑 시설들이 있는 상업 지역도 있습니다. 봅시다… 산업 지역에는 공장, 창고, 그리고 항만 시설이 있으며, 레크레이션 지역에는 공원, 경기장, 그리고 실외 활동을 즐길 수 있는 장소가 있습니다. 아, 그리고 도시 인근 지역에는 농사를 지을 수 있는 농업 지역이 있을 수 있습니다.

학생: Jackson 교수님, 교외 지역은 어떤가요? 이들도 일종의 지역인가요?

교수: 아니에요, Jim, 그렇지 않아요. 교외 지역은 보다 큰 대도시 지역의 경계 밖에서 생긴 작은 마을이나 도시입니다. 초기의 대다수 교외 지역들은 계획된 것이 아니었지만, 지난 수십 년 동안 많은 교외 지역들은 광범위한 계획을 통해 조성되었습니다. 이로써 보다 편리한 위치에 쇼핑 및 교육 시설을 짓는 일이 더 쉬워지고 있죠.

자, 오늘날 도시 계획에 있어서 고려해야 할 매우 중요한 사항이 하나 더 있습니다. 바로 환경적 요인들에 대한 고려입니다. 도시의 높은 인구 밀도, 도시 내 수많은 산업 시설, 그리고 도시에서 이용하는 차량들 때문에 오염은 모든 도심지에서 문제가 되고 있습니다. 또한 도시에는 좁은 지역에 많은 고층 건물들이 있기 때문에 — 마치, 어, 뉴욕 시의 맨하튼과 같이 — 음, 공기의 흐름이 부족해서 오염 물질들이 도시에서 빠져나가지 못할 수가 있습니다. 이와 같은 건물들은 도시 열섬이라는 효과 때문에 도시의 온도를 상승시키는 원인이 될 수도 있습니다. 하지만 그러한 점은 잠시 후에 알아보도록 하죠. 어쨌든, 도시 계획자들은 고층 건물들을 서로 떨어뜨리고, 나무를 심고 옥상에 녹지 공간을 만들고, 그리고 바람의 흐름을 연구함으로써 환경적인 우려를 감소시키기 위해 노력하고 있습니다. 항상 성공하는 것은 아니지만 점차 나아지고 있는 중입니다.

> **WORD REMINDER**
> urban center 도심지 compatible 양립할 수 있는 urban planning 도시 계획 modernize 현대화하다 geographical 지리(학)적인 terrain 지형 waterborne trade 해상 무역 stability 안정성 infrastructure 기반 시설 prone to ~에 취약한 have access to ~에 접근하다, ~을 이용하다 vital 필수적인, 중요한 residential 주거의 portion 부분 take ~ into account ~을 고려하다 zoning law 토지사용제한법 metropolitan 대도시의 density 밀도

PART 2

Conversation   p.46

사서: 안녕하세요, Anna. 드디어 학생과 만날 기회를 갖게 되다니 기쁘군요.

학생: 저도 그래요, Geller 선생님. 그리고 저와 이야기하기 위해 시간을 내 주셔서 정말 고맙습니다. 학교 도서관을 관리하느라 틀림없이 매우 바쁘실 것이라고 생각하기 때문에 정말로 감사를 드려요.

사서: 음, 물론 바쁘긴 하지만 총학생회장과 이야기를 나눌 시간을 내는 것은 괜찮아요. 그래서, Anna, 지난 번 제 메일로 학생의 모든 질문에 답이 되었나요?

학생: 음… 꼭 그렇지는 않았어요.

사서: 좋아요. 그런 경우라면 조금 더 자세히 말을 해 줄래요?

학생: 네, 그럴게요… 우선, 발표된 도서관 리모델링 공사의 계획과 관련하여 확신이 서지 않아요. 제 말은, 음, 학교에 이용할 수 있는 자금이 그처럼 많은 것은 아닌데, 이번 리모델링 공사에는 막대한 비용이 들 것이라는 점이죠. 금액이 130만 달러였던 것 같아요, 그렇죠? 저와 이야기를 나누었던 많은 학생들이 그러한 비용에 대해 불만을 표시했어요. 비용이 너무 많이 든다고 생각하고 있죠. 그리고 그들에 의해 선출된 대표로서, 그에 대해 알고, 이를 다시 학생들에게 알려 주기 위해 선생님과 그러한 비용에 대해서 이야기하는 것이 제 일이고요.

사서: 학생들에게 책임감을 느끼면서 행동하는 것 같아 보기가 좋군요. 이러한 문제와 관련해서 과거의 모든 학생회장들이 저를 만나려는 수고를 한 것은 아니었거든요. 어쨌든, 그래요, 학생이 말한 수치가 맞아요. 130만 달러예요.

학생: 좋아요. 그러면, 음, 그처럼 많은 돈을 써서 도서관에 정확히 어떠한 종류의 리모델링 공사가 진행될 것인지 말씀해 주실 수 있나요?

사서: 물론이죠. 먼저, 도서관 전체의 모든 책걸상들을 교체할 예정이에요. 교체되는 책상들은 학생들이 앉기에 훨씬 더 편할 거예요. 또한 시청각실의 기기들을 최신 기기들로 교체하고, 컴퓨터도 새로 구입할 거예요. 마지막으로, 도서관 전체에 페인트칠을 할 예정이에요. 도서관 내부를 말씀드리고 있는 것이죠. 외부는 하지 않을 것이고요.

학생: 컴퓨터 및 시청각실의 기기들을 교체해야 할 필요성은 확실히 이해가 가요. 하지만 책걸상에 대한 불만 사항들은 들은 적이 없어요. 그래서, 어, 왜 그것들을 교체하려고 하시나요?

사서: 실은, 학생과 교직원들 모두로부터 그에 대한 불만이 많았어요. 그 때문에 도서관 이용객 모두에게 보다 편안한 환경을 만들어 주어야겠다고 생각했죠.

학생: 그 돈을 다른 목적을 위해 사용하는 것은 어떨까요?

사서: 예를 들면요?

학생: 도서관을 확장시킬 수도 있을 거예요. 제 말은, 우리 학교가 정말로 세계적인 대학이 되기를 바란다면 훨씬 더 큰 도서관이 필요할 거예요. 물론 제 말에 악의는 없어요.

사서: 악의로 생각하지 않아요. 학생의 아이디어가 마음에 든다는 점은 믿어 주세요. 저도 정말로 도서관이 확장되었으면 해요. 하지만 그렇게 하기 위해서는, 오… 천만 혹은 2천만 달러가 필요하죠. 저희에게는 백만 달러가 약간 넘는 돈이 있을 뿐이라서 이곳을 확장하는 일은 생각할 수도 없어요.

학생: 오, 그렇게 많은 비용이 드는지는 모르고 있었네요.

사서: 네. 보세요. 우리가 지불해야 할 금액이 항목별로 적혀 있는 목록을 보여줄 텐데, 그러면 제가 무슨 말을 하는지 알 수 있을 거예요.

학생: 좋아요. 그렇게 하면 돈이 정확히 어디에 사용될 것인지에 대한 이해가 보다 빨라질 것 같아요.

> **WORD REMINDER**
> in person 직접, 몸소 president of the student body 총학생회장 elect 선출하다 representative 대표 audiovisual 시청각의 patron 후원자; 고객 institution 기관 no offense 악의는 없다

Lecture · Environmental Science   p.48

교수: 식물이 생존하기 위해서는 세 가지가 필요합니다. 햇빛, 물, 그리고 좋

은 토양입니다. 이번 시간에 제가 논의하고자 하는 것은 세 번째 요소인 토양입니다. 답이 필요한 두 가지 중요한 질문이 있습니다… 우선 토양의 어떤 성분이 식물에게 이로울까요…? 그 다음으로 식물은 어떻게 토양에게 혜택을 줄까요…?

제가 물어본 순서대로 질문들을 살펴봅시다. 토양의 영양소는 13개가 있습니다. 이들 모두는 두 개의 그룹으로, 즉 다량 영양소와 미량 영양소로 구분될 수 있습니다. 다량 영양소는 더 나아가 1차 다량 영양소와 2차 다량 영양소로 나누어집니다. 1차 다량 영양소에는 세 가지가 있습니다. 질소, 인, 그리고 칼륨이 그것이죠. 모든 식물의 성장에 이들이 필요합니다. 안타깝게도 토양에서 영양분을 뽑아가고는 아무것도 되돌려 주지 않는 식물들로 토양이 꽉 차면 이러한 세 다량 영양소들은 빠르게 고갈될 수 있습니다. 2차 다량 영양소에 대해 말씀을 드리면, 이들은 칼슘, 마그네슘, 그리고 황입니다. 식물의 성장에 그렇게 필수적인 것은 아니며, 토양에서 고갈되는 경우도 별로 없습니다. 그건 그렇고, 미량 영양소는 붕소, 구리, 철, 염화물, 망간, 몰리브덴, 그리고 아연입니다. 이들은 식물에 의해 소량이 이용됩니다. 실제로 너무나 적은 양이 활용되기 때문에 사실상 토양에서 완전히 없어지는 일은 결코 일어나지 않습니다.

모든 영양분은 식물의 성장을 도우며 식물이 튼튼하고 건강하게 지내는 데 일정한 역할을 합니다. 그 중 몇몇에 대해 말씀을 드리면… 아마도 식물의 성장에 가장 중요한 영양분은 질소일 것입니다. 광합성을 하기 위해 식물들이 사용하는 엽록소의 필수 성분이죠. 질소는 또한 빠른 성장 및 식물들의 잎, 과실, 그리고 씨앗의 크기 증대에 필수적입니다. 인은 식물의 뿌리 발달과 식물 자체의 건강 유지에 기여합니다. 이들 모두는, 어, 식물을 지면에 고정시키고 식물이 자신의 무게로 인해 쓰러지는 것을 방지해 준다는 점에서 중요합니다. 그리고 칼륨은 광합성에서 일정한 역할을 하고, 또한 식물이 질병과 싸우는데 도움을 줍니다.

칼-칼-칼슘은… 죄송합니다. 반면에 칼슘은 식물의 세포벽 구조에서 중요하며, 식물이 염분과 산을 너무 많이 흡수하는 것을 예방해 줍니다. 마그네슘 역시 광합성 및 식물 성장에 필요한 영양분입니다. 황은 여러 가지 역할을 합니다. 봅시다… 식물과 씨앗의 성장에 도움을 주고, 뿌리를 튼튼하게 하며, 추운 날씨를 견딜 수 있게 해 주고, 기타 몇 가지 기능들도 수행합니다. 미량 영양소들 역시 중요한 역할을 합니다. 여러분 교재의 203페이지에서 살펴볼 수 있습니다. 아시겠죠?

학생: Reed 교수님, 영양분들은 어디로부터 나오는 것인가요?

교수: 대부분은 토양에서 자연적으로 생성됩니다. 또한 자연적인 방법으로 다시 채워지죠. 예를 들면, 질소는 토양의 유기물이 식물에게 필요한 질소로 변환되는 순환 과정을 통해 다시 채워집니다. 콩과에 있는 여러 식물들은, 여기에는 콩이 포함되는데, 자신들이 지니고 있는 박테리아를 통해 토양에 있는 질소를 교체해 줄 수 있습니다. 하지만 현대의 첨단 농법에서는 많은 영양분들이 화학 비료로부터 나오고 있습니다. 효과적이긴 하지만, 문제는 그들이 단지 화학 물질일 뿐이라는 점인데, 따라서 과도하게 사용된다면 장기적으로 환경 문제를 일으킬 수 있습니다.

하지만 비료가 필요한 경우도 종종 있습니다. 너무 많은 식물들이 아무 것도 주지 않은 채 토양으로부터 너무 많은 영양분을 빼앗아갈 때가 그렇습니다. 아시겠지만, 음, 동일한 농경지에 매년 같은 식물을 심으면 — 가령 밀이나 옥수수라고 합시다 — 이러한 식물들은 영양분이 거의 없거나 전혀 없는 경우가 될 때까지 많은 영양분을 추출해 갈 것이고, 따라서 식물들이 제대로 자라지 못하게 될 것입니다. 역사적으로 농부들은 시행착오를 통해 토양의 영양분을 어떻게 다시 채워 넣는지를 알게 되었습니다. 수 세기 동안 농부들은 통상적으로 윤작을 시행해 왔습니다. 세 곳 중 한 곳의 경작지를 휴한해

서… 어, 곡식을 심지 않았다는 의미입니다… 그렇게 하면 경작지는 원기를 회복할 시간을 갖게 되는 것이죠. 하지만 이러한 관행은 비경제적이었는데, 그 이유는 이러한 윤작을 시행하는 농부들이 밭의 1/3을 그냥 내버려두어야 했기 때문입니다. 시간이 지남에 따라 농부들은 밭을 휴한하게 놔두는 대신 토끼풀과 같이 영양분을 다시 채워 주는 작물을 심는 법을 알아냈습니다. 토끼풀은 가축용 먹이로도 사용될 수 있었기 때문에 이를 기르는 것은 농부에게 이득을 가져다 주었습니다.

윤작보다 더 뛰어난 방법은 같은 경작지에 특정한 작물들을 함께 기르는 것입니다. 예를 들면 유럽 사람들이 신세계에 도착했을 때, 그들은 미 원주민들이, 음, 옥수수, 콩, 그리고 호박을 활용한 삼모작을 발전시켜 왔다는 점을 알게 되었습니다. 이들은 각 식물들이 다른 식물에게 도움을 줄 수 있도록 하나의 경작지에 이들 셋 모두를 심었습니다. 옥수수는 콩 식물들이 타고 오를 수 있는 기다란 줄기를 지니고 있어서 콩 식물들은 더 많은 햇빛을 받을 수 있었습니다. 옥수수는 토양으로부터 질소를 제거시켰지만, 콩 식물들이 손실된 질소의 상당 부분을 채워 주었습니다. 호박에는 지면을 따라 뻗어 자라는 수많은 덩굴이 달렸고, 이들이 만들어 낸 그늘은 토양이 수분을 유지하는데 도움이 되었습니다. 반면에 유럽에서 온 식민지 주민들은 종종 해마다 같은 밭에 담배를 재배했는데, 이로써 토지의 영양분들이 빠르게 고갈되었습니다. 그렇게 하면 안 된다는 것을 알게 된 것은 한참 후의 일이었습니다.

WORD REMINDER

phosphorus 인   potassium 칼륨, 포타슘   oversaturated 과포화된, 꽉 찬   extract 뽑아내다, 추출하다   sulfur 황   boron 붕소   chloride 염화물   manganese 망간   molybdenum 몰리브덴   zinc 아연   chlorophyll 엽록소   photosynthesis 광합성   replenish 다시 채우다   legume family 콩과   crop rotation 윤작, 돌려짓기   fallow 휴한의   recuperate (원기 등을) 회복하다   clover 토끼풀, 클로버   three-crop system 삼모작   squash 호박   sprawl 제멋대로 퍼져나가다

Lecture · Geology

교수: 종종 지각이 구부러지고 접힘에 따라 그 결과로서 나타나는 것을 우리 지질학자들은 폭포선이라고 부릅니다. 그리고, 어, 아닙니다, 남성 및 여성의 최신 가을 패션을 말씀드리는 것이 아니에요. 대신, 음, 폭포선은 낭떠러지와 같은 경계에 의해 단단한 암석과 보다 무른 암석이 구분되는 지역과 관련이 있습니다. 바로 그러한 경계가 폭포선입니다. 단단한 암석은 보통 변성암이나 화성암이며, 보다 무른 암석은 주로 퇴적암의 일종입니다.

낭떠러지와 같은 경계는 두 가지 요인이 작용한 결과로 나타납니다. 먼저 단층이 일어납니다. 지면이 구부러지거나 접히는 것이죠. 지진을 다루었던 수업 내용을 기억해 보면, 단층은 갑자기 일어날 수도 있고, 혹은 보다 장기간에 걸쳐 일어날 수도 있습니다. 단층이 일어나면 보다 단단한 암석은 위로 밀려나고 보다 무른 암석은 원래의 위치에 남게 됩니다. 이러한 일이 발생한 후에는 이 두 유형의 암석의 높이 차이를 크게 만드는 두 번째 요인이 작용합니다. 두 번째 요인은 바로 침식입니다. 침식은 양쪽에 있는 암석들을 모두 마모시키지만, 보다 무른 퇴적암에서 마모가 빨리 진행되기 때문에 퇴적암의 높이가 보다 더 낮아지게 됩니다.

침식의 속도는 물의 흐름에 의해서, 어, 즉 강이나 시내에 의해서 빨라질 수 있습니다. 이는 실제로 폭포선의 주목할 만한 측면 중 하나입니다. 낭떠러지와 같은 경계가 있는 장소에서는, 강이나 시내가 폭포선을 가로지르는 경우, 많은 폭포가 있을 수 있습니다. 때때로, 음, 낭떠러지와 같은 폭포선의 가장자리로부터 떨어져 있는 암석들은 천천히 침식되기 때문에, 이러한 폭포들은 구부러진 형태를 나타냅니다. 자, 제가 "낭떠러지와 같은"이라는 용어

를 계속해서 사용하고 있지만, 이러한 경계가 가파른 절벽의 경사면처럼 항상 급경사를 이루는 것은 아니라는 점을 기억해 주세요. 사실, 훨씬 더 완만할 수도 있습니다. 이러한 경계는 또한 비교적 길이가 짧을 수도 있고, 혹은 수백 킬로미터까지 이어져 있을 수도 있습니다.

북미의 동쪽에 유명한 폭포선들이 몇 개 있습니다. 이들은 대략 4억 년… 어, 아니죠… 4억 4천만 년 전 거대한 산들이 형성되었던 시기가 지난 후 그 결과로서 형성되었습니다. 이 시기에 기다란 산맥이 동부 해안가에 형성됨에 따라 육지가 계속해서 접히고 구부러지면서 위쪽으로 밀려났습니다. 침식 작용으로 인해 이러한 대부분의 산들의 크기는 상당히 작아졌고, 현재 이들은 예전에 높았던 흔적만을 보이고 있습니다. 하지만 그와 같은 산이 형성되었던 시기의 한 가지 유산으로서 수많은 폭포선이 형성되었습니다. 눈에 띄는 사례 중 하나가 나이아가라 폭포에 위치해 있는 폭포선입니다. 가파른 경사를 따라 상부의 단단함 암석과 하부의 무른 암석 사이에 명확한 차이가 보이는 극적인 사례입니다. 퀘벡과 뉴잉글랜드에서도 또 다른 폭포선을 찾아볼 수 있습니다. 하지만 북미에서 가장 유명한 폭포선은 미국의 동부 해안가를 따라 있습니다. 뉴저지에서 캐롤라이나에 이르기까지 끊임없이 이어져 있는데, 그 거리가 1,400킬로미터에 이릅니다. 그곳에서는 평탄한 해안가 평지가 매우 가파른 폴 라인에서 애팔래치아 산맥과 만납니다.

여러분 책에 있는 지도를 봐 주세요… 82페이지에 있습니다. 폭포선이 어디에 위치해 있는지를 보여 줄 것입니다. 보다 높은 경사면은 빨간색으로 되어 있고… 해안가의 평지는 노란색으로 되어 있습니다. 자, 지도를 보면 알 수 있는 중요한 점을 누가 말해볼까요…? 그래요, Louise.

학생: 많은 마을과 도시들이 폭포선에 위치해 있는 것처럼 보이는군요.

교수: 관찰력이 좋군요, Louise. 상당히 빨리 알아냈네요. 맞습니다, 여러분. 지도를 보시면… 트렌턴, 뉴어크, 필라델피아, 볼티모어, 조지타운, 리치먼드, 그리고 기타 몇몇 도시들이 폭포선을 따라 있습니다. 이러한 점에는 이유가 있습니다. 아시다시피 미 동부에 있는 이러한 폭포선에서는 상당히 많은 수의 시내와 강들이 교차하는데, 여기에는 몇몇 주요한 강들이 포함되어 있습니다. 이 중에는 뉴저지의 래리턴 강 및 델라웨어 강, 매릴랜드와 버지니아의 경계에 있는 포토맥 강, 그리고 버지니아의 래퍼해넉 강이 있습니다. 이러한 거대한 강들이 — 그리고 보다 작은 많은 강들이 — 수많은 폭포를 만들어 냅니다. 왜 그렇게 폭포가 중요한지 물어볼 수 있겠죠…? 음, 17세기와 18세기 식민지 주민들이 미국에서 마을과 도시를 건설하기 시작했을 때 그들에게는 동물, 바람, 그리고 물 이외의 동력원은 없었습니다. 따라서 폭포는 중요한 자원이 되었죠. 제재소를 작동시킬 수 있었고, 곡식을 빻을 제분소도 작동시킬 수 있었습니다. 이후 폭포는 초창기 직물 공장을 가동시키기 위해서도 쓰였습니다. 따라서 식민지 시기에는 많은 산업체들이 — 그리고 마을과 도시 또한 — 폭포선을 따라 폭포가 존재하는 곳 근처에서 발전했습니다.

기억해야 할 또 다른 점은 선박들이 폭포선을 넘어 상류로 이동할 수가 없었다는 점입니다. 따라서 폭포선은 식민지 시기 동안 미국의 미개척지를 꿰뚫었던 가장 깊은 지점이 되었습니다. 마침내, 몇몇 장소에 배를 올리고 내릴 수 있는 갑문이 지어짐으로써 선박들은 내륙의 더 깊은 곳으로 들어갈 수 있게 되었습니다. 하지만 주로, 어, 이전 세기에는 배로 이동할 수 있는 뱃길의 마지막 종착지가 폭포선이었습니다.

WORD REMINDER

separate 분리하다, 구분하다 metamorphic 변성암의 igneous 화성암의 sedimentary 퇴적암의 fault 단층 come into play 활동하기 시작하다, 작동하기 시작하다 erosion 침식 waterfall 폭포 edge 가장자리, 끝부분 steep 가파른 drop 가파른 비탈 mountain range 산맥 escarpment 가파른 경사지, 급경사면 sawmill 제재소 mill 제분소 wilderness 황무지, 미개척지 lock 수문, 갑문

Actual Test 03

PART 1

Conversation   p.58

학생: Taylor 교수님, 아직 계셨군요. 좋은 소식이네요. 저는, 어, 3시 반 약속 때문에 왔어요.

교수: 아, 네, Margaret. 학생이 오늘 오지 않을지도 모른다고 잠시 생각했어요. 학생이 잊고 있을 것 같아 걱정을 했죠.

학생: 오, 예. 어… 그 점에 대해서는 죄송해요. 그리스 역사 수업이 끝나고 Madison 교수님과의 이야기가 길어져서 지금에서야 오게 되었어요. 죄송합니다.

교수: 괜찮아요. 학업에 관해 다른 교수님과 이야기를 하고 있었다고 하니 일리 있는 변명이라고 생각해요.

학생: 그렇게 말씀해 주셔서 정말 고맙습니다.

교수: 좋아요. 이제 자리에 앉아서 이야기를 시작해 볼까요?

학생: 좋아요.

교수: 자, 오늘은 특별한 이유 때문에 학생과 이야기를 하고 싶었어요.

학생: 네?

교수: 조금 전 수업에서 학생이 한 발표와 관련이 있어요. 궁금한데… 그에 대한 아이디어를 어디에서 얻었나요? 잡지에서 얻었나요? 아니면 아마도 웹 사이트에서?

학생: 어, 아니에요. 정말 솔직히 말씀을 드리면 저 혼자서 생각해 냈어요. 음… 제 발표는 괜찮았죠, 그렇지 않나요?

교수: 정말 훌륭했어요. 실제로 수업에서 가장 높은 점수를 받았죠… 그건 그렇고 제가 말한 것은 아무한테도 말하지 말아요. 다음 주까지는 점수를 알려 주지 않을 거예요. 하지만 본인이 얼마나 잘했는지를 학생이 알고 싶어할 거라고 생각했어요.

학생: 정말 알고 싶었어요. 제가 잘했다니 믿을 수가 없군요.

교수: 음, 사실이니까 믿으세요. 자, 학생에게 또 다른 질문이 있는데… 미술사 전공이 아니죠, 그렇죠?

학생: 아니에요, 교수님. 저는 현재 영문학을 전공하고 있어요. 전문 분야는 르네상스 시기의 작가들에 관한 것이지만, 다른 시기의 작품들을 읽는 것도 좋아해요. 왜 물으시는 건가요?

교수: 영어를 얼마나 잘하는지는 모르겠지만, 학생은 미술사에 있어서 탁월해요. 전공을 바꿔볼 생각을 해 본 적이 있나요? 제 말은, 학생이 수업에서 한 발표로 학생에게 예술에 대한 안목이 있다는 점은 확실해졌어요. 그뿐 아니라 발표한 그림에 대해 상당히 정교한 해석도 했고요. 학생의 해석은 수업을 듣는 다른 학생의 해석보다 훨씬 더 좋았는데, 학생들 중 일부는 미술사를 전공하고 있는 대학원생들이죠.

학생: 와, 그렇게 말씀해 주시다니 정말 친절하시군요. 하지만 교수님의 질문에 대답을 드리면, 아니에요, 미술사를 전공하는 것에 대해서는 정말로 생각해 본 적이 없어요. 하지만 미술은 제가 늘 좋아하는 것이었어요. 저는 시간이 있을 때마다 미술관을 찾아가고, 미술 서적을 살펴보는 것도 좋아해요. 하지만 전공을 한다? 아니에요, 그런 생각은 결코 해 본 적이 없어요.

교수: 음, 제 생각에 학생은 훌륭한 미술사가가 될 수 있기 때문에 그런 생각을 해 보았어야 해요. 말해 보세요… 이번이 첫 번째 미술사 수업은 아니죠, 맞나요?

학생: 맞아요. 이곳에서 1학년 때 이후로, 저는, 음… 세 번…? 아니군요, 네 번 미술사 수업을 들었어요.

교수: 3학년이죠, 맞나요?

학생: 맞아요.

교수: 그러면 미술사를 전공하는 것이 불가능하겠군요. 하지만, 이러한 점은 모르고 있겠지만, 현재 미술사를 부전공으로 삼을 수 있어요. 부전공을 하기 위해서는 5개의 수업만 들으면 되는데, 학생이 이미 거의 다 들어 둔 상태죠. 그 분야를 부전공으로 삼는 방법에 관한 정보를 알려 줄까요?

학생: 어, 물론이에요. 살펴볼 수 있을 것 같아요.

> **WORD REMINDER**
>
> get caught up ~에 휘말리다 outstanding 뛰어난 have an eye for ~을 보는 눈이 있다, ~에 대한 안목이 있다 browse 둘러보다, 훑어보다

Lecture · Anthropology

p.60

교수: 다음으로 여러분과 함께 다루고 싶은 것은 인도네시아 군도의 작은 섬 중 하나인 발리입니다. 현재에는 멋진 경치와 해변으로 잘 알려진 아시아의 주요 관광지이죠. 하지만 그에 대해 말하려는 것은 아닙니다. 대신 발리 섬 사람들의 역사를 살펴보려고 하는데, 그렇게 하기 위해서는 먼 과거로 거슬러 올라가야 합니다.

인류학자들은 약 만 년 전 원시적인 형태의 인류의 조상이 발리에서 살았다는 점을 밝혀냈습니다. 이러한 원인들은 기초적인 석기 도구를 사용했고, 섬에 있는 동굴에 거주했습니다. 이들은 커다란 자바 섬 근처에서 발견된 자바 원인의 표본과 관련이 있을 가능성이 높습니다. 이들 원인들이 어떻게 발리에 도착했는지에 대해 말씀을 드리면, 간단합니다. 오늘날에는 섬이지만, 과거 여러 차례 해수면이 보다 낮았을 때에는 발리가 인근의 다른 섬들과 연결되어 있었습니다. 바로 이와 같은 시기에 몇몇 무리의 원시 원인들이 걸어서 발리로 왔던 것이죠. 수십 만 년에 걸쳐 이들은 보다 지적인 존재로 진화했고, 사냥 및 채집 기술도 모두 발전하게 되었습니다. 발리에서 발견된 몇몇 유물에서 도끼 형태의 석기, 화살 및 창끝, 그리고 골각기가 포함되어 있었기 때문에 그러한 사실을 알 수 있습니다.

수천 년 동안 이러한 원인들이 발리 주변 지역을 지배했습니다. 그 후 약 4만 년이나 5만 년 전에 해부학적으로 현대 인류에 해당되는 이들이 이 지역에 도착했습니다. 점차적으로 이들은 그곳에 살던 원시 원인의 후손들과의 경쟁에서 그들을 앞서게 되었습니다. 실은, 그러한 일이 일어났다고 생각됩니다. 하지만 그러한 원인들은 그 당시에 이미 멸종해 있었을 수도 있습니다. 그에 관한 화석 기록이 명확하지 않습니다. 어쨌든 그곳에 도착했던, 해부학적으로 현대 인류에 해당되는 이들은 또한 뉴기니와 호주에도 가게 되었고, 그들의 자손이 아직까지도 그곳에 살고 있습니다. 그 후 약 5천 년 전 새로운 무리의 사람들이, 발리를 포함하여, 인도네시아의 섬들로 이주했습니다. 고고학자들은 이러한 사람들을 오스트로네시안이라고 부릅니다. 오스트로네시안들은 피부색이 보다 밝았고 직모를 지니고 있었으며 최초로 발리에 살았던 사람들보다 동양적인 외모를 가지고 있었는데, 최초로 발리에 살았던 사람들은 피부가 어둡고 곱슬 머리를 지니고 있었습니다. 이러한 오스트로네시안들은 중국 본토에 기원을 두고 있었었다고 생각됩니다. 이후 이들은 대만으로 갔고, 그 후에는 필리핀으로, 그 다음에는 남쪽으로 가서 인도네시아에 도착했습니다. 그곳에서부터는 여러 태평양 섬들로 이동을 했고요.

이들 오스트로네시안들은 쌀을 경작하는 방법을 포함하여 농사에 대한 지식을 가지고 왔고, 또한 길들여진 돼지와 닭도 가지고 왔습니다. 도달한 모든 인도네시아 섬에서, 이들은 제가 방금 말씀드렸던 해부학적으로 현대 인류에 해당되는 이들을 경쟁에서 물리쳤습니다. 그들은 점차 동쪽으로 밀려났고, 결국 솔로몬 반도의 섬에 정착하게 되었습니다. 하지만 뉴기니에 있던 사람들은 이미 농사에 대해 알고 있었기 때문에 오스트로네시안이 섬을 완전히 점령하는 일을 막을 수 있었습니다. 특히 섬의 안쪽 산악 지대에 살던 사람들이 그랬습니다. 또한 오스트로네시안들은 호주와 제한적으로만 접촉을 했는데, 따라서 유럽 사람들이 도착하기 전까지, 약 4만 년 전 정착한 호주 원주민들이 호주를 지배할 수 있었습니다.

발리에서 이들 새로운 정착민들은 상당할 정도로 농업을 발전시켰습니다. 발리는 화산섬이었기 때문에 작물을 기르기에 토양이 좋았고, 이로써 생산성이 꽤 높았습니다. 이들 정착민들은 발리에 도착했을 당시 여전히 석기 시대의 도구들을 사용하고 있었습니다. 하지만 기원전 600년경에 점차적으로 청동으로 된 도구 및 무기를 획득하게 되었습니다. 청동은 주석과 구리로 만들어지지만 발리에서는 이들 중 어떤 금속도 이 사람들에게 알려진 바가 없기 때문에 "획득하게 되었다"라고 말씀드렸습니다. 그러면 이들은 어떻게 청동 도구 및 무기를 얻게 되었을까요? 일부 사람들은 완성된 제품이 수입되었다고 생각하는 반면, 주석과 구리가 수입되어 발리 사람들 스스로 청동기를 만들었다고 주장하는 사람들도 있습니다. 아무도 확실한 것은 모릅니다. 하지만 발리의 청동기 제작 기술은 베트남의 기술과 유사했는데, 이러한 사실은 인도네시아 사람들과 베트남 사람들 사이에 무역이 존재했다는 점을 암시합니다.

대략 기원전 600년을 시작으로 발리 사람들은 천 년 동안 비교적 평화로운 시기를 보냈습니다. 하지만 시간이 지나면서 외부와의 접촉이 그들에게 영향을 미치기 시작했습니다. 발리인들은 주로 인도의 영향을 받았습니다. 불교와 힌두교를 가장한 종교가 인도로부터 수입되었고, 문자 역시 인도로부터 수입되었습니다. 오, 확실히 여러분 중 다수는 오늘날 인도네시아가 이슬람 국가라고 알고 있을 것입니다. 그럼에도 불구하고 발리에는 여전히 힌두교와 불교의 영향력이 강하게 남아 있습니다. 그곳의 많은 사람들이 아직도 인도의 의식과는 약간 다른 형태의 힌두교 의식을 거행하고 있습니다. 하지만 이 문제는 추후 인도네시아의 다양한 종교에 대해 이야기할 때 자세히 다룰 수 있는 문제라고 생각합니다. 종교가 아니라 발리에서 발전된 청동 문화에 대한 논의를 계속하고 싶군요… 오, 이런. 시계를 보니 시간이 다 되었네요. 오늘은 이만하고 목요일 수업에서 발리에 대한 이야기를 계속하는 것이 어떨까요? 모두들 어떻게 들리나요?

> **WORD REMINDER**
>
> archipelago 군도 tourist destination 관광지 humanoid 인간과 비슷한 존재, 원인 artifact 유물 dominate 지배하다 anatomically 해부학적으로 outcompete 경쟁에서 이기다, 물리치다 remnant 나머지, 생존자 descendant 자손, 후손 domesticated 길들여진 takeover 인수, 접수 tin 주석 speculate 사색하다, 생각하다 in the guise of ~을 가장하여 wrap ~ up ~을 마무리하다

PART 2

Conversation

p.64

학생: 안녕하세요, Chapman 선생님. 제 이름은 Ray Sanders예요. 지금 이 시간에 선생님하고 약속이 되어 있죠.

상담 교사: 아, 그래요. 안녕하세요, Ray. 사무실로 들어와서 앉으세요.

학생: 정말 감사합니다.

상담 교사: 천만에요. 그러면, Ray, 정확히 무엇에 관해 저와 이야기하고 싶은가요?

학생: 제 장래에 대해서요… 저는, 어… 좋아요. 제 상황에 대해서 잠깐 말씀을 드릴게요. 저는 4학년으로 역사를 전공하고 있어요. 지난 4번의 학기 동안 장학생 명단에 올랐고, 우등으로 졸업을 하게 될 예정이죠. 특별히 대학원에 가고 싶지는 않아요. 그 대신 졸업을 하자마자 취직을 하고 싶어요. 그리고 다음 달에 이곳 교내에서 취업 박람회가 두 차례 열릴 것이라는 이야기를 들었는데…

상담 교사: 그래요, 맞아요. 말해 보세요, Ray… 어떤 종류의 일자리를 찾고 있나요?

학생: 솔직히 말씀드리면… 저-저-저는 잘 모르겠어요.

상담 교사: 음, 그러면 결정한 것이 없다고 생각해도 될까요?

학생: 꼬박꼬박 월급이 들어오는 한 어떤 일이라도 기꺼이 하겠어요.

상담 교사: 그래요. 그에 대해서는 생각이 열려 있어서 다행이네요. 자, 어떤 일을 하고 싶어하는지에 대한 생각을 가지고 있어야만 해요.

학생: 흠… 금융 쪽이 좋을 것 같아요. 아니면 컨설팅 회사의 일자리도 받아드릴 용의가 있고요.

상담 교사: 좋아요. 범위가 좁혀지고 있군요. 그런 경우라면 이번 주 토요일로부터 2주 후에 있을 취업 박람회에 꼭 참석하도록 하세요. 두 차례의 박람회 중 규모는 더 작지만, 금융업계의 상당수 기업들이 담당자들을 보낼 거예요. 규모가 더 큰 박람회에도 참석할 수 있겠지만, 그곳은 엔지니어, 컴퓨터 프로그래머, 그리고 과학 전공자들을 뽑으려는 기업들로 가득할 거예요.

학생: 어… 그러면 그 박람회는 가지 말아야겠네요.

상담 교사: 그래요. 그게 좋을 것 같아요. 자, 취업 박람회에 대한 준비를 하기 위해 몇 가지 해야 할 일이 있어요. 제일 먼저 — 그리고 가장 중요한 것인데 — 이력서를 작성해야 하죠.

학생: 오, 얼마 전에 이력서를 만들어 놓았어요. 그 점에 대해서는 걱정할 필요가 없어요.

상담 교사: 전문가를 통해 작성했나요? 정말 중요해서 그래요. 자기 자신을 미래의 고용주에게 소개하는 것이기 때문에 이력서에 실수가 없어야 하고 최대한 좋아 보여야 하죠. 물론 약간의 돈이 들겠지만 취직이 된다면 투자한 만큼의 가치는 있을 거예요.

학생: 전혀 생각하지 못했던 점이군요. 좋아요. 조언에 감사를 드립니다. 업체에 연락해서 처리하도록 할게요. 그 밖에 해야 할 일이 또 있나요?

상담 교사: 네, 있어요. 취업 박람회에 그와 같은 옷을 입고 갈 계획은 아니죠, 그런가요?

학생: 면 바지와 단추가 달린 셔츠가 잘못이라는 건가요?

상담 교사: Ray, 취업 박람회에는 반드시 정장에 넥타이를 매고 가야 해요. 또한 최대한 단정하게 보여야 하고요. 첫인상이 좋게 보이기를 원한다면 가능한 옷을 잘 차려 입어야 해요.

학생: 그러면 정장을 한 벌 사야 할 것 같군요. 조언해 주셔서 고마워요. 말씀 주신 모든 것에 정말로 감사를 드립니다.

WORD REMINDER

Dean's List 우등생 명단   graduate with honors 우등으로 졸업하다
regular salary 본봉, 고정급   open minded 마음이 열린   as to ~에
관한   finance 금융, 재정   decent 적절한, 온당한   land a job 취직하
다   slacks (정장) 바지   well groomed 단정한, 말쑥한

교수: 수업을 마치기 전에 시장 조사로 관심을 돌려 보도록 하겠습니다. 괜찮죠…? 좋습니다. 시장 조사는 사람들에 관한 정보를 수집하는 한 가지 방법으로, 기업이 보다 우수한 제품을 만들거나 보다 많은 제품 및 서비스를 판매하는데 도움을 줍니다. 시장 조사에서는 온갖 질문들을 묻습니다. 일부 질문들은 예컨대, 음, 성별, 인종, 수입, 혼인 유무, 직업, 그리고 교육 정도와 같은 개인적인 정보에 관해 묻습니다. 개인의 소비 성향, 일반적으로 사용하는 제품 및 서비스, 그리고 신제품에 대한 구매 의향과 관련된 질문도 있을 수 있습니다. 당연하게도, 시장 조사에서는 기업이 제공하는 특정 제품 및 서비스에 대한 질문을 합니다. 시장 조사에는 여러 가지 유형이 있기 때문에, 그 중 일부에 대해 여러분들과 함께 간략히 검토하도록 하겠습니다.

첫 번째는 소매점 조사입니다. 이는 고객이 매장의 제품 및 서비스에 만족하는지, 그리고 특정 고객 서비스에 대해 만족하는지를 알아내고자 할 때 사용됩니다. 매장 내 만족도 조사에서는 소비자에게 일정 제품을 테스트해 볼 것을 요청하고, 그에 대한, 어, 피드백을 요청을 할 수 있습니다. 여기에는 식품이나 음료수를 시식하고 그에 대한 의견을 밝히는 것이 포함될 수 있습니다. 여러분 중에 정기적으로 대형 슈퍼마켓에서 쇼핑을 하는 사람이 있다면 아마도 이러한 종류의 조사에 참여해 보았을 것이라고 생각합니다.

또 다른 일반적인 유형의 시장 조사는 전화 조사입니다. 이는 조사를 실시하는 기업에게 몇 가지 이점을 가져다 줍니다. 현재 전화 요금이 대부분 상당히 저렴한 편이기 때문에 비용이 비교적 적게 듭니다. 물론 조사를 실시하기 위해서는 기업이 사람들을 고용해서 이들을 교육시키거나, 혹은 전문 조사 기관에 도움을 요청해야 하는데, 그렇게 하면 약간 많은 비용이 들 수도 있습니다. 그럼에도 불구하고 기업들은 전화 조사를 통해 인종 및 경제적 배경이 다를 뿐만 아니라 인구통계학적으로 다양하게 구성된 남녀를 조사 대상으로 삼을 수 있습니다. 또한 즉각적인 피드백이 제공됩니다. 이와 관련된 주된 문제는 사람들이 종종 응답을 거절한다는 점입니다. 조사원이 전화를 걸면 그냥 전화를 끊는 경우가 빈번합니다. 당황스러운 일이죠. 여러 해 전에 제가 학생이었을 당시 저도 그랬습니다. 두 번째 문제는 일부 사람들이 솔직한 답변을 하지 않는다는 점입니다. 어떤 사람들은 가능한 조사를 빨리 끝내기 위해서 머릿속에 떠오르는 아무 말이나 합니다. 세 번째 단점은 이러한 조사가 청각적으로만 진행되기 때문에 개인이 제품을 테스트하거나 볼 수는 없다는 점입니다.

다음으로 우편 조사가 있습니다. 사람들에게 우편으로 설문지가 보내지고, 어, 앙케이트죠. 설문지가 작성되면 수취인 부담 봉투로 설문지가 다시 발신자에게 보내지게 됩니다. 이러한 종류의 조사는 비교적 비용이 적게 들지만, 어느 정도의 노력과 많은 양의 용지 및 봉투가 필요합니다. 한 가지 주요한 단점은, 모든 설문지가 다시 회사로 돌아오기까지 몇 주 혹은 심지어 몇 개월이 걸릴 수도 있다는 점에서, 응답 시간이 느리다는 점입니다. 그리고 많은 사람들이 설문지를 채우려는 수고를 하지 않고 그냥 내던져 버립니다. 제 자신도 그런 적이 많았다는 점을 고백해야겠군요. 이를 막기 위해 오늘날 기업들은, 사람들이 설문지를 작성해서 돌려보내야 한다는 의무감을 느끼기를 바라면서, 우편으로 무료 샘플 제품을 제공하고 있습니다. 사람들이 설문지를 작성해서 보내는 경우, 리베이트나 쿠폰을 제공해 주는 기업들도 있습니다.

최근에는 온라인 조사가 인기를 얻고 있습니다. 여러분 대부분은 인터넷 서핑을 하면서 매일같이 이러한 것들을 보고 있을 것입니다. 작은 팝업창이 화면에 나타나서 시간을 내어 몇 가지 질문에 대답해 달라는 요구를 합니다. 이러한 조사 유형의 주된 장점은 다양한 소비자들에게 접근할 수 있다는 점입니다. 또한 설치만 하면 되기 때문에 비교적 비용이 적게 들며, 설치한 다

음에는 데이터를 수집해서 숫자를 처리할 수 있는 시스템을 만들어야 합니다. 온라인 조사에 참여하는 사람들은 조사용 팝업창을 클릭하여 질문에 대한 답을 선택할 수 있으므로 전화 조사에 참여하는 사람보다 더 솔직하게 대답하는 경향이 있습니다. 이러한 사람들은 종종 시간을 갖고 신중히 답을 하는데, 이로써 답변의 가치가 높아집니다. 게다가 온라인 조사가 특정 웹사이트에서 진행되면 틈새 시장과 직접 연결될 수 있습니다. 주된 문제점은 모든 계층에 접근하지는 못한다는 점입니다. 컴퓨터나 인터넷을 사용할 수 없는 사람들, 예컨대 많은 노년층들의 의견은 온라인 조사에서 항상 제대로 반영되지 않습니다.

학생: 전화가 없거나 인터넷을 사용하지 못하는 사람들, 그리고 우편 조사를 거부하는 사람들은 조사원이 어떻게 접촉할 수 있나요?

교수: 마지막 기회가 있습니다. 바로 가정 방문 조사입니다. 이를 위해 조사원들은 집집마다 돌아다니며 사람들에게 조사에 응해 줄 것을 요청합니다. 이러한 조사의 주된 장점은 얼굴을 마주하고 조사에 참여한 사람들이 보다 솔직한 반응을 나타내는 경향이 있다는 점입니다. 하지만 조사를 진행하는 사람들이 교육을 받고 보수를 받아야 해서 상당히 많은 비용이 듭니다. 그리고 많은 사람들이 낯선 사람에게 문을 열어 주는 것을 좋아하지 않기 때문에 조사에 대한 참여를 거부합니다. 좋아요. 시간이 다 되었군요. 질문이 있나요?

Lecture · Zoology   p.69

교수: 동물들은 먹는 음식과 전반적인 식습관에 의해 더 세분화될 수 있습니다. 여러분들께서 아셔야 할 몇 가지가 있는데… 일부 동물들은 식물만 먹고, 일부는 고기만을 먹으며, 두 가지를 모두 먹는 동물들도 있습니다. 많은 동물들이 사실상 아무것이나 먹는 반면, 보다 까다로워서 특정 종류의 먹이만을 먹는 동물들도 있습니다. 일부 동물들은 밤에만 사냥을 해서 먹이를 먹지만, 낮에 그러한 행동을 하는 동물들도 있죠. 그리고 많은 동물들이 먹이를 구한 곳에서 먹이를 먹지만, 먹이를 다른 장소로 가져간 후에 먹이를 먹는 동물들도 있습니다. 이러한 모든 유형의 행동에는 장점과 단점이 있는데, 이제 그에 대해서 자세히 살펴보도록 하겠습니다.

그러면, 어, 동물들을 구분할 수 있는 가장 손쉽고도 일반적인 방법은 그들이 먹는 먹이에 따른 것입니다. 우리는 동물을 초식 동물, 육식 동물, 그리고 잡식 동물로 구분할 수 있습니다. 초식 동물은 식물만을 먹습니다. 그러한 예에는 다양한 포유류, 예컨대 말, 소, 양, 사슴, 그리고 토끼가 포함됩니다. 다른 강의 동물들 중 순수한 초식 동물은 보다 드문 편으로, 대부분의 어류, 파충류, 조류, 그리고 양서류들은 충분한 양의 에너지를 얻기 위해 고기를 섭취해야만 하기 때문입니다. 육식 동물은, 물론, 고기를 먹습니다. 이에 해당되는 예는 모든 강의 동물들에서 찾을 수 있습니다. 종종 대다수 사람들의 머릿속에 떠오르는 육식 동물로 사자, 호랑이, 늑대, 그리고 상어가 있는데, 이를 모두는 몸집이 큰 포식 동물입니다. 잡식 동물은 식물과 고기를 모두 먹는 동물입니다. 이들은 사실상 아무것이나 먹기 때문에 기회주의적 포식자로 여겨집니다. 쥐, 돼지, 곰, 침팬지, 그리고 많은 종의 조류들이 잡식성입니다. 인간 또한, 잘 알고 계시듯이, 잡식성이죠.

동물들이 낮에 먹이를 구하는지 혹은 밤에 구하는지에 따라 동물들을 한 번 더 나눌 수 있습니다. 주행성 동물은 낮에 활동하는 동물이며, 야행성 동물은 밤에 활동해서 밤에 사냥을 하고 먹이를 먹는 동물입니다. 올빼미와 뱀은 많은 이들에게 친숙한 야행성 동물 중 하나입니다. 이러한 동물들은 어떻게 어둠 속에서 볼 수 있을까요? 음, 올빼미는 — 다른 여러 야행성 동물들과 마찬가지로 — 뛰어난 시력 덕분에 어둠 속에서도 볼 수가 있습니다. 뱀에 대해 말하자면, 이들은 온도 변화를 감지할 수 있기 때문에 생물체의 체온을 느낌으로써 그들에게 접근하여 공격을 합니다.

동물들은 또한 어디에서 먹이를 먹는지에 따라 다르게 행동합니다. 일부 동물들은 먹이를 구한 바로 그 장소에서 먹이를 먹습니다. 예를 들면 먹이를 잡은 육식 동물은 일반적으로 그 현장에서 먹이를 잡아먹습니다. 아마도 여러분 모두는 텔레비전 다큐멘터리 프로그램에서 사자가 동물을 쓰러뜨린 후 먹이를 잡은 바로 그 자리에서 먹이를 먹는 모습을 본 적이 있을 것입니다. 늑대도 이와 같은 행동을 하죠. 하지만 붙잡은 먹이의 일부를 자신의 무리나 가족이 살고 있는 곳으로 가져와서 사냥을 하지 않은 구성원들도 이를 먹을 수 있도록 하는 동물들도 있습니다. 초식 동물에 대해 말씀을 드리면, 이들 대부분은 먹이를 발견한 곳에서 먹이를 먹습니다. 풀을 먹는 동물들, 예컨대, 어, 예컨대 말, 소, 그리고 양들은 음식을 다른 곳으로 가져갈 수가 없기 때문에 선택의 여지가 거의 없습니다. 하지만 먹이를 다른 곳으로 가져가는 초식 동물들도 있습니다. 캥거루쥐가 이러한 행동을 하죠. 이들은 포식자의 공격에 대한 두려움을 느끼지 않고 먹이를 먹을 수 있는 비밀 장소로 먹이를 가지고 갑니다. 많은 종의 새들은 새끼들을 위해 먹이를 구해서 둥지로 가지고 갑니다. 일부 조류들은 새끼들에게 먹이를 먹이기 위해 먹었던 음식을 토해 낼 수도 있습니다.

동물과 먹이에 관해 마지막으로 구분해 볼 수 있는 점은 다양한 종류의 먹이를 먹는 동물과 특정한 종류의 먹이만을 먹는 동물과 관련이 있습니다. 먹을 수 있는 먹이가 많은 동물들은 다양한 환경에서 살아남을 수 있습니다. 또한 하나의 먹이가 소진되면 다른 먹이를 먹을 수가 있기 때문에 이러한 동물들은 보다 쉽게 먹이를 확보할 수 있습니다. 예를 들면 곰은 베리 및 다양한 식물들을 먹지만, 물고기 및 기타 종류의 고기도 먹습니다. 그래서 한 가지 먹이의 공급량이 적어지면 곰은 다른 먹이를 찾으면 됩니다. 하지만 한 가지 종류의 먹이만을 먹는 동물들은 그러한 먹이가 소진될 경우 참사를 겪을 수도 있습니다. 유칼립투스 잎만을 먹는 코알라가 그러한 동물 중 하나입니다. 유칼립투스 잎이 없다면 한 지역에 사는 코알라들은 굶어 죽을 것입니다. 실제로 코알라는 전적으로 유칼립투스 잎에만 의지하도록 진화가 되었습니다. 코알라에게는 불행한 일인데, 유칼립투스 잎은 코알라에게 단백질 및 에너지를 거의 공급해 주지 못하기 때문에 코알라는 하루에 3시간에서 5시간 정도만 돌아다닐 수 있으며, 그것도 먹이를 먹기 위해서만 그렇게 합니다. 이들은 나머지 대부분의 시간을 움직이지 않고 지내거나 잠을 자는데 사용합니다.

학생: 그들이 그렇게 할 때는 일종의, 어, 일종의 동면을 하는 동물들과 같은가요?

교수: 흠… 비슷한 행동을 한다고 말할 수는 있을 것 같지만, 그들이 동면을 하는 것은 아닙니다. 하지만 좋은 지적이었어요, Claudia. 동면을 하는 많은 동물들, 가령 곰과 박쥐 같은 동물들은 동면을 하기에 앞서 많은 먹이를 먹어서 살을 찌웁니다. 음식을 먹을 수 없는 장기간의 비활동 시즌에서 살아남기 위해 그들의 신진대사는 느려집니다. 좋아요. 이제까지 동물의 식습관에 있어서 주요한 차이점들을 알아보았습니다. 다음으로 넘어가기 전에 질문이 더 있을까요?

PART 3

Conversation

p.74

학생: Gregg 교수님, 잠깐 시간을 내실 수 있는지 궁금하군요. 지금 바쁘신가요?

교수: 전혀 그렇지 않아요, Tim. 무슨 일이죠?

학생: 오늘 수업에서 대체 에너지에 관한 교수님의 논평이 정말로 마음에 들었어요. 특히 태양광 발전에 관해 말씀하신 부분에서 흥미를 느꼈죠.

교수: 고마워요. 수업에서 학생들이 배운다는 점뿐만 아니라 제 강의를 좋아한다는 점을 알게 되면 항상 기분이 좋아지죠.

학생: 그런데 두 가지 질문이 있어요.

교수: 그래요.

학생: 먼저 저는 태양 전지가 그다지 효율적이지 않다는 점에 깊은 인상을 받았어요. 제가 알기로 그러한 점은 태양광 발전의 주요한 단점 중 하나이죠.

교수: 주요한 단점이라고 한 점은 맞아요. 하지만 최근에 태양광 전지의 효율이 크게 증가하고 있다는 점은 알아야 해요. 1970년대와 1980년대 당시에는 효율 등급이 약 10%정도였죠. 알겠지만 이는 태양광 전지가 이용 가능한 에너지의 10%만을 생산할 수 있다는 뜻이에요.

학생: 오늘날에는 얼마나 높은가요?

교수: 시중에 나와 있는 태양 전지들의 효율성은 약 22% 정도예요. 실험실 테스트에서는 두 개의 태양 전지가 25% 이상을 달성했죠. 하지만 그건 극도로 이상적인 환경에서였어요. 현재에는 29%의 효율성에 도달하는 것이 목표예요.

학생: 허, 그 정도로 개선되었다는 점은 제가 모르고 있었네요.

교수: 분명히 개선되었죠. 더 많은 연구가 진행되면 계속해서 더욱 개선될 것이고, 보다 우수한 태양 전지가 개발될 것으로 생각해요.

학생: 그렇군요, 고맙습니다. 질문이 하나 더 있어요.

교수: 그래요.

학생: 사람들이 태양광 도로를 개발하고 있다는 것이 사실인가요? 진짜로 존재할 리가 없잖아요. 제 말은, 어, 그건 유명한 공상 과학 소설에서나 나올 법한 이야기로 들리거든요.

교수: 알겠지만, 음, 공상 과학 소설에서 처음 다루어진 많은 아이디어들이 최근에 현실이 되고 있어요. 그리고, 어, 그래요, 실제로 태양광 도로가 개발 중이라는 말은 사실이에요. 태양광 도로는 낮 동안 에너지를 생산할 수 있을 뿐만 아니라 밤에는 조명을 제공할 수도 있으며, 열을 발산함으로써 도로에 내린 눈을 녹일 수도 있어요.

학생: 와, 정말 근사하게 들리는군요.

교수: 근사하죠, 그렇죠? 하지만 현재로서는 태양광 도로의 건설 비용이 극도로 높아요. 도로 1킬로미터당 수백만 달러를 얘기하고 있는 거예요. 기본

적으로 에너지를 생산할 수 있고 밤낮없이 운행하는 차량에도 부서지지 않는, 보다 우수하고 단단한 재료가 필요하죠.

학생: 미래에는 수많은 태양광 도로가 존재할 것으로 생각하시나요?

교수: 저는 미래에 대해 매우 낙관적인 편이에요. 사실 앞으로 수십 년 이내에 태양광 발전 기술이 훨씬 더 일상적이 될 만큼 크게 발전할 것이라고 생각해요. 학생도, 어, 제가 오늘 수업에서 언급했으니 알겠지만, 전 세계 정부들이 대체 에너지원을 장려하고 있다는 사실에도 불구하고, 대체 에너지원은 화석 연료와 비교해 볼 때 여전히 매우 조금만 사용되고 있어요. 하지만 기술이 발전하고 비용이 저렴해지면 태양광 발전이 급격히 증가해서 화석 연료는 서서히 사라지는 광경을 보게 될 거예요.

학생: 저도 분명 그렇게 되기를 바라요. 그것이 바로 제가 살고 싶어하는 미래이고요. 시간을 내 주셔서 감사합니다. Gregg 교수님. 이번 대화는 정말로 유익했어요.

Lecture • Marketing

p.76

교수: 여러분도 저와 같다면, 쇼핑을 하러 가기 전에 필요한 물건의 목록을 작성해 둘 것입니다. 보통 저는 목록에 모든 것을 적어둔 다음, 가능하면 목록에 따라 쇼핑을 하려고 하죠. 하지만 집에 돌아오면 제 쇼핑 가방에는 거의 언제나 제가 구입하려고 생각했던 것보다 많은 물건들이 들어 있습니다. 그래서 문제는 다음과 같습니다. 제가 왜 이렇게 불필요한 물품들을 구입할까요? 기억력 결함을 겪고 있어서 쇼핑 목록에 물품을 추가해야 한다는 점을 잊고 있었던 것일까요? 음, 몇몇 경우에는 그렇기도 합니다. 예전만큼 머리가 돌아가지는 않으니까요. 하지만 제가 구입하는 대부분의 불필요한 물품들은 정말로 제게 필요한 것들이 아닙니다. 그럼에도 불구하고 결국 쇼핑 카트에 놓여지고, 저는 그에 대한 값을 지불하게 되죠. 제가 이렇게 불필요한 물품들을 구입하는 주된 이유는 충동 구매 때문입니다. 이는 여러 가지 심리학적인 요인들에 의해 일어나는 것입니다. 그리고 가장 좋지 못한 것은 다음과 같은 점입니다. 체인점들은 이러한 요인들을 알고 있으며, 쇼핑객들로 하여금 자신의 충동에 넘어가서 불필요한 물건을 사도록 만드는 방법들을 알고 있습니다.

그러면… 충동 구매 뒤에 감춰져 있는 심리는 무엇일까요? 우선, 사람들은 종종 기분이 좋아지기 위해 물건을 구입합니다. 다양한 물품들을 보고 그러한 제품을 감당할 여유가 없다는 점을 알면서도 구입을 하죠. 일부 개인들은 자존심을 높이기 위해 제품을 구입하는데… 어, 아시겠지만, 자신들에게 멋진 소유물이 있다는 것을 보여 주고자 하는 것입니다. 그리고 어떤 사람들은 스트레스를 풀기 위해 물건을 구입합니다. 어쨌거나 자발적인 구매 행위는 많은 사람들의 스트레스를 줄여 주는 기능을 합니다.

음, 그러한 사람들에게는 불행한 일이지만 사업체들은 점점 더 특정한 심리학적 요인을 이용하여 보다 많은 쇼핑객들이 충동 구매를 하도록 만들고 있습니다. 기업들은 충동적으로 무언가를 구매하는 일이 부정적인 것이 아니라는 점을 보여 주기 위해 노력합니다. 대신 쇼핑객들이 무엇을 구입하던 좋은 기분을 느끼도록 만들려고 하죠. 이와 같은 일을 하기 위해 기업들이 이용하는 여러 가지 방법들이 있습니다. 그 중 몇 가지를 알려 드리죠. 그러면 제 생각에, 음, 여러분들이 좋아하는 매장에서 다음 번 쇼핑을 하는 경우, 제가 여러분에게 말씀드리려고 하는 것이 그곳에서 어떻게 이루어지고 있는지 알게 될 것입니다.

먼저, 사업체들은 소비자들이 물품을 구입하고 싶도록 매장 내 환경을 조성하려고 합니다. 이러한 매장에서는 충동 구매의 부정적인 측면들이 크게 느껴지지 않는 반면, 긍정적인 측면들은 강조됩니다. 어떻게…? 봅시다… 매장들은 그 중에서도 쇼윈도의 화려한 상품 진열, 특정 제품을 사용하는 사람들의 즐거운 모습을 보여 주는 광고, 그리고 판촉을 위한 슬로건들을 이용합니다. 이러한 것들은 사람들이 물품을 구매할 때 좋은 기분을 느끼도록 만드는 역할을 합니다. 매장들은 또한 영업 시간을 늘리고, 쇼핑객들의 신용 거래를 보다 용이하게 만들고, 구매한 제품에 대해 불만을 갖는 경우 쇼핑객들에게 교환을 해 줌으로써 충동 구매를 부추깁니다. 이에 대한 예가 하루 24시간을 영업하는 슈퍼마켓과 편의점입니다. "100% 만족하지 않으면 환불해 드립니다"와 같은 슬로건들도 마찬가지죠. 이러한 선전 구호들은 사람들로 하여금 아무런 위험 없이 물건을 구입해도 된다는 기분을 느끼도록 만듭니다. 생각해 보세요… 그와 같은 특정 슬로건들을 몇 번이나 들어보셨나요? 물론 사업체를 운영하는 사람들은, 어, 구입한 제품에 만족하지 않더라도 대부분의 사람들이 환불하려는 수고를 하지 않을 것이라는 점을 알고 있습니다.

또 다른 중요한 요인은 매장에서 — 오프라인 매장과 온라인 매장에서 모두 — 세일을 하는 것입니다. 어쨌거나 누가 세일을 거부할 수 있을까요…? 세일은 사람들로 하여금 종종 평소 같으면 사지 않았을 제품들을 구매하고 싶도록 만듭니다. 다음에 슈퍼마켓에 갈 때 주의해서 보세요. "한 개 구매 시 하나가 공짜"라고 알려 주는 할인 내용을 찾아보십시오. 사람들에게 이러한 제품 중 한 개 조차 필요하지 않는 경우가 많지만, 한 개 가격으로 두 개를 얻는 것은 꽤 괜찮은 거래처럼 보이기 때문에 사람들은 결국 구매를 하게 됩니다. 기업들이 세일 품목에서 수익을 내지 못하는 과도한 할인이 진행되는 경우도 있습니다. 하지만 이러한 매장을 방문하는 고객들은 일반적으로 다른 불필요한 물품들을 정가로 구입하기 때문에 매장은 다른 제품을 판매함으로써 이윤을 얻게 됩니다.

매장들이 충동 구매를 자극하는 세 번째 중요한 방식은 상품 진열을 통해서입니다. 왜 보석과 화장품은 항상 대형 백화점의 입구 근처에 있는지 궁금해 본 적이 있나요? 그러한 특정 제품들은 종종 충동적으로 구매되기 때문에 그곳에서 판매되고 있는 것입니다. 슈퍼마켓 역시 상품 진열에 크게 의존하고 있습니다. 많은 쇼핑객들은 빵, 우유, 고기, 야채, 그리고 과일을 구입하기 위해 슈퍼마켓에 갑니다. 하지만 사이다, 과자, 초콜릿, 그리고 아이스크림과 같은 맛있는 제품들이 그러한 상품 근처에 놓여 있기 때문에 고객들이 이들 제품을 살 가능성이 높아집니다. 네, Cindy?

학생: 계산대에서 이루어지는 일도 그런 것이 아닌가요 — 아시겠지만, 초코바와 기타 정크 푸드들 모두 항상 계산대 근처에 있잖아요?

교수: 저도 그보다 더 잘 말씀드릴 수는 없을 것 같군요. 바로 그겁니다. 그 품목들은 사람들의 주위를 끌기 위해 그러한 곳에 있는 것이죠. 계산을 하기 위해 기다리는 동안 쇼핑객들은 눈을 아래로 향해 그러한 제품들을 보게 되고, 마침내 사이다나 초코바를 집을 수도 있을 것입니다. 저와 마찬가지로, 사실상 여러분 모두가 이러한 광고 술수의 먹잇감이 된 적이 있을 것이라고 확신합니다.

WORD REMINDER

stick to ~에 달라붙다; ~을 고수하다   faulty 결함이 있는   impulse shopping 충동 구매   psychological 심리(학)적인   succumb to ~에 굴복하다   boost 증대시키다, 북돋우다   ego 자존심, 자부심   possession 재산, 소유물   spontaneous 자발적인   implement 시행하다   downplay 경시하다, 대단치 않게 생각하다   obtain credit 신용을 얻다, 신용 거래를 하다   catchphrase 유명 문구, 선전 구호   resist 저항하다   trigger 촉발시키다, 유발하다   wind up -ing 결국 ~으로 끝나다   staple 주요 산물, 중요 상품   gimmick 술책, 술수

PART 1

Conversation   p.82

학생: Douglas 교수님, 미리 연락을 드리지 못했는데 만나자고 하셔서 정말 고맙습니다. 오늘 사무실 근무 시간이 없는 것으로 알고 있는데, 이렇게 뵐 수 있도록 시간을 내 주시다니 정말 감사합니다.

교수: 전혀 문제될 것이 없어요, Mandy. 은퇴하시는 교직원 한 분을 위한 오찬에 참석하기 전까지 약 10분 정도의 시간이 있거든요. 그 정도 시간이면 학생에게 충분할까요?

학생: 오, 물론이에요. 다음 주에 제출하기로 한 에세이에 관해서 일이 분 정도만 이야기하면 될 것 같아요.

교수: 아, 그래요. 에세이요. 그것이 어떻다는 것이죠?

학생: 솔직히 말씀드리면, 에세이를 작성하는데 약간의 문제를 겪고 있어요.

교수: 좋아요. 학생의 주제가 무엇인지 다시 한번 제게 알려 주세요. 학생이 주제를 제출했고 제가 그것을 승인한 것은 알고 있지만, 그것이 무엇인지는 생각나지가 않네요. 그 점에 대해서는 미안해요.

학생: 천만에요, 교수님. 학생들이 꽤 많은 수업이니까요.

교수: 그렇게 말해 주니 고맙군요. 어쨌든, 계속해 보세요.

학생: 그럴게요. 음, 조지 워싱턴의 생애에 대해서 에세이를 쓸 계획이었는데, 하지만, 음, 그에 대한 약간의 문제가 있어요.

교수: 왜 그렇죠? 제 말은, 학생이 도서관에서 찾을 수 있는 정보가 분명 충분히 많을 것이라는 뜻이에요. 자료를 찾는 일은 문제가 없을 거예요, 아닌가요?

학생: 오, 아니에요. 그것은 전혀 문제가 되지 않아요. 워싱턴에 관한 책은 수없이 찾아 두었어요. 문제는, 음, 그에 대해 새로운 것을 쓸 수가 없을 것 같아서 걱정이 들어요. 어찌되었든 그의 생애에 대한 책들은 수백 권이 — 아마도 수천 권이 될 수도 있는데 — 쓰여져 있기 때문에, 그래서…

교수: 그래서요?

학생: 그래서, 어, 워싱턴이 일생 동안 무엇을 했는지에 관한 글을 쓰면 지루한 보고서가 되지 않을까요?

교수: 흠… 그래요, 무슨 말인지 알겠어요. 그렇게 되면 상당히 재미없는 보고서가 될 것이고, 학생이 쓸 수 있는 워싱턴 전기에서 제가 전에 읽어본 적이 없는 내용은 분명 많지 않겠죠. 그런 경우라면, 주제를 바꾸는 것도 생각해 보았나요?

학생: 네. 실은 그것 때문에 제가 여기에 온 것이에요. 문제는 제가 워싱턴에 대해 이미 많은 조사를 해 두었다는 점인데, 따라서 주제를 그에 대한 것에서 다른 것으로 바꾸고 싶지는 않아서요. 게다가, 그러한 시기의 또 다른 역사적 인물에 대한 조사를 할 수 있는 시간도 충분하지 않은 것 같고요. 그래서, 음, 제가 어떻게 하면 좋을까요, Douglas 교수님?

교수: 이렇게 하면 어떨까요…? 워싱턴의 일반적인 삶에 대한 글은 쓰지 마세요. 그의 생애에서 특별했던 한 가지 사건에 대해 글을 쓰고 그에 대한 학생의 의견을 제시해 보세요.

학생: 예를 들면요?

교수: 오, 많이 있죠. 제 말은, 워싱턴에게 자녀가 없었다는 점은 학생도 알 거예요, 그렇죠? 음, 미 독립 혁명이 끝난 후 그는 왕이 될 것을 거부했는데 — 아마 쉽게 될 수도 있었을 거예요 — 몇몇 사람들은 그 이유가 그에게 자식이 없어서 그가 죽은 뒤 왕권 계승 문제가 생길 수 있기 때문이라고 생각하죠. 그에 대한 학생의 의견을 제시할 수 있을 거예요. 워싱턴이 전시 상황을 관리한 능력이나 대통령으로서 외교 정책을 다룬 점에 대해서도 글을 쓸 수 있을 것이고요. 학생이 할 수 있는 것은 여러 가지가 있어요.

학생: 와. 그러한 주제 중 어떤 것도 생각해 보지 못했어요. 좋아요. 정말 고맙습니다, Douglas 교수님. 교수님께서 말씀하신 것에 대해 생각해 보고 무언가 새로운 것을 떠올려 보도록 할게요.

교수: 좋아요. 또 다른 문제가 생기는 경우, 개의치 말고 제게 이메일을 보내거나 사무실에 들리도록 해요, Mandy.

Lecture · Astronomy   p.84

교수: 강의 계획서도 살펴보고 이번 학기에 하게 될 일에 대해서도 이야기를 했기 때문에 바로 첫 번째 주제로 넘어가고자 합니다. 처음으로부터 — 모든 것의 처음으로부터 — 이야기를 시작해서 우주의 생성에 대해 논의하는 것이 좋을 것 같군요. 우주가 어떻게 생성되었는지에 관해 꽤 훌륭한 아이디어가 존재하기는 하나, 아직 해결해야 할 문제들이 많다는 점을 언급함으로써 이번 강의를 시작하도록 하겠습니다. 이 점을 명심해 두세요. 좋아요, 어, 우주의 기원에 관한 유력한 이론은 빅뱅 이론입니다. 먼저 그에 대한 설명을 한 다음, 두어 가지 경쟁 이론에 관해 살펴볼 수 있을 것입니다.

빅뱅 이론은 1920년대에 만들어진 수많은 이론 및 관찰의 결과로서 등장했습니다. 벨기에 출신 성직자인 조지 레메트르는, 명문 대학에서 연구를 하던 과학자이기도 했는데, 1920년 우주가 팽창하고 있다고 주장했습니다. 그의 이론은 알버트 아인슈타인 등 당시 저명한 학자들에 의해 회의적으로 다루어 졌습니다. 하지만 그의 이론을 뒷받침하는 강력한 증거들이 발견되자 이후에 레메트르의 이론을 지지하는 사람들이 생겨나기 시작했죠. 20세기 전에는, 아시겠지만, 그렇게 큰 망원경이 존재하지 않았기 때문에 우리가 살고 있는 우리 은하의 작은 부분 바깥에 있는 우주에 대해서는 거의 알려진 바가 없었습니다.

하지만 1900년대에 보다 크고 성능이 뛰어난 망원경들이 만들어지면서 천문학자들은 마침내 우주를 상당히 정확하게 관찰할 수 있었습니다. 이들은 우리 은하 이외에도 더 많은 은하들이 존재하고 있다는 점을 알아냈습니다. 1929년, 미국인 천문학자 에드윈 허블은 우주 내 은하들이 지구에서뿐만 아니라 서로 간에도 점차 멀어지고 있다는 사실을 발견했습니다. 여러분도 알다시피, 이러한 발견은 허블 이외의 다른 사람들에 의해서도 이루어진 바가 있었습니다. 하지만 허블은 확신을 갖고 그와 같은 일이 실제로 일어나고 있다는 점을 증명할 수 있었습니다. 그러나 이러한 발견으로 인해 새로운 질문이 제기되었습니다. 모든 은하가 서로로부터 멀어지고 있고 우주가 팽창하고 있다면 우주가 시작된 지점은 어디였을까요? 천문학자들은, 우주가 정말로 팽창하고 있다면, 우주는 반드시 어딘가로부터 시작되었으며, 한때 우주 전체가 모여 있던 시작점이 있었을 것이라는 점을 알아냈습니다.

2년 후인 1931년에 레메트르가 급진적인 이론을 제시했습니다. 그는 과거 어느 시점에 우주 내 모든 물질들이 하나의 뜨겁고 밀도가 높은 지점에 압축되어 있었다고 주장했습니다. 그것이 무엇으로 만들어져 있었는지, 어떻게 존재하게 되었는지, 그리고 그 이전에는 무엇이 존재했는지는 아무도 모릅니다. 아마도 결코 답을 알아낼 수 없을 것입니다. 하지만 어느 시점에 이르자 이러한 지점이 폭발했고… 다시, 어떻게 혹은 왜 그러한 일이 일어났는지는 아무도 모릅니다. 이러한 폭발은 빅뱅이라고 명명되었으며, 그와 관련된 이론은, 꽤 적절하게도, 빅뱅 이론이라고 불리게 되었죠.

이 이론을 지지하는 사람들과 비판하는 사람들 모두가 존재했지만, 1964년 천문학자들이 우주 전체에 우주배경복사라고 불리는 마이크로파 에너지의 잔재가 존재한다는 점을 발견하면서, 이러한 이론은 지지를 얻게 되었습니다. 많은 천문학자들은 이러한 방사선이 빅뱅이 일어난 때부터 남아 있던 것이라고 믿었습니다. 자, 보다 현명한 사람들이었던 이러한 천문학자들은 방사선을 측정할 수 있었고, 그로써 지구가 얼마나 오래 되었는지를 알아냈습니다. 학자들은 빅뱅이 약 1,300억 년 전에 일어났다는 점을 계산해 냈습니다.

빅뱅이 일어난 후 우주는 확장되고 냉각되기 시작했습니다. 그런 다음 최초의 원소들이 — 아마 수소와 헬륨이었을 텐데 — 생겨났습니다. 막대한 양의 이 두 원소가 우주 전체에서 발견된다는 사실은 그들이 공통된 기원을 가지고 있다는 점을 암시해 주며, 이러한 점은 빅뱅이 일어났다는 또 다른 증거로 받아들여지고 있습니다. 어쨌든 빅뱅 이후 수십억 년이 걸린 과정을 통해 최초의 은하들이 생겨났고, 최초의 항성이 태어났으며, 그 다음에는 행성들이 생성되었습니다. 매우 복잡한 과정을 제가 단순화시켜서 말씀드리고 있다는 점을 알아 주세요. 빅뱅 직후 일어난 모든 일에 대해 확신할 수는 없지만, 우주의 생성에 관해서는 이것이 가장 훌륭한 모델이라고 저는 생각합니다. 네? 앞줄인가요? 질문이 있나요?

학생: Hudson 교수님, 암흑 물질은 어떤가요? 우주의 생성에 관한 그 모델에 암흑 물질과 암흑 에너지의 존재가 필요하지는 않나요?

교수: 아, 그래요, 빅뱅 이론의 아킬레스건을 지적했군요. 확실히 이 이론에는 모순되는 부분이 많습니다. 하지만 일부 천문학자들은 두 가지 알려지지 않은 요인이 — 암흑 물질과 암흑 에너지가 — 이 모든 모순을 설명해 줄 수 있을 것이라고 주장합니다. 안타깝게도, 아직 암흑 물질과 암흑 에너지가, 음, 실제로 존재한다는 점은 증명되지 않았습니다. 그리고 이러한 문제점 때문에 일부 천문학자들은 우주의 생성에 관한 다른 이론들을 제시해 왔습니다. 이제 그 중 두어 가지 이론에 대해 말씀을 드릴 것인데, 여러분들은 이들이 빅뱅 이론과 어떻게 비교되는지 알 수 있을 것입니다.

Lecture · Art History   p.87

교수: 사진이 발명되기 이전, 사람의 이미지를 포착하기 위해 사용되었던 주된 방법은 그림이었습니다. 그 결과, 부유하고 권력 있는 사람들은 종종 자신의 초상화를 의뢰했습니다. 이러한 초상화들은 캔버스에 그려졌고, 크기가 컸으며, 집, 궁전, 그리고 미술관 벽에 걸기 위해 그려졌습니다. 하지만 자신

의 가족이나, 어, 왕과 왕비의 그림을 가지고 다니고 싶었던 사람들은 어땠을까요? 일반적인 초상화는 너무나 무거워서 쉽게 가지고 다닐 수가 없었습니다. 따라서 작은 초상화를 거래하는 시장이 16세기 유럽에서 발달해서 19세기까지 지속되었는데, 19세기에는 카메라가 발명됨으로써 세밀 초상화를 그리는 일은 쇠퇴하게 되었습니다.

방금 언급했듯이 세밀 초상화의 역사는 16세기 유럽에서 시작되었습니다. 몇몇 미술사가들은 세밀 초상화의 기원이 초상 메달에 있다고 믿습니다. 초상 메달은, 여러분이 모르고 있는 경우를 위해 말씀을 드리면, 사람의 이미지가 새겨져 있는 둥근 형태의 메달이었습니다. 하지만 최초의 세밀 초상화는 책을 위한 것이었다고 주장하는 미술사가들도 있습니다. 어떠한 경우이던 최초의 세밀 초상화는 그렇게 사실적이 아니었는데, 하지만 시간이 지남에 따라 화가들은 사람의 이미지를 재현할 수 있는 보다 뛰어난 방법들을 익히게 되었습니다. 어, 16세기 동안에는 르네상스가 지속되고 있었다는 점을 기억해 주시고, 이후 화가들은 재발견된 고대 그리스 및 로마의 회화 기법을 활용하여 그림 속 인물들을 보다 해부학적으로 정확하게 그리기 시작했습니다. 이는 당연하게도 그들이 그린 작품의 질을 향상시켜 주었습니다.

자, 음, 세밀 초상화를 그리는 과정은 쉽지 않았습니다. 그렇게 작은 크기에 사람의 모습을 똑같이 그리기 위해서는 숙련된 손과 예리한 눈이 필요했습니다. 물감을 칠하기 위한 특별한 붓이 필요했고, 미세한 붓놀림 역시 요구되었습니다. 거친 붓놀림을 하면 작은 이미지가 망쳐질 것이었기 때문에 화가들은 매우 주의를 기울여야 했습니다. 수 세기를 거치면서 일부 화가들은 전문적으로 작은 그림을 그리게 되었고, 따라서 자신의 초상화가 그런 식으로 그려지길 바라는 사람들이 이들을 많이 찾게 되었습니다.

학생: Nordy 교수님, 질문이 있습니다.

교수: 그래요. 어떤 질문인가요?

학생: 그러한 화가들을 많이 찾았다고 하셨는데요. 누구에 의해서였나요? 제 말은, 어, 사회 내 어떤 사람들이 자신의 초상화가 작게 그려지기를 원했나요?

교수: 흠… 그러한 초상화는 유럽에서, 그리고 몇 년 후에는 미국과 기타 지역에서 모든 계층의 사람들 사이에서 인기가 높았습니다. 어떤 사람들이 그림을 그리도록 했을까요? 음, 종종 여행을 하거나 고향을 멀리 떠나 있는 사람들은 사랑하는 사람들의 이미지를 항상 소지하고 싶어했습니다. 일반적으로 긴 항해를 하는 선원들도 가족의 세밀 초상화를 지니고 다녔고요. 고국을 떠나 타지로 간 식민지 사람들도 부모와 기타 친척들의 모습을 잊지 않기 위해 통상적으로 그들의 초상화를 가지고 다녔습니다. 몇몇 아버지들은 자신의 딸과 결혼하게 될지도 모르는 예비 사위에게 딸을 보여 주기 위해 딸의 사진을 가지고 있기도 했죠.

이러한 초상화들은 로켓, 브로치, 그리고 팔찌에 넣어져 휴대되었고, 보통은 타원형 형태로 되어 있었습니다. 일부는 정사각형 혹은 직사각형 형태였지만, 대부분은 타원형 형태였죠. 세밀 초상화는 종종 보석과 결합되었는데, 이들은 특히 배우자의 사진을 가지고 다니는 남편과 아내들을 위해 제작되었습니다. 그건 그렇고, 이러한 초상화들은 통상 인물의 머리와 어깨만을 보여 주었습니다. 머리는 약간 오른쪽이나 왼쪽으로 살짝 돌아가 있어서 부분적으로 옆모습이 보였습니다.

학생: 괜찮으시다면 질문이 하나 더 있는데요.

교수: 물론이에요.

학생: 감사합니다. 그러한 그림들은 대부분의 커다란 초상화와 마찬가지로 캔버스 위에 유화 물감으로 그렸나요?

교수: 아니요, 그렇지 않았습니다. 대신 다른 다양한 재료가 사용되었어

요. 몇몇 화가들이 유화 물감과 에나멜을 사용하기는 했지만, 대부분의 세밀 초상화들은 수채화 물감으로 그려졌습니다. 구리는, 캔버스가 아니라, 많은 소형 초상화 화가들이 선택했던 재료였지만, 피지와 판지를 사용한 화가들도 있었습니다. 18세기 무렵에는 상아에 수채화 물감을 칠하는 방법이 광범위하게 사용되었습니다. 상아는 피부색을 빛나게 해 주었고 머리카락을 윤기나게 보이도록 만들었는데, 이로써 그림의 질이 향상되었습니다. 물론 다양한 국가의 사람들은, 어, 다양한 기호를 가지고 있었습니다. 예를 들면 에나멜은 프랑스 및 스위스에서 흔하게 사용되었고, 구리에 유화 물감을 사용하는 방법은 독일과 이탈리아에서 일반적이었으며, 영국과 미국에서는 상아에 수채화 물감을 사용하는 것이 지배적이었습니다. 하지만 이는 주로 개개의 화가들과, 당연하게도, 그림을 의뢰한 개인들에게 달려 있었죠.

어쨌든, 19세기 말 경, 세밀 초상화의 시대는 종말을 맞이하게 되었습니다. 사진이 질적으로 향상되었고, 사진은 값싸고 사실적인 인물 이미지를 제공해 주었습니다. 또한 그림을 그리는 것보다 사진을 찍는 일이 더 빠르고 더 수월했습니다. 오늘날, 과거에 그려졌던 많은 세밀 초상화들은 매우 귀중한 예술 작품으로 여겨지고 있습니다. 다행히 학교에도 몇몇 작품이 소장되어 있는데, 오늘 우리가 살펴볼 수 있도록 제가 가지고 왔습니다. 자, 이쪽으로 와서 이것들을 봐 주세요. 하지만 만지지는 마시고요. 손상되기 쉽습니다. 아무런 일도 일어나지 않았으면 좋겠네요.

WORD REMINDER

commission 위임하다, 위탁하다 portrait 초상화 miniature 소형의, 작은 medallion 큰 메달 etch 식각하다, 새기다 anatomically 해부학적으로 duplicate 복제하다, 복사하다 brushstroke 붓놀림 potential 잠재적인 suitor 구혼자 locket 로켓 (사진 등을 넣고 다닐 수 있는 작은 상자) brooch 브로치 bracelet 팔찌 oval 타원형의 incorporate 합체하다, 합병하다 spouse 배우자 profile 옆모습 oil paint 유화 물감 vellum 고급 피지 cardboard 판지 luminosity 광도, 밝기 sheen 광택, 윤 heyday 전성기

PART 2

Conversation

p.92

학생 활동 센터 직원: 안녕하세요. Melissa겠군요. 저쪽에 앉겠어요?

학생: 고맙습니다, 선생님. 안녕하세요.

학생 활동 센터 직원: 뭐라도 갖다 줄까요? 커피, 물, 아니면 다른 거라도 마실래요?

학생: 괜찮아요, 선생님. 말씀만으로도 감사합니다.

학생 활동 센터 직원: 좋아요, Melissa. 만나고 싶다는 학생의 요청은 받았어요. 하지만 무엇을 논의하고 싶은지는 밝히지 않았더군요. 제게 자세히 말을 해 보는 것이 어떨까요?

학생: 그럴게요. 저는 학교를 졸업하기 위해 모든 학생들이 해야 하는 의무적인 자원 봉사 서비스에 대해 논의하고 싶어요.

학생 활동 센터 직원: 네? 그게 어쨌다는 말인가요?

학생: 저는, 음, 저는 자원 봉사를 하게 될 장소를 변경하는 것이 가능한지가 궁금해요.

학생 활동 센터 직원: 흠… 가끔 그런 경우가 있기는 하지만, 제가 결정을 내리기 위해서는 더 많은 정보가 필요해요. 자세히 말을 해 볼래요?

학생: 물론 그럴게요. 음, 2주 전 저는 Jefferson 초등학교에서 자원 봉사로 수업을 하겠다고 신청했어요. 그곳 1학년 학생들에게 수업을 하기로 했

죠. 제 친구이자 현재 룸메이트인 Rebecca Moore도 그곳에서 수업하는 것에 동의했어요. 아시다시피, 어, 그 학교는 캠퍼스에서 30분 정도 떨어진 곳에 있기는 하지만, Rebecca가 차를 가지고 있기 때문에 그곳까지 차를 타고 갈 계획이었어요. 음, 어, 함께 차를 타고 가는 동안에는 그녀가 운전할 예정이었고요.

학생 활동 센터 직원: Rebecca와 관련된 문제가 생겼다고 생각해도 될까요?

학생: 맞아요, 선생님. 어젯밤에 Rebecca가 제게 주의 다른 지역에 있는 대학으로 전학을 갈 계획이라고 말하더군요. 그녀가 살고 있는 곳이죠. 그녀는, 어, 그녀는 정말로 집을 그리워하기 때문에 고향에 있는 학교에 전학 신청을 했고, 그곳에 다니게 되면 집에서 지낼 수 있을 거예요.

학생 활동 센터 직원: 그곳에 갈 수 있는 방법이 없어졌다는 말이죠?

학생: 맞아요.

학생 활동 센터 직원: 이용할 수 있는 버스가 있나요?

학생: 확인해 봤어요. 두 차례 환승을 해야 하고, 캠퍼스에서 학교까지 가는 데 대략 한 시간 10분이 걸릴 것 같아요. 일주일에 세 번씩 거의 두 시간 반 정도 걸리는 이동 시간을 제가 감당할 수는 없을 것 같아요.

학생 활동 센터 직원: 그래요, 그다지 유쾌하게 들리지는 않는군요. 흠… 혹시 그곳에서 자원 봉사로 수업을 할 학생들이 또 있는지 알고 있나요? 만약 있다면 아마도 그들 중 한 명과 차를 같이 탈 수도 있을 것 같아요.

학생: 실은 오늘 아침에 학교 교장 선생님께 전화를 해서 상황을 설명드렸어요. 다음 학기에 그곳에서 자원 봉사를 하려고 한 학생은 Rebecca와 저뿐이었다고 말씀하시더군요. 그래서 선생님께서 하신 제안은 선택이 불가능해요.

학생 활동 센터 직원: 그래요, 학생이 할 수 있는 일은 없는 상황인 것 같군요. 그런 경우라면 제 권한으로 학생이 자원 봉사를 할 장소를 바꾸는 것을 허락할게요. 자, 어, 혹시 그 대신 어디에서 자원 봉사를 할 수 있을지 생각해 둔 곳이 있나요?

학생: 사실, 네, 있어요. 듣자 하니 캠퍼스 아래쪽에 초등 학교가 있더라고요. 저는, 어, 어젯밤에 기숙사의 어떤 친구가 알려 주기 전까지는 결코 그에 대해 모르고 있었어요.

학생 활동 센터 직원: 아, Madison 초등학교를 말하는 건가요? 제가 그곳 교장 선생님을 알고 있기 때문에 학생은 운이 좋은 편이네요. 이 학교의 졸업생이시고 학생들을 돕는 일에 항상 열정적이시죠. 제가 지금 바로 Hanson 선생님께 전화를 해 볼까요?

학생: 그렇게 해 주시면 정말 좋겠어요.

WORD REMINDER

fill in ~에게 자세히 알려 주다　mandatory 강제적인, 의무적인
commute 통학하다, 통근하다　be authorized to ~할 권한이 있다

Lecture • Environmental Science　p.94

교수: 그러면, 음, 어떻게 차량에서 나오는 해로운 배기가스를 감소시킬 수 있을까요? 현재 연구 중인 한 가지 가능한 해결 방안은 바이오 연료입니다. 이는 식물과 같은 유기물들로 만들어지는 연료입니다. 사실상 모든 형태의 식물이 바이오 연료로 전환될 수 있지만, 특히 옥수수, 사탕수수, 그리고 콩이 이상적인 선택이 되는데, 그 이유는 사용된 에너지에 비해 이들이 가장 많은 에너지를 되돌려 주기 때문입니다. 이 말은 만들어진 연료가 연료를 만들

기 위해 사용되는 에너지보다 더 많은 양의 에너지를 가지고 있다는 뜻입니다.

우선 바이오 연료가 어떻게 만들어지는지에 대해 초점을 맞추도록 하죠. 옥수수를 예로 들어 봅시다. 옥수수로 바이오 연료를 만드는 것은, 가정에서 옥수수로 위스키를 만들기 위해 오랫동안 이용해 왔던, 동일한 원리에 기반하고 있습니다. 기본적으로 커다란 증류 장치에 옥수수를 끓여서 증기로부터 알코올 성분을 제거합니다. 그것이 바로 에탄올입니다. 현재, 에탄올은 그 자체로서 자동차의 연료로 사용될 수 있지만, 또한 다양한 비율로 가솔린과 혼합될 수도 있습니다. 미국에서는 주로 에탄올 85%, 가솔린 15%의 형태로 에탄올과 가솔린이 혼합됩니다. 그건 그렇고, 이는 E85라고 불립니다. 들어본 적이 있으시죠, 그렇죠…? 좋아요. 어쨌든, 그러한 혼합물은 해로운 배기 가스를 일반 가솔린보다 22% 더 적게 방출합니다.

바이오 연료의 자원으로 옥수수를 이용하는 것과 관련된 주요 문제는 옥수수 에탄올을 만드는데 막대한 양의 에너지가 필요하다는 점입니다. 실제로 에탄올 증류소는 다른 유기 물질, 천연 가스, 혹은 석탄을 사용하여 옥수수를 가열해야만 하는데, 이러한 연료들을 연소시키면 다량의 유해 물질이 방출됩니다. 게다가, 옥수수 에탄올에 의해 생산되는 에너지는 그것을 만드는데 필요한 에너지보다 약간 더 많을 뿐입니다. 또 다른 문제는 옥수수가 식품용으로도 그리고 연료용으로도 사용되고 있기 때문에 그 가격이 현재 상승하고 있다는 점입니다. 지난 몇 년 간 이 작물이 기록적인 가격으로 판매됨으로써 옥수수를 기르는 농부들은 이익을 보고 있지만, 에탄올 소비자들은 전혀 혜택을 받지 못하고 있습니다. 마지막으로, 옥수수 에탄올은 사실상 주요 연료원인 석유와 가스를 결코 대체할 수 없습니다. 미국 내의 옥수수 전부를 에탄올을 만드는데 사용하더라도 연료를 필요로 하는 곳의 12%에만 연료를 제공해 줄 수 있을 것입니다. 그것만으로는 충분하지가 않죠.

하지만 보다 유망한 바이오 연료의 에너지원은 사탕수수로, 이는 브라질에서 수십 년 동안 자동차 연료를 만드는데 사용되어 왔습니다. 사실 사탕수수는 바이오 연료의 에너지원으로서 옥수수를 뛰어넘는 몇 가지 눈에 띄는 장점들을 가지고 있습니다. 우선, 사탕수수에서 나오는 부산물들은… 어, 잎, 잎대, 그리고 줄기는… 사탕수수 증류소를 가동시키는 연료로서 사용될 수 있습니다. 이로써 화석 연료를 연소시킬 필요성이 줄어듭니다. 둘째, 사탕수수 에탄올에는 그것을 만드는데 사용되는 에너지의 약 8배의 에너지가 포함되어 있습니다. 기억하신다면 옥수수의 경우보다 훨씬 더 많은 양입니다. 마지막으로, 사탕수수 한 대는 옥수수 한 대보다 에이커당 두 배가 많은 에탄올을 생산해 낼 수 있습니다. 자, 어, 옥수수가 있는 1에이커의 땅은 3백에서 4백 갤런의 에탄올을 생산해 낼 수 있는 반면, 사탕수수가 있는 1에이커의 땅은 6백에서 8백 갤런을 생산해 낼 수 있습니다.

2005년에 브라질은 거의 40억 갤런에 달하는 사탕수수 에탄올을 생산했습니다. 경이로운 양입니다. 그리고 브라질 내 대부분의 차량에는, 가솔린과 에탄올 모두로 작동될 수 있는, 이중 기능 엔진이 장착되어 있습니다. 사탕수수의 또 다른 장점은 사탕수수 에탄올이 가솔린보다 56% 정도 적은 유해 물질들을 배출한다는 점입니다. 하지만 사탕수수도 자체적인 문제를 가지고 있습니다. 대부분의 사탕수수는 농장에서 힘든 나날을 보내는 저임금 노동자들의 손으로 수확됩니다. 또한 처음에는 종종 밭을 태우는 경우가 있는데, 이렇게 함으로써 사탕수수 수확이 보다 쉬워집니다. 밭을 태우면, 당연하게도, 환경 오염이 발생합니다.

세 번째 선택은 바이오디젤로, 독일에서는 주로 카놀라유로, 미국에서는 콩으로 이를 만듭니다. 바이오디젤은 일반 디젤에 비해 해로운 배기가스를 68%만 배출하기 때문에 매우 친환경적입니다. 안타깝게도 만드는데 상당히 많은 비용이 들며, 주유 가격 또한 일반 디젤에 비해 약간 더 비쌉니다. 따라

서 환경에는 보다 좋은 선택임에도 불구하고, 일반 디젤보다 더 높은 가격을 바이오디젤에 지불하려는 사람은 거의 없습니다.

여러분들도 알 수 있듯이, 제가 말씀드린 세 가지 유형의 바이오 연료 모두 장점과 단점을 가지고 있습니다. 매우 흥미롭게도 바이오 연료의 미래는 이들에게 없을 수도 있습니다. 대신 저는 바이오 연료의 미래가 해조류에 있다고 생각합니다. 네, 맞습니다. 연못, 호수, 강, 그리고 바다에서 발견되는 초록색의 끈적끈적한 해조류가 유해한 배기가스의 경감에 핵심이 될 수 있습니다. 해조류 바이오 연료에 대한 과학은 비교적 시작된지 얼마 되지 않았지만, 해조류로 만들어지는 바이오 연료는 에이커당 5천 갤런까지 생산될 것으로 예측되고 있습니다. 해조류는 또한 사실상 어디에서나 자랄 수 있고, 넓은 면적의 토지나 많은 양의 비료를 필요로 하지 않는 인공적인 환경에서도 자랄 수 있습니다. 하지만 해조류 바이오 연료에 대한 연구는 현재 진행 중이며 실험 단계에 머물러 있을 뿐입니다. 하지만 미래에는 많은 사람들이 이를 연료로 차량을 운전하게 될 것이라고 저는 확신합니다.

> **WORD REMINDER**
> emission 방출물, 배기가스 in particular 특히 distill 증류하다 siphon (사이펀으로) 옮기다, 뽑아내다 combination 조합 promising 유망한 mitigate 완화하다, 경감시키다 phenomenal 경이로운 backbreaking 힘든, 고된 algae 해조류 slimy 끈적끈적한, 점액질의 prediction 예상, 예측

Actual Test 05

Conversation
p.100

학생 서비스 센터 직원: 안녕하세요. 제가 도울 일이라도 있나요?

학생: 정말로 도와 주시면 좋겠어요. 동아리와 관련된 몇 가지 일에 대해 알아보려고 왔어요.

학생 서비스 센터 직원: 이곳 캠퍼스에 어떤 동아리들이 있는지를 말하는 건가요?

학생: 오, 아니에요. 죄송해요. 제가 애매하게 말씀드린 것 같아요. 저는 컴퓨터 디자인 동아리의 회장인데, 하지만, 음, 몇 가지 사항들이 확실하지가 않아서요. 아시겠지만, 이번 학기에 동아리를 새로 만들었는데, 음, 솔직히 말씀드려야 할 것 같군요… 제가 무엇을 해야 하는지 전혀 모르겠어요.

학생 서비스 센터 직원: 음, 최소한 그 점에 대해서는 솔직하군요. 그리고 학생이 기꺼이 질문을 하려고 하다니 좋은 징조고요. 자, 대부분의 동아리들이 무엇을 하는지 알려 드릴게요.

학생: 네, 좋은 시작이 될 것 같아요.

학생 서비스 센터 직원: 이곳 대다수의 동아리들은 상당히 왕성한 활동을 하고 있죠. 하지만 제가 왕성한 활동이라고 하는 것은 최소한 한 달에 한 번 모임을 갖는다는 점을 의미한다는 것에 주의해 주세요.

학생: 그것이 왕성한 활동이에요?

학생 서비스 센터 직원: 어, 그래요. 알겠지만, 많은 학생들이 두 개 이상의 동아리에 가입해 있어요. 게다가 학생들에게는 수업도 있고, 아르바이트도 있고, 그리고 사회 활동도 있죠. 따라서 대부분의 학생들이 한 달에 한 번이

나 두 번 이상 만나는 것에 그다지 흥미를 느끼지 않아요.

학생: 어, 그 점은 몰랐네요. 사실 일주일에 한 번 정도 모임을 갖겠다는 계획이 있었거든요.

학생 서비스 센터 직원: 흠… 그럴 수도 있을 것이라고 생각해요. 하지만 그렇게 자주 만난다면 회원수가 줄어들 거예요. 물론, 매번 모임에 나타나는 사람들도 몇몇 있을 수 있겠죠. 정말로 헌신적인 회원들일 거예요. 하지만 보다 일반적인 회원들은 — 어, 컴퓨터 디자인에는 관심이 있지만 헌신적이지는 않는 회원들은 — 곧 동아리를 탈퇴하게 될 거예요.

학생: 알겠어요. 그 점은 생각해 보지 못했네요. 그러면 2주마다 한 차례 모임을 가져야 할 것 같아요.

학생 서비스 센터 직원: 아마도 꽤 적절한 절충안이 될 것 같군요. 자, 모임을 가질 수 있는 방이 있나요?

학생: 아니요, 없어요. 제가 여쭤보고 싶었던 것 중의 하나예요. 어떻게 방을 예약하나요?

학생 서비스 센터 직원: 음, 몇 가지 방법이 있어요. 물론 제게 말을 해도 되고요. 학생을 위해 제가 교내 건물 중 한 곳의 방을 예약해 드릴 수 있어요. 하지만 몇몇 동아리들은 대안이 될 수 있는 장소를 선택하기도 해요. 예를 들면 학생 회관 내의 카페에서 모일 수도 있죠. 날씨가 좋으면 야외에서 모이기도 하고요. 심지어 일부 동아리들은, 어, 인근 지역 내 식당과 술집에서 만나기도 해요.

학생: 이곳 캠퍼스의 방을 예약해야겠다는 생각을 유지해야겠네요. 적어도 제가 하고 있는 일에 더 익숙해지기 전까지는 그렇게 할래요.

학생 서비스 센터 직원: 처음에는 그것이 분명 최선의 방법이죠.

학생: 감사합니다. 어떻게 해야 선생님께서 방을 예약해 주시나요?

학생 서비스 센터 직원: 아, 좋은 질문이에요. 이곳으로 와서 양식을 작성하면 되는데… 여기에 있어요. 일반적인 경우, 평일 기준으로 최소한 방을 원하는 날 3일 전에는 오도록 하세요. 만약 월요일에 방이 필요하면 그 전 주의, 금요일이 아니라, 수요일에 요청을 하세요. 3일 전에만 알려 주면 캠퍼스 어디에선가 확실히 방을 구해 드릴 수 있어요.

학생: 좋아요. 감사합니다.

학생 서비스 센터 직원: 질문이 더 있나요?

학생: 네, 한 가지 더요. 지원금에 대해 알고 싶어요. 제 말은, 동아리들이 이용할 수 있는 지원금에는 어떤 종류가 있으며, 그리고 지원금은 어디에 사용할 수 있나요?

학생 서비스 센터 직원: 좋아요. 돈에 대해 관심을 가질 줄 알았어요. 사전 승인을 받으면 돈을 사용할 수 있는 것들이 꽤 많이 있어요.

> **WORD REMINDER**
> vague 모호한, 애매한 membership 회원 자격; 회원수 dedicated 전념하는, 헌신적인 devoted 헌신적인 reserve 예약하다 venue 장소 stick to ~을 고수하다 business day 평일, 영업일 get around to ~에 관심을 갖다, ~을 고려하다 prior approval 사전 승인 quite a few 상당수의, 꽤 많은

Lecture • Physics
p.102

교수: 우리 주변에는 빛의 속도로 움직이는 전자기 스펙트럼이 있습니다. 이는 막대한 거리를 파동 형태로 이동하는 에너지 광자로 이루어집니다. 이러한 에너지는 때때로 전자기 방사선이라고도 불립니다. 우주에 있는 물체들

과 이곳 지구에 있는 물체들은 전자기 방사선을 방출합니다. 이러한 방사선은 파동 형태를 띠는데, 이러한 파동은 빛의 속도로 움직이는 광자들이 진동하는 것입니다. 이러한 에너지는 파장과 주파수에 의해 측정됩니다. 상기시켜 드리면, 파장은 진동하는 광자들의 두 정점 사이의 거리이며, 주파수는 초당 발생하는 파장의 횟수입니다. 어떤 파동들은 파장이 길고 주파수가 낮으며, 파장이 짧고 주파수가 높은 파동들도 있습니다.

자, 모두들 수업을 시작하면서 제가 나누어 드린 유인물을 봐 주세요. 거기에서 전자기 스펙트럼 표를 보실 수 있습니다. 이 표에서는 제가 방금 말씀드린 여러 가지 파장 및 주파수를 다양한 방식으로 살펴볼 수 있습니다. 표의 가운데 부분을 봐 주세요. 가시 광선입니다. 가시 광선의 파장과 주파수는 우리 눈으로 색을 볼 수 있는 영역 내에 있습니다. 표의 왼쪽 끝에는 가장 파장이 짧고 가장 주파수가 높은 것들이 있습니다. 자외선, X선, 그리고 감마선입니다. 이들은 모두 막대한 양의 에너지를 지니고 있으며 생물에게 장기간 노출될 경우 피해를 끼칩니다. 표의 오른쪽에는 보다 파장이 긴 것들이 존재하는데, 이들은 주파수가 낮고 가지고 있는 에너지 양도 적습니다. 이들은, 왼쪽에서 오른쪽 방향으로, 적외선, 마이크로파, 그리고 전파입니다.

학생: 전자기 스펙트럼은 처음에 어떻게 생성되나요?

교수: 흠… 지금이 그것에 대해서 설명하기 가장 좋은 때인 것 같군요. 질문에 대답을 하면, 전자기 스펙트럼은 두 가지 방법으로 생성됩니다: 열방출과 비열방출에 의해서죠. 열방출은 흑체 복사와 스펙트럼선 방사로 이루어집니다. 비열방출은 싱크로트론 복사, 펄서, 그리고 메이저로 이루어지고요. 대부분의 전자기 방사선은 흑체 복사에 의해 생성되기 때문에, 이를 예로서 살펴봅시다. 흑체 복사는 가장 단순한 형태의 방사선입니다. 절대영도보다 높은 온도를 가지고 있는 모든 물체는, 그 내부에서 움직이고 있는 분자를 포함하고 있습니다. 분자들이 움직임에 따라 이들은 서로 충돌하게 되는데, 이로써 일부 입자들의 속도가 빨라집니다. 입자의 속도가 빨라지면, 입자는 전자기 방사선을 방출합니다. 이것이 흑체 복사입니다. 온도가 높고 움직임이 많아지면 보다 많은 양의 전자기 방사선이 생성됩니다. 우주 공간 내의 모든 물체들은 이러한 방식으로 전자기 방사선을 방출합니다. 모든 항성, 행성, 그리고 심지어 이 강의실 내의 물체들도, 어, 모두 일정한 형태의 에너지를 방출하고 있습니다.

다음으로, 어, 계속해서 전자기 스펙트럼의 각각의 부분에 대해 이야기를 해 보고 싶군요. 전파에 관한 이야기로 시작해 봅시다. 전파는 전자기 스펙트럼에서 파장이 가장 길고 주파수가 가장 낮습니다. 또한 가장 적은 양의 에너지를 가지고 있습니다. 그 결과 이들은 전자기 스펙트럼에서 가장 무해한 부분입니다. 또한 우리에게 상당히 유용한 것이기도 한데, 음, 그 이유는 전파가 20세기 초반부터 통신의 목적으로 활용되었기 때문입니다. 물론 전파를 듣기 위해서는, 이러한 파동을 귀로 들을 수 있는 소리로 변환시키는 장치를 사용해야 합니다. 전파의 주파수는 서로 다른 파장으로 구성된 주파대로 측정됩니다. 우리는 이러한 파장들을 헤르츠로 측정하는데, 헤르츠는 초당 파장의 숫자로 표현됩니다. 또한 주파수가 매우 높은 파장을 나타내기 위한 킬로헤르츠, 메가헤르츠, 그리고 기가헤르츠라는 용어들도 있죠. 전파에 대해 이야기하면, 이들은 3에서 300기가헤르츠 사이에 있습니다. 각각의 주파대는 이러한 범위 내에 있으며, 각 대역은 서로 다른 목적의 통신을 위해 사용됩니다. 여러분들이 서로 다른 대역의 목록을 확인할 수 있도록 한번 더 유인물에 주목해 주세요.

가장 아랫부분에는 3에서 300헤르츠의 범위에 있는 극초저주파와 상초저주파가 있습니다. 이러한 주파수들의 유일한 목적은 잠수함과의 통신입니다. 잠수함은 수중에서 임무를 수행하는데 전파는 물속을 잘 통과하지 못하기 때문에 이처럼 낮은 주파수로만 통신이 가능합니다. 그 다음은 300에서

3,000헤르츠에 해당되는 초저주파입니다. 이 대역은 광산에서의 통신에 이용되는데, 이곳에서는 전파가 암석과 흙을 통과해야 합니다. 다음으로 초장파와 저주파가 있으며, 이들은 항해 신호, 라디오 방송, 그리고 아마추어 무선 통신에서 사용됩니다. 이러한 대역들은 3에서 300킬로헤르츠 사이에 있습니다. 그 위에는 주로 AM 라디오 방송에서 사용되는 중주파가 있습니다. 이 대역은 300에서 3,000킬로헤르츠 사이에 있습니다.

이러한 단계 위에는 통신에서 가장 흔하게 사용되는 세 가지 주파수가 있습니다: 바로 고주파, 초단파, 그리고 극초단파입니다. 이러한 세 가지 대역은 3에서 300메가헤르츠 사이에 있습니다. 대부분의 TV 방송이 이 범위에 있으며, 개인 무선 송수신기, 블루투스 시스템, 휴대폰 송신, GPS 시스템, 그리고 FM 라디오 방송도 마찬가지입니다. 상당히 높은 주파수인, 어, 3에서 300기가헤르츠 사이에 있는 주파수는 레이더 시스템, 위성 전송, 그리고 마이크로파 전송 장치에서 사용됩니다.

WORD REMINDER

electromagnetic spectrum 전자기 스펙트럼   photon 광자   oscillate 진동하다   packet 꾸러미, 통   frequency 진동수, 주파수   crest 정점, 최고조   scale 저울; 등급표   visible light 가시 광선   expose 노출시키다   in the first place 우선, 제일 먼저   thermal 열의   blackbody radiation 흑체 복사   absolute zero 절대영도   bump into ~와 부딪히다, 충돌하다   accelerate 가속하다   band (무선) 주파대, 밴드   penetrate 관통하다, 뚫다   citizen band radio 시민 라디오, 개인 무선 송수신기

Lecture · Music
p.105

교수: 계속해서 고대 그리스 음악에 대한 이야기를 하고자 합니다. 우리에게는 안타까운 일인데, 매우 단편적인 그리스 음악만이 음표 형태로 전해져 오고 있습니다. 이를 가지고 현대의 음악가들이 그리스 음악의 일부를 해석하고 있죠. 몇몇 사람들이 고대 그리스 음악을 재현하려고 시도해 왔지만, 그들의 해석이 얼마나 정확하게 본래의 소리를 들려 줄 수 있는지는 결코 알 수 없을 것입니다. 어쨌든, 제가 주목하고자 하는 것은 고대 그리스인들이 어떠한 용도로 음악을 사용했고, 어떤 악기들을 사용했으며, 그리고 그리스 음악 양식이 어떻게 변화했는지에 관한 것입니다.

고대 그리스 음악은, 현대 음악과 마찬가지로, 다양한 목적을 가지고 있었습니다. 예컨대 올림픽과 같은 다양한 행사에서 사용되었습니다. 무대 공연에서 사용되었고요. 장례식과 같은 의식에서 일정한 역할을 수행했습니다. 또한 많은 사람들의 일상 생활 중 일부이기도 했습니다. 그리스 사람들은 종종 음악과 신화를 연관시켰고, 많은 고대 그리스 신화에서 음악은 중요한 역할을 담당했습니다. 아시겠지만, 고대 그리스 사람들에게 음악은 상당히 중요한 것이었습니다.

자, 음, 그리스 음악이 어떻게 들렸는지는 알 수 없다고 말씀드렸습니다. 사실입니다. 하지만 그리스 음악이 단선율 곡이었다는 점은 알려져 있습니다. 따라서 그리스인들은 한 번에 하나의 멜로디만 연주했습니다. 그리스인들이 이에 대한 몇 가지 예외를 두었다는 증거가 일부 존재합니다: 그렇지만 대부분의 경우, 그리스 음악은 단선율이라고 생각해야 합니다. 그러한 이유는 음악에 대한 그리스인들의 철학과 관련이 있는데, 이에 대해서는 잠시 후에 알아보도록 하겠습니다.

고대 그리스 사람들은 세 개의 기본적인 악기를 연주했습니다. 관악기, 현악기, 그리고 타악기입니다. 이쪽 화면을 보시면 이들 악기의 사진을 볼 수 있습니다. 우선 팬파이프 사진이 있습니다. 이 악기는 그리스인들에 의해 시링크스라고 불렸습니다. S－Y－R－I－N－X이고요. 구멍에 바람을 불어넣어서가 아니라 구멍 윗부분을 횡으로 가로지르며 바람을 넣어 연주합니다. 다

양한 길이의 관에 주목하시면… 팬파이프가 다양한 소리를 낼 수 있도록 그렇게 되어 있었습니다. 고대 그리스인들은 또한 황동으로 만든 트럼펫을 사용했는데, 여기에는 뼈로 된 마우스피스가 있었습니다. 이러한 트럼펫은 구부러진 형태였고, 트럼펫을 연주하는 음악가의 신체를 감싸고 있는 모습은 종종 그리스 시에서 묘사되어 있습니다. 여기 사진이 있습니다… 꽤 흥미롭죠, 그렇지 않나요? 또 다른 관악기는 *아울로스*로, 이것은 오늘날의 플루트와 비슷했습니다. 두 가지 형태가 있었습니다. 하나는 마우스피스로부터 이어진 한 개의 파이프를 가지고 있었습니다. 이렇게 생겼고요… 그리고 다른 하나는 두 개의 파이프를 가지고 있었습니다. 여기에서 파이프가 두 개인 *아울로스*를 보실 수 있습니다…

현악기에 대해 말씀을 드리면, 리라가 가장 흔했습니다. 여기를 봐 주세요… 현이 7개인 것에 주목해 주시고… 각각의 현은 서로 다른 소리를 낼 수 있도록 다르게 조율되었습니다. 고대 그리스에서 리라는 보편적으로 사용되었는데, 종종 그룹에서, 독주용으로, 그리고 심지어는 시 낭송회의 반주용으로도 사용되었습니다. *키타라*는, 어, 소리기 나는 대로 철자를 쓰시면 됩니다… 또 다른 현악기로서 연주자가 원하는 소리를 낼 수 있도록 도움을 주는 나무 상자를 가지고 있었습니다.

학생: 잠시만요. 그 악기는 일종의 기타처럼 보이는군요.

교수: 어, 그래요, 현대의 기타와 동일한 원리에 기반하고 있었는데, 현대의 기타는 스페인에서 개발되었죠. *키타라*와 기타 간의 연관성 여부에 대해 말씀을 드리면… 음, 확실하지는 않지만, *키타라*가 최초로 기타를 만든 사람에게 영향을 주었다고 해도 그리 놀라울 일은 아닌 것 같군요.

그러면, 음, 그리스인들이 연주했던 음악은 어땠을까요? 여러분이 흥미롭다고 생각할 만한 것이 있습니다: 초기 그리스 음악은 수학에 기반하고 있었으며, 어느 정도 그리스 수학자인 피타고라스에 의해 발전되었다고 생각됩니다. 그는 화음과 배음에 대한 개념을 만들어 낸 인물로, 이들이 수학적인 방식으로 서로 어떻게 연관되는지를 보여 주었습니다. 피타고라스의 발견으로 몇몇 음악 형태의 기준이 만들어 졌습니다. 하지만 그리스의 여러 도시 국가들의 사람들 또한 이러한 개념에 기반하여 자신들의 독특한 음악을 발전시켰습니다. 여러분들이 기억해야 할 사항입니다. 고대 그리스 음악은 상당히 다양했습니다. 따라서 도리스 스타일, 아테네 스타일, 그리고 기타 스타일들에 대해 이야기를 할 수가 있습니다.

그리스의 철학자인 플라톤도 종종 자신의 글에서 음악을 언급했습니다. 몇몇 대화에서 그는 그리스 음악이 본래 상당히 고루한 것으로, 관객들은 단지 즐거움을 위해 음악을 들을 뿐이고, 이들이 음악의 수준과 관련해서 박수를 치거나 환호를 하지 않을 것이라고 말했습니다. 플라톤의 글에서는 그리스 음악이 엄격하게 통제되고 있으며, 관객들이 기대한 것을 변형시키거나 크게 바꾼 연주자에게는 불만이 쏟아질 것처럼 쓰여 있습니다. 하지만 플라톤이 살았던 기원전 약 400년경 고대 그리스 음악은 몇 가지 변화를 겪기 시작했습니다. 우리에게는 다행스러운 일인데, 우리는 이러한 변화가 어떠했는지를 알고 있습니다. 어떤 일이 있었는지 알려 드리죠.

WORD REMINDER

fragment 조각, 파편 **note** 음, 음표 **interpret** 해석하다 **recreate** (과거의 것을) 되살리다, 재현하다 **concentrate on** ~에 집중하다 **purpose** 목적 **funeral** 장례식 **monophonic** 단선율의, 단선율 곡의 **brass** 황동, 놋쇠 **lyre** 리라, 수금 **tune** 조율하다, 조정하다 **ubiquitous** 어디에나 있는, 매우 흔한 **accompany** 수반하다, 동반하다; 반주를 하다 **recital** 발표회, 연주회 **overtone** 배음 **staid** 재미없는, 고루한 **rigorously** 엄격히, 엄밀히

PART 2

Conversation

p.110

학생: 실례지만 Clemons 선생님이신가요?

극장 관리자: 네, 저예요. 제가 도와 드릴 일이 있나요?

학생: 어, 네, 도와 주셨으면 해요. 선생님이 이곳 극장 관리자이시죠, 맞나요?

극장 관리자: 맞아요. 연극을 준비 중인 극단에 속해 있는 학생이라고 생각해도 될까요?

학생: 네, 그래요. 저는 지금부터 약 한 달 후에 *햄릿*을 공연하게 될 극단에 속해 있어요.

극장 관리자: 좋아요. 알겠어요. 무엇을 도와 드릴까요? 예행 연습 시간을 조정하는 일 등이 필요한가요?

학생: 아니에요, 전혀 그렇지 않아요. 사실 저희 모두는 선생님께서 정해 주신 시간에 매우 만족하고 있어요.

극장 관리자: 그런 말을 들으니 좋군요.

학생: 하지만 저희가 모르는 점이 하나 있어요. 아시겠지만, 공연을 위한 소품들이 많은데 그것들을 놓아둘 곳이 없어요.

극장 관리자: 창고 예약을 신청하지 않았다고 말하는 건가요?

학생: 어…

극장 관리자: 그래요. 하지 않았다는 것으로 받아들이죠. 극단에 있는 어느 누구도 소품, 의상, 그리고 그와 같은 것들을 보관 하기 위해서는 창고를 예약해야 한다는 점을 모르고 있었다고 생각해도 될까요?

학생: 그런 것 같아요. 음, 우리 극단의 대부분의 사람들에게 이번이 첫 번째 연극이라서, 어, 저희가 아직 절차를 잘 모르는 것 같아요. 창고 이용에 대해서 저희에게 이야기해 준 사람은 없었어요.

극장 관리자: 음, 극단의 지도 교수님이 어떤 분이시던 간에 그에 대해서는 알려 주셨어야 했는데요. 교수님의 성함을 제게 알려 주면 제가 그러한 실수에 대해 무언가 조치를 취할 수 있어요. 어쨌거나, 모든 소품들은 현재 어떻게 하고 있나요?

학생: 음, 당분간 여러 배우들의 기숙사에 보관해 두고 있어요.

극장 관리자: 농담이죠…? 그래요, 음, 아마도 농담은 아닌 것 같군요.

학생: 죄송해요. 저희는 그것이 일반적인 경우라고 생각했지만, 아시다시피, 소품 중 일부는 정말로 크기가 크거든요. 그래서 학생들이 예행 연습을 하기 위해 소품을 끌고 캠퍼스를 가로질러 기숙사로부터 이곳 건물까지 오기가 힘들어요. 그런 다음에는 물론 다시 숙소로 가지고 가야 하죠. 게다가, 현재 몇몇 사람들의 기숙사는 정말로 비좁아요.

극장 관리자: 상상이 가는군요.

학생: 그래서, 음, 지금 당장 사용할 수 있는 창고가 있나요? 창고 한 곳을 이용할 수 있다면 정말 좋을 것 같아요.

극장 관리자: 엄밀히 말하면 없어요. 다른 극단들이 모두 예약해 두었죠.

학생: 오…

극장 관리자: 하지만 제 개인 창고가 현재 절반만 차 있어요. 그리고 학생의 교수님께서 충분히 도움을 주지 않으신 것 같으니 제가 하려고 하는 것을 알려 드리죠. 제 창고에 학생의 물건들을 보관할 수 있도록 하겠지만, 학생이

창고의 열쇠는 받지 못할 거예요. 그곳에는 제 개인적인 물건들도 약간 있거든요. 그것이 이유예요. 창고 문을 열고 소품을 꺼내거나 다시 그곳에 넣으려면 저와 이야기를 해야 할 거예요. 하지만 적어도 학생의 물건들을 모두 놓아둘 수 있는 공간은 마련될 것이에요. 괜찮나요?

학생: 완벽해요. 감사합니다. 정말로 친절하시군요.

극장 관리자: 아, 별말씀을요. 제가 해 드릴 수 있는 최소한의 일인데요. 어쨌든, 학생과 학생의 극단이 어디로 가면 되는지 알 수 있도록 창고가 어디에 있는지 제가 알려 줄게요. 이쪽으로 저를 따라오세요.

WORD REMINDER

take it that ～이라고 믿다, ～이라고 생각하다   troupe 극단   put on (공연 등을) 상연하다   prop (연극 등에서의) 소도구, 소품   outfit 옷, 의상   learn the ropes 요령을 터득하다   oversight 실수, 간과   for the time being 당분간   cramped 비좁은, 갑갑한   technically 기술적으로; 엄밀히 말하면   arrange with ～와 합의하다

Lecture • Zoology

p.112

교수: 동물도 사람처럼 기억을 할까요? 오늘 수업에서 답을 구하고자 하는 질문입니다. 동물들도 기억을 형성한다는 아이디어는, 주로 그들과의 커뮤니케이션 문제 때문에 많은 논쟁을 일으켜 왔습니다. 동물들과 말을 할 수가 없는데 그들이 무언가를 기억하는지 혹은 기억하지 않는지를 동물들이 어떻게 우리에게 말해 줄 수 있을까요? 이러한 문제를 해결하기 위해 과학자들은 동물들에게 기억력이 있는지 없는지를 밝혀 줄 수 있는 실험을 진행했습니다. 대부분의 학자들이 도달한 결론은 일부 종의 동물들에게 장기 및 단기 기억력이 존재한다는 것입니다.

우선, 과학자들에게 장기 및 단기 기억이 무엇을 의미하는지에 대해 분명히 하도록 하겠습니다. 단기 기억은 몇 초 동안 지속되는 기억을 가리킵니다. 대부분의 과학자들은 20초를 그 한계로 생각하고 있습니다. 장기 기억은 그보다 더 오래 지속되는 기억입니다. 자, 우리가 장기 기억이라고 부르기에는 터무니없이 짧은 시간으로 비춰질 수도 있겠지만, 우리 인간은 단기간에 사소한 사건들을 기억할 수 있는 반면, 보다 중요한 사건들은 장기에 걸쳐, 때로는 일생 동안 기억한다는 점을 이해해야 합니다. 이렇게 생각해 보세요… 여러분들은 아마도 수업이 시작하기 10분 전에 무엇을 했는지 잊어버렸을 텐데, 그 이유는 그것이 너무나 사소한 일이었기 때문입니다. 하지만 여러분은 첫 데이트, 고등학교 졸업, 그리고 사랑하는 사람이 사망한 일에 대해서는 쉽게 기억을 떠올릴 수 있을 것인데, 그 이유는 그러한 일들이 보다 중요한 기억이기 때문입니다.

학생: 그러면 동물들도 인간과 마찬가지로 중요한 사건들을 기억할 수 있다는 말씀이신가요?

교수: 어… 아니에요, 꼭 그런 것은 아닙니다. 제 말은, 동물들이 장기 기억을 형성할 수 있다고 할 때, 인간의 장기 기억에 있어서 그런 것처럼, 몇 년 혹은 몇 십 년을 생각해서는 안 된다는 것입니다. 대신 분이나 날을 생각해야 합니다. 상대적인 것이죠. 예컨대 개와 고양이들은 인간보다 훨씬 더 일찍 죽습니다. 그들에게 장기라고 하는 것이 우리에게도 반드시 그런 것은 아니죠.

자, 주제로 다시 돌아가서… 어떤 동물들을 실험했고, 그들의 기억력을 테스트하기 위해 어떤 실험이 이루어졌을까요? 음, 이야기하고 싶은 첫 번째 동물은 서양의 덤불어치입니다. 음식을 구한 다음 이를 다양한 장소에 숨겨두는 작은 새죠. 동물 행동주의자들이 도달한 첫 번째 결론은 덤불어치들이 음식을 저장함으로써 차후의 식사를 계획한다는 점이었습니다. 이들에게는 여분의 식량이 있었기 때문에, 이를 땅에 묻어 미래에 이용했습니다. 또한 과학자들이 주목한 점은, 이 새들이 음식을 어디에 감추었는지를 기억하고 있

는 것처럼 보였고, 음식이 상한다는 점을 알고 있었기 때문에 음식이 상하기 전에 이를 꺼내 먹는다는 사실이었습니다. 이러한 행동은 그들이 음식을 숨긴 시기와 장소에 대한 일종의 장기 기억을 형성하고 있다는 점을 암시해 주었습니다.

행동주의자들은 벌레와 견과를 가지고 덤불어치에 관한 실험을 설계했습니다. 견과는 부패가 잘 되지 않는 반면 벌레는 빨리 상했습니다. 행동주의자들은 덤불어치가 그 차이를 알 수 있는지 확인하고자 했습니다. 이 새로 하여금 견과와 벌레 중에서 하나를 선택할 수 있도록 했습니다. 처음에는 벌레를 선택하는 경우가 많아서 이들이 벌레 먹는 것을 더 좋아하는 것처럼 보였습니다. 하지만 선택한 벌레 중 일부는 저장해 두었습니다. 어느 정도 시간이 지난 후 덤불어치는 벌레를 무시하고 견과만을 선택하기 시작했습니다. 과학자들은 새들이 나중에 먹기 위해 벌레를 저장했을 때 벌레가 상했다는 점을 알게 되었습니다. 따라서 이 새들은 훨씬 더 오래 지속될 수 있는 견과를 선택한 것이었습니다. 이러한 점은 과학자들이 믿기에 기억의 증거였습니다.

여러분이 알아야 할 덤불어치의 또 다른 측면은 이 새들이, 음, 도둑이라는 점입니다. 야생에서 이 새들은 거리낌 없이 다른 덤불어치를 감시하고, 그들이 음식을 어디에 숨기는지에 주목한 다음, 다른 새의 음식을 훔쳐서 나중에 먹기 위해 이를 또 다른 곳에 숨겨 놓습니다. 하지만 한 마리의 덤불어치가 음식을 숨기는 동안 다른 새가 자신을 보고 있다는 점을 알아차리면 이 새는 음식을 새로운 장소로 옮겨다 놓을 것입니다. 왜 이런 일을 할까요? 행동주의자가 내린 결론은 덤불어치가 도둑질을 기억하고 있고, 다른 새들도 유사한 행동을 할 것이라는 점을 알기 때문이라는 것입니다.

덤불어치에 관한 이러한 실험 및 관찰로부터 추론할 수 있는 것은 무엇일까요? 가장 중요한 결론은 이 새들이 과거의 특정 사건을 기억해 낼 수 있다는 점입니다. 이들은 자신이 음식을 어디에 숨겼는지 알고 있으며, 언제 그것을 다시 가지고 와야 할지도 알고 있습니다. 과거에 음식을 저장해 두었다는 점을 알고 있으며, 이런 행동을 다른 덤불어치도 할 수 있다고도 생각하죠. 이는 종종 일화 기억이라고 불립니다. 어떤 종이 머릿속으로 시간을 거슬러 올라가 특정 사건을 기억해 낼 수 있을 때만 일어날 수 있는 일입니다.

틀림없이 여러분들도 짐작할 수 있을 텐데, 이러한 연구는 많은 비판을 받아 왔습니다. 일부 전문가들은 덤불어치의 행동이 본능적인 것이며, 이 새가 기억 같은 것을 형성하지는 않는다고 주장합니다. 모든 동물에게는 시간 관념이 없다고 주장하는 사람들도 있습니다. 동물들은 과거, 현재, 그리고 미래를 인식할 수 없기 때문에 기억을 할 수가 없는 것입니다. 저는 이러한 사람들의 의견에는 동의하지 않으며, 동물들도 기억을 할 수 있다는 점을 확고하게 믿고 있습니다. 여러분들을 설득할 수 있다고 생각되는, 영장류들의 기억력에 관한 몇몇 연구 사례들을 알려 드리죠.

WORD REMINDER

spark 불꽃이 튀다, 불러일으키다   clarify 분명하게 하다   retain 지니다, 보유하다   ridiculously 우습게, 어리석게   trivial 사소한, 하찮은   perspective 원근법의   scrub-jay 덤불어치, 스크럽제이   spoil (음식 등이) 상하다   retrieve 회수하다, 회복하다   devise 고안하다, 만들어 내다   perishable 썩기 쉬운, 부패하기 쉬운   spy on ～을 염탐하다, 몰래 감시하다   deduce 연역하다, 추론하다   episodic memory 일화 기억   conceive of ～을 상상하다, 마음에 그리다

PART 3

Conversation

p.116

교수: Alice, 잠깐 얘기를 해야 할 것 같아요.

학생: 그래요, Watson 교수님. 무슨 일이시죠?

교수: 아직까지 실험 보고서를 하나도 제출하지 않았더군요. 지금까지 두 차례의 실험을 했고 이번 주에 세 번째 실험을 할 예정인데, 저는 아직 학생으로부터 어떤 것도 받지 못했어요. 무슨 일이 있나요?

학생: 오, 보고서를 쓰는 일이 중요하다고 생각하지 않아서 신경을 쓰지 못했어요. 그것이 문제가 되나요?

교수: 큰 문제죠.

학생: 정말인가요? 하지만 왜 그렇죠? 제 말은, 어, 이미 우리가 하고 있는 실험실 실험의 결과는 알고 계시잖아요.

교수: 음… 네, 그건 그렇지만 학생이 실험을 했다는 점과 학생이 실험 과정과 관련된 모든 내용을 이해했다는 점을 제가 알 수 있도록 학생은 실험 보고서를 제출하기로 되어 있어요. 게다가, 어, 학생은 제출한 실험 보고서에 따라 성적을 받게 되는데, 현재 학생은 두 차례 0점을 받은 상태죠. 최종 점수에 도움이 되지 않을 거예요.

학생: 오…

교수: 그러면 이번에는 실험 보고서를 제출할 건가요?

학생: 네, 교수님. 그렇게요. 이전의 두 차례 실험에 대한 실험 보고서를 제출해도 되나요?

교수: 아니요, 그럴 수는 없어요. 마감일이 이미 지났고, 수업을 듣는 다른 학생들이 받지 못한 추가 시간을 학생에게만 주는 일은 공정하지 않을 거예요.

학생: 그렇군요. 알겠습니다. 하지만, 음, 하지만 아직도 이해가 가지 않아요. 먼저 실험 보고서는 왜 쓰는 건가요? 무엇이 그렇게 특별한가요?

교수: 고등학교 화학 수업에서 실험을 할 때 실험 보고서를 써 본 적이 없나요?

학생: 어… 고등학교 때 화학 수업을 들어본 적이 없어요. 저희 학교에서는 수업이 없었어요.

교수: 좋아요, 이제 설명이 되는 것 같군요. 생각을 해 보면… 우리가 왜 실험을 하는지 알고 있나요?

학생: 어, 화학 물질들을 섞으면 어떤 일이 일어나는지 보기 위해서요?

교수: 그건 일부예요. 기본적으로 우리가 실험실에서 하는 일은 강의에서 배운 내용을 실험에서 적용시키는 것이죠. 실험을 진행함으로써 강의에서 다루어진 내용을 더 잘 이해할 수 있어요. 자, 어, 실험을 하기 전에는 가설을 세우게 될 거예요. 실험에서 일어날 것으로 생각되는 일에 대한 이론이죠. 그 후에 실험을 진행하고 그 결과를 분석해서 가설이 맞는지 맞지 않았는지를 알게 되어요.

학생: 그리고 그것이 제가 써야 하는 것인가요?

교수: 네, 맞아요. 실험 보고서에 그러한 내용들을 전부 포함시켜야 해요. 학생이 취한 모든 조치를 하나씩 쓰고 실험 결과를 적으세요. 그렇게 하면 학생이 실험을 올바르게 했는지 아닌지를 제가 알 수 있죠. 만약 올바르게 했다면 학생이 적은 조치를 정확히 따름으로써 누구든 똑같은 결과를 얻을 수 있을 거예요.

학생: 알겠어요, 그렇게 할 수 있어요.

교수: 실험 보고서에 관해 할 말이 하나 더 있어요. 기본적으로 보고서를 쓰면 다른 능력을 향상시키는데 도움이 될 거예요. 글을 더 잘 쓰는 법을 알게 될 거예요. 생각을 정리하는 법도 배우게 될 것이고요. 세부적인 사항에 면밀한 주의를 기울여서 가설을 세우고 실험을 하는 법도 알게 될 거예요.

학생: 정말로 맞는 말씀인 것 같아요, 교수님. 제게 그러한 이야기를 해 주셔서 감사합니다. 이번 학기에 하게 될 나머지 실험에서는 반드시 보고서를 쓰도록 할게요.

WORD REMINDER

in the first place 먼저, 우선   **hypothesis** 가설   **analyze** 분석하다
replicate 복제하다   **pay close attention to** ~에 면밀한 주의를 기울이다   **remainder** 나머지

Lecture • Art History   p.118

교수: 콜럼버스가 미대륙을 발견하기 이전의 예술에 대해 다음으로 논의할 측면은 마야 제국의 예술입니다. 마야 예술 중 오늘날까지 남아 있는 작품은 주로 조각과 도자기이나, 회화도 일부 존재합니다. 마야 예술은 다양한 재료, 음, 주로 사암, 대리석, 비취, 그리고 흑요석과 같은 특정 종류의 석재들로 만들어졌습니다. 하지만 마야인들은 진흙을 사용해 도자기를 만들기도 했으며, 나무로 조각을 하기도 했고, 금속으로 장신구를 만들기도 했습니다. 하지만 마야인들은 야금술에 대해 아는 바가 없었고 금속 자원도 가지고 있지 못했기 때문에 금속으로 작품을 만드는 경우는 흔하지 않았다는 점을 주목해 주세요. 아, 마야인들은 또한 종이를 사용하여 그림을 그렸고 벽에 회반죽을 칠해서 치장 벽토와 테라코타 작품들을 만들기도 했습니다. 이들의 다양한 예술은 수많은 도시 국가의 통치자들이 위탁하여 만들어진 것이었으며, 전형적으로는 통치자의 업적을 과시하고 그들의 통치를 찬양하기 위한 의도로 제작되었습니다.

먼저 마야의 조각에 대해 보다 자세히 이야기하고 싶군요. 그들이 만들었던 가장 일반적인 형태의 조각은 석비였습니다. 철자는 S-T-E-L-A예요. 여기 화면에서 몇 가지 사례를 볼 수 있는데… 그리고 여기에서도… 그리고 여기에 있는 이것도 봐 주세요… 석비는 거대한 석판의 표면에 새겨진 조각으로, 새겨진 다음에는 수직으로 세워집니다. 마야인들이 만들었던 대부분의 석비는 폭과 높이가 수 미터에 이르렀습니다. 또한 석비들은 제작된 장소로부터 먼 거리를 이동하여 마야의 궁전과 사원들로 옮겨졌고, 이곳에 전시되었습니다. 일반적으로 석비는 마야의 신 혹은 통치자들을 묘사하고 있었으며, 많은 석비에 글이 새겨져 있었습니다. 마야 조각의 기타 유형에는 이와 같은 흑요암 조각상과… 비취로 된 조각상들… 그리고 나무로 된 조각들이 포함되어 있었습니다. 아름답습니다, 그렇지 않나요? 아, 마야 조각들이 획일적인 특징을 가지고 있지는 않았다는 점을 아셔야 합니다. 어떤 유형의 조각인지에 따라, 제작되었던 시기에 따라, 그리고 그것들이 제국의 어디에서 만들어졌느냐에 따라 다양한 특성을 지니고 있었습니다. 하지만 대체로 마야의 조각가들은 작품 속 인물들을 사실적으로 조각했습니다. 특히 통치자들을 묘사할 때 그러했는데, 이러한 점 때문에 우리는 일부 통치자들의 실제 모습에 대한 아이디어를 얻을 수가 있습니다.

마야인들은 많은 건물에서 치장 벽토를 사용했습니다. 특정 나무에서 발견되는 유기 화합물과 석회암 및 기타 재료들을 태운 것을 섞어 치장 벽토를 만들었습니다. 그들이 사용했던 유기 화합물은 치장 벽토에 점착력을 부여했고, 이로 인해 혼합물은 돌로 만들어진 벽에 잘 붙었습니다. 그런 다음 마야인들은 축축한 치장 벽토를 벽에 발랐고, 자신들이 원하는 문양을 새겨 넣었으며, 그 후에는 단단해지도록 놔두었습니다. 여기를 봐 주세요… 그리고 여기도요…

마야의 회화는 어떨까요? 안타깝게도 오늘날까지 남아 있는 마야의 회화는 거의 없습니다. 중앙 아메리카의 축축하고 습한 기후는 회화의 보존에 적합하지 않습니다. 실제로 남아 있는 몇 안 되는 회화들은 주로 석재로 지어진 건물이나 동굴 안쪽의 벽화로 제작되었습니다. 여기를 보시고… 이 그림의 화려한 색상에 주목해 주세요… 현존하는 회화들이 얼마나 아름다운지

를 고려하면 남아 있는 그림이 거의 없다는 점은 매우 안타까운 일입니다. Teresa, 질문이 있나요?

학생: 네, 교수님. 마야인들이 사용했던 물감이 궁금합니다. 무엇으로 물감을 만들었나요?

교수: 아, 좋은 질문이군요. 마야인들이 사용했던 안료는 식물과 광물질에서 나온 것이었습니다. 마야인들은 이러한 성분들을 혼합하여 다양한 색조의 안료를 만들었습니다. 가장 아름다운 것 중의 하나가 마야 블루라는 것입니다. 여기 스크린 위쪽을 봐 주세요… 멋집니다, 그렇지 않나요? 마야 블루는 터키석의 색깔입니다. 마야인들만이 그것을 어떻게 만드는지 알고 있었죠. 마야 블루는 벽화, 조각, 그리고 도자기를 포함하여 모든 종류의 예술 작품에서 찾아볼 수 있습니다. 그것을 제작하는 비법은 16세기에 사라졌지만, 다행스럽게도 그 제작 과정이 최근에 재발견되었습니다. 마야 블루에 관해 주목할 만한 점은 그것이 풍화에 매우 잘 견디고 오랜 기간 지속된다는 점입니다.

다음으로 살펴볼 형태의 예술은 자기입니다. 여기에는 자기로 된 형상과… 도자기… 꽃병… 그리고 평범한 가정용 접시들이 포함됩니다… 마야인들은 또한 자기를 사용하여 유골 단지를 제작하기도 했습니다. 대부분의 자기와 마찬가지로 이들도 진흙을 구워서 모양을 만들고 색을 칠함으로써 만들어졌습니다. 마야인들은 화산재와 진흙을 혼합했습니다. 도자기 조각과 기타 자기로 만들어진 형상을 연구함으로써 진흙 혼합물 중 약 20%가 화산재라는 점이 밝혀졌습니다. 여러분들에게는 흥미로운 정보가 될 것 같군요. 마야의 예술가들은 종종 매우 독창적인 스타일의 자기를 만들었고, 현대의 예술가처럼 작품에 자신의 이름을 새겨 넣는 경우가 많았습니다. 가장 뛰어난 자기 제작자들은 귀족들이 많이 찾았습니다. 자기는 종종 교환의 수단 및 선물 수단으로서 사용되었기 때문에 최상의 자기를 구하는 일은 마야 귀족들에게 중요한 일이었습니다. 그림이 들어 있는 자기에 대해 이야기를 하면, 마야 예술가들은 자신의 상상력을 자유로이 풀어 놓았습니다… 이들은 신과 통치자들의 모습을 그렸지만, 평범한 사람들의 일상 생활을 그리기도 했습니다. 이제 제가 가장 좋아하는 그림들을 몇 개 보여 드리겠습니다.

WORD REMINDER

ceramic 도기   jade 비취, 옥   obsidian 흑요석, 흑요암   trinket (자질구레한) 장신구   metallurgy 야금술   plaster 회반죽, 벽토   stucco 치장 벽토   terra cotta 테라코타   show off 과시하다, 자랑하다   glorify 찬양하다   stela 석비, 기념 석주   slab 평석, 석판   chisel (끌로) 새기다   figurine 작은 조각상   limestone 석회암   adhesiveness 점착력, 접착성   mural 벽화   vibrant (색깔이) 강렬한, 화려한   extant 현존하는   fabulous 멋진, 굉장한   hue 색조   turquoise 터키석; 청록색   urn 단지, 항아리   shard 파편, 조각   trivia 하찮은 것, 사소한 정보   medium 매개물   commoner 평민, 서민

Actual Test 06

PART 1

Conversation

p.124

학생: 괜찮으시면, 교수님, 떠나기 전에 교수님과 한 가지 더 이야기를 나누고 싶어요. 잠시 시간을 내 주실 수 있나요, 아니면 지금 다른 수업에 가셔야 하나요?

교수: 학생을 위한 시간은 많아요, Matt. 그 밖에 또 어떤 것을 논의해야 하죠?

학생: 2주 전 수업에서 교수님께서 특별 과제에 대해 언급하신 걸로 기억하고 있어요 — 어, 추가 점수를 위한 것이요. 추가 점수를 얻기 위해 정확히 어떤 특별 과제를 해야 하나요?

교수: Matt, 정말로 제 수업에서 추가 점수를 받는 일이 필요하다고 생각하나요?

학생: 받아서 나쁠 건 없죠.

교수: 중간고사 성적이 어땠는지 다시 한번 알려 주세요.

학생: 97점이었는데, 하지만, 어, 교수님께서는 결코 모르실 거예요. 제가 기말고사를 망칠 수도 있고, 혹–혹–혹은 그 밖에 다른 좋지 않은 일들이 일어날 수도 있죠. 저는 단지 성적에 대해 확신을 갖고 싶어요.

교수: 좋아요, 무슨 말인지 알겠어요. 그리고 학생의 질문에 대한 대답은 '그렇다'인데, 제 수업에서 추가 점수를 얻기 위해 학생이 할 수 있는 프로젝트는 아주 많아요.

학생: 잘 되었군요. 제가 어떻게 하면 되나요?

교수: 도서관에 가서 프로젝트에 대해 알아보세요. 대출대로 가서 수업에 대한 파일을 보겠다고 요청하세요. 파일 안에 — 음, 실제로 고리가 세 개인 바인더인데 — 어쨌든, 파일 안에서 "공학 72 수업을 위한 보너스 프로젝트"라는 라벨이 붙어 있는 부분을 발견하게 될 거예요. 수업을 듣는 각각의 학생들이 학기 마다 하나의 보너스 프로젝트를 할 수 있어요. 하지만 프로젝트를 한다고 해서 추가 점수를 얻는 것은 아니에요. 선택한 프로젝트를 제가 만족할 만한 방법으로 완성시켜야 하죠.

학생: 맞는 말씀인 것 같아요. 파일에는 어떤 종류의 프로젝트들이 있나요?

교수: 학생이 찾아내야 해요, Matt. 하지만 학생이 파일을 확인하기 전에 두 가지만 이야기할게요: 파일에 들어 있는 프로젝트들은 쉽지 않아요. 이번 수업에서 배운 내용을 이용해서 프로젝트를 해결해야 하는데, 하지만 다른 수업에서 배운 지식도 필요할 거예요. 간단히 말해서, 성공적으로 프로젝트를 수행할 수는 있겠지만 많은 노력과 시간이 필요할 거예요. 게다가 프로젝트를 혼자서 수행할 수도 있고, 최대 2명의 학생들과 협력을 할 수도 있어요. 프로젝트를 시작하기 전에 어떠한 프로젝트를 수행할 것인지, 그리고 누구와 함께 할 것인지에 대해 알려만 주면 되죠. 됐나요?

학생: 완벽한 것 같아요. 오, 질문이 하나 더 있어요.

교수: 말해 보세요.

학생: 이 프로젝트에 대해 수업 시간에 말씀을 해 주시는 것이 어떨까요?

교수: 흠… 대체로, 그것은 적극성과 관련된 일이에요. 학생과 같은 학생들은 — 다른 소수의 학생들은 — 적극성을 띠고 이곳에 찾아와서 제게 특별 프로젝트에 대한 질문을 하죠. 그렇게 하면 제가 그들이 이용할 수 있는 기회에 대해 말을 해 주고요. 하지만 질문을 할 정도의 관심도 없는 학생들에게는… 음, 알려 줄 필요는 없을 것 같아요. 추가 점수라는 점을 기억하세요. 적극성을 지닌 학생들은 점수를 얻으려 할 것이고, 반면에 적극성이 없는 학생들은 그렇게 하지 않을 거예요.

학생: 무슨 말씀인지 알겠어요. 이해가 가는군요. 좋아요. 이제 파일을 확인해 볼게요.

WORD REMINDER

spare (시간, 돈 등을) 내다, 할애하다   mess up 엉망으로 만들다, 망치다   reserve desk 대출대   in short 짧게 말해서, 즉   take initiative 주도권을 갖다, 적극성을 띠다   enlighten 계몽하다, 깨우치게 하다

Lecture · Physiology
p.126

교수: 인간의 눈은 어떻게 서로 다른 색을 볼 수 있을까요? 우선 설명하기에 앞서 색이 무엇인지에 대해 이야기를 해야 할 것 같군요. 색은 빛으로부터 나옵니다. 주로 이러한 빛은 소위 백색광이기 때문에, 우리는 이를 볼 수가 없습니다. 백색광은, 아시겠지만, 스펙트럼상의 모든 색으로 구성됩니다. 아이작 뉴턴은 프리즘에 백색광을 투과시켰을 때 그러한 사실을 알아냈고, 이것이 무지개 색깔로 나뉘어진다는 점에 주목했습니다. 하지만 뉴턴은 이러한 색이 입자이며 각각의 색은 각기 다른 색 입자에 의해 구성된다고 믿었습니다. 명백하게도, 그에 대해서는 뉴턴이 틀렸습니다. 색은 입자로 구성되어 있지 않습니다: 대신 각각의 색은 전자기 스펙트럼상 고유한 파장을 지니고 있습니다. 우리가 색으로 인식하는 것이 바로 이러한 파장입니다.

색에 대해 더 많이 알게 되었으니까 다시 한번 질문을 할 수 있겠군요: 인간의 눈은 어떻게 서로 다른 색을 인식할까요? 백색광이 물체에 부딪히면 스펙트럼상의 대부분의 색은 그러한 물체에 의해 흡수됩니다. 하지만 일부는 흡수되지 않습니다. 대신 반사됩니다. 예를 들어 제가 쥐고 있는 이 연필을 봐 주세요. 아시다시피 노란색입니다. 이는 노란색을 제외한 스펙트럼상의 모든 색이 연필에 의해 흡수되었다는 점을 의미합니다.

학생: Venters 교수님, 하얀색과 검정색 물체는 어떤가요?

교수: 하얀색 물체는 스펙트럼상의 모든 색을 흡수하기 때문에 어떠한 색도 가지고 있지 않습니다. 반면에 검정색 물체는 어떤 색도 흡수하지 않고 어떤 색도 반사하지 않기 때문에 하얗지도 않으며 색깔을 띠지도 않습니다. 이는 검정색이 색이 아니며 실제로 색이 없는 경우를 의미한다고 주장하는 사람들도 있습니다.

앞서 논의했듯이 눈의 망막에는 다수의 추상체 및 간상체가 포함되어 있습니다. 이러한 추상체와 간상체 때문에 우리가 빛을 볼 수 있습니다. 간상체는 저조명 상태에서 빛을 인식합니다. 이것이 암소시입니다. 추상체는 매우 밝을 때 색을 인식합니다. 이것이 명소시고요. 빛이 희미한 경우에는 간상체가 사용되는데, 이들은 상당히 민감해서 빛의 약한 파장도 감지할 수 있습니다. 반면에 간상체는 색을 인식하는데 있어서 아무런 역할을 하지 못합니다. 하지만 추상체가 색을 인식하는데 중요한 역할을 합니다.

추상체가 어떻게 색을 인식하는가에 관한 두 가지 주요 이론이 있습니다. 첫 번째는 삼원색 이론입니다. 이 이론은 눈이 추상체에 기반하여 색을 인식한다고 주장하는데, 추상체에는 세 가지 유형이 존재합니다: 장파장, 중파장, 그리고 단파장 추상체입니다. 각각의 추상체는 세 가지 주요 파장의 색상, 즉 빨간색, 파란색, 그리고 초록색의 각기 다른 파장에 맞춰져 있습니다. 이 이론은 1800년대에 처음으로 제기되었고, 그 후로 널리 인정을 받아 왔습니다. 또 다른 주요 이론은 대립 과정 이론입니다. 이 이론은 세 가지 종류의 추상체가 색의 차이를 추구한다고 주장합니다. 추상체 수용기들이 볼 수 있는 세 가지 주요 색에서 중첩되는 부분이 있기 때문에 그런 것이죠. 따라서 추상체들은 색 정보를 처리할 때 세 쌍의 대립되는 색을 설정합니다. 이들 세 쌍은 청-황, 적-녹, 그리고 백-흑입니다.

수십 년 동안 색 인식에 관한 이 두 개의 대립되는 이론들은 각기 독자적인 것이며 서로 간에 아무런 관련성도 없다고 생각되었습니다. 하지만 오늘날 과학자들 사이에서의 지배적인 견해는 이 이론들이 본질적으로 동일한 과정의 일부라는 것입니다. 현재 많은 사람들이 생각하기로, 세 가지 종류의 추상체가 삼원색 과정을 이용하여 먼저 색의 파장을 감지합니다. 그 후 추상체가 대립 과정을 이용해 다양한 색을 해석합니다. 또한 과학자들은 추상체의 다양한 부분들이 각각의 과정을 담당한다고 생각합니다. 대립 과정은 망막 신경절 세포에 의해 이해될 수 있다고 생각되는데, 망막 신경절 세포는 망막에서 발견되는 신경 세포입니다. 각각의 망막에는 백만 개가 약간 넘는 망막 신경절 세포가 존재하며, 이들은 각 망막에서 발견되는 수십억 개의 추상체 수용기와 연결되어 있습니다. 따라서 각각의 망막 신경절 세포는 대략 100개의 추상체 수용기와 연결되어 있는 것이죠.

색의 파장 신호는 망막 신경절 세포에 도달한 후 시각 신경에 의해 뇌로 보내지는데, 시각 신경은 눈과 연결되어 있습니다. 뇌는 이러한 신호를 어떻게 해석할까요? 신호들은 뇌의 일차 시각 피질 센터로 보내집니다. 이는 후두엽의 뒷부분에 위치해 있습니다. 이곳에서 시각 신호는 극도로 복잡한 과정을 통해 뇌에 의해서 해석됩니다. 어떻게 그런 일이 일어나는지를 설명하고 싶지만, 오늘은 그럴 시간이 없군요. 하지만 여러분들이 수업 웹사이트를 방문해서 "시각 피질" 제목 아래에 있는 내용을 찾아보길 바랍니다. 반드시 그곳에 있는 내용을 읽고 도표들을 확인해 보세요. 그러면 다음 번 강의를 이해하는 것이 훨씬 더 쉬워질 것입니다. 좋아요, 오늘 수업은 여기서 끝내야 할 것 같네요. 오늘부터 일주일 후에 중간 고사를 본다는 점을 기억하시고, 시험 시간 전까지 두 번의 수업이 더 남아 있습니다. 여러분이 저를 찾는 경우를 대비해서 제가 4시까지는 사무실에 있을 것입니다.

> ### WORD REMINDER
> white light 백색광 electromagnetic spectrum 전자기 스펙트럼 reflect 반사하다 retina 망막 cone 추상체 rod 간상체 scotopic vision 암소시 photopic vision 명소시 trichromatic theory 삼원색 이론 attune 조율하다, 맞추다 opponent process theory 대립 과정 이론 receptor 수용체 overlap 겹침; 공통 부분 isolated 고립된 prevailing 우세한 mindset 사고방식, 태도 essentially 본질적으로 detect 탐지하다 retinal ganglion cell 망막 신경절 세포 neuron 신경 세포, 뉴런 optic nerve 시각 신경 visual cortex 시각 피질 occipital lobe 후두엽 call a halt 정지시키다

Conversation
p.130

학생 식당 관리자: Nick, 오늘 근무 시간이 끝났군요, 그렇지 않나요? 하고 있는 일이 없으면 잠시 이쪽으로 올래요?

학생: 물론이죠, Carter 선생님. 방금 일이 끝났어요. 무엇에 관해 이야기를 나누어야 하죠?

학생 식당 관리자: 다음 학기 학생의 근무 시간에 관해서요.

학생: 벌써 봄 학기의 근무 시간표를 작성하고 계신 건가요? 그러기에는 약간 이르지 않나요?

학생 식당 관리자: 그렇지 않아요, Nick. 제 말은 이미 12월 중순이고, 1월 중순에 겨울 방학이 끝난 직후에 이곳 학생 식당에서 일을 할 수 있는 학생이 충분한지 확인해야 하거든요.

학생: 예, 말이 되는 것 같군요. 학기의 첫 주나 둘째 주에 일손이 부족한 것을 원하지는 않으실 테니까요.

학생 식당 관리자: 바로 그거예요. 그래서 첫 번째 질문이… 다음 학기에도 여기에서 일을 할 생각인가요?

학생: 그럼요. 이곳 학생 식당에서 일을 하는 것이 정말 마음에 들어요. 시간도 좋고, 급여도 정말 좋고, 그리고 함께 일하는 사람들도 모두 다 좋아요.

학생 식당 관리자: 다음 학기부터 학생을 학생 매니저로 임명하기로 결정했기 때문에 그런 이야기를 들으니 좋군요, Nick. 학생은 승진을 하게 될 거예요.

학생: 매니저요? 제가요?

학생 식당 관리자: 네, 학생이요. 축하해요. Nick, 학생은 제가 같이 일해 본 사람 중에서 가장 근면한 학생 직원이고, 저는 학생이 훌륭한 매니저가 될 것이라고 믿어요. 하지만 이 일에 대해 학생이 알아야 할 것이 두어 가지 있어요… 먼저, 일주일에 20시간을 근무해야 할 거예요. 음, 20시간에서 30시간 동안 어디에서든 일을 해야 하죠. 받아드릴 수 있나요?

학생: 20시간이요? 흠… 현재 18시간 근무를 하고 있기 때문에 제 생각에는 두 시간 더 일을 해서 업무량이 늘어난다고 하더라도 그렇게 힘들 것 같지는 않아요. 제가 근무할 시간을 선택할 수 있나요?

학생 식당 관리자: 어느 정도까지는 가능해요. 하지만 학생이 최소한 일주일에 4일은 저녁에 일을 하면 좋겠어요. 어, 알겠지만, 저녁 식사 시간이죠. 점심 식사 시간 때 보다 그 시간에 학생이 더 필요할 것 같아요.

학생: 저녁 때에는 아무런 문제가 없어요. 실은 다음 학기에 낮 12시 전후로 수업이 몇 개 있어서 점심 때 일을 하는 것 대신 그 시간에 일을 하겠다고 여쭤볼 생각이었거든요.

학생 식당 관리자: 오, 좋아요. 그러면 근무 시간에 있어서는 아무런 문제가 없겠군요. 자, 좋은 점이 있어서… 아마 짐작할 수 있을 텐데, 매니저로 승진하면 급여가 인상되죠. 매니저로서 학생은 시간당 2달러를 추가로 받게 될 거예요. 그리고 저녁 근무 시간에 일을 하면 5시 이후로 일을 한 것에 대해 시간당 1달러를 더 받게 될 것이고요. 다음 학기에는 학생이 많은 돈을 벌게 될 것 같네요.

학생: 잘 되었군요. 정말 고맙습니다, Carter 선생님. 그처럼 저를 믿고 계시다니 기쁘네요.

학생 식당 관리자: 제가 더 기쁘죠. 아, 한 가지가 더 있어요… 겨울 방학 동안 이곳 인근에 있을 계획인가요? 학교 식당은 문을 열 예정인데, 그때 일을 할 수 있는 사람들이 몇 명 필요하거든요.

학생: 오, 죄송해요. 방학 동안 집에 가서 가족들을 만날 예정이기 때문에 그에 대해서는 도움을 드릴 수가 없어요. 하지만 Karen Cooke이 여기에 남아 있을 것이라고 알고 있어요. 그녀에게 한번 물어보세요.

학생 식당 관리자: 그 점은 몰랐네요. 알려 줘서 고마워요.

WORD REMINDER

shift 교대 근무 (시간)　　get off work 일을 끝내다, 퇴근하다　　come to an end 끝나다　　shorthanded 일손이 부족한　　as of ~ 일자로　　workload 업무량, 작업량　　strenuous 몹시 힘든　　buck 달러

Lecture • History of Science

p.132

교수: 아이작 뉴턴은 역사상 가장 위대한 과학 정신을 지니고 있었던 사람 중 한 명이었습니다. 중력, 운동의 법칙, 광학, 그리고 색에 관한 그의 연구는 17세기 이후 과학계에서 초석과 같은 역할을 했습니다. 하지만 그의 연구의 한 가지 측면에서, 주요한 논쟁거리가 하나 있습니다. 미적분학의 발전과 관련된 것이죠. 즉, 누가 최초로 그것을 발전시켰을까요? 뉴턴과 그의 지지자들은 뉴턴이 미적분학을 이론화하고 발전시킨 최초의 인물이라고 주장했지만, 다른 이들은 — 지금도 마찬가지로 — 독일의 고트프리트 라이프니츠가 최초였다고 주장했습니다. 증거를 철저히 조사해 보면 두 사람 모두 각기 동일한 아이디어에 관해 연구를 했고 동일한 결론에 이르렀다는 결론을 얻게 됩니다.

자, 미적분학이나 그 이면에 있는 이론에 관해 본격적으로 토론을 벌이고 싶지는 않습니다. 대신 이 두 인물을 둘러싼 논쟁에 대해서만 검토를 하

고자 합니다. 먼저, 여러분들은 두 사람 모두 전적으로 미적분학을 발전시킨 것은 아니라는 점을 알 필요가 있습니다. 어찌되었든 미적분학이 기반하고 있는 아이디어 중 일부는 고대부터 존재해 왔던 것이니까요. 봅시다… 이집트인, 그리스인, 그리고 중국인들 모두 미적분학과 관련된 연구를 했습니다. 하지만 뉴턴과 라이프니츠 이 두 사람이 한 것은, 어, 음, 이러한 아이디어들을 취합해서 통합한 후, 하나의 통일된 이론을 만들어 낸 것이었습니다. 뉴턴은 1666년에 미적분학에 관한 연구를 시작했다고 주장했지만, 1693년 이후가 되어서야 자신의 아이디어들을 책으로 발표했습니다. 반면 라이프니츠는 1674년에 자신의 이론에 대한 연구를 시작해서 1684년에 첫 번째 책을 발간했습니다. 라이프니츠가 대수학에 관한 뉴턴의 미출간 원고를 본 것은 1676년 그가 런던을 방문했을 때였습니다. 또한 그와 뉴턴은 서신을 주고받았고, 이로써 라이프니츠는 아마도 뉴턴이 무엇에 대한 연구를 하고 있었는지에 관해 어느 정도 단서를 가지고 있었을 것입니다. 이러한 일들은 뉴턴을 지지하는 사람들에게 좋은 정보를 제공해 주는데, 그와 같은 사람들은 확고 부동하게 라이프니츠가 표절자라고 주장합니다. 하지만 라이프니츠를 지지하는 사람들은 뉴턴이, 먼저 출간된 라이프니츠의 연구를 입수했다고 주장합니다.

음, 라이프니츠는 1699년에 처음으로 표절에 따른 비난을 받았지만 1711년이 되어서야 문제가 크게 불거지게 되었습니다. 비난의 말이 라이프니츠의 귀에 들어가자 그는 런던 왕립학회에 비난 철회 및 문제에 대한 조사를 요청했습니다. 왕립학회는, 모르는 경우를 위해 말씀을 드리면, 당시 가장 권위 있던 과학 단체였습니다. 학회는 조사를 진행했고, 음, 그에 대한 결과가 — 입증된 것은 아니지만 — 학회 회원 중 한 명에 의해 쓰여진 것으로 전해지고 있습니다. 그 사람은 다름 아닌 뉴턴 자신이었죠. 그 결과가 어떠했는지 여러분들도 상상할 수 있으리라고 확신합니다. 그렇죠? 이러한 편파적인 보고서는 뉴턴의 편을 들고 있었고, 그의 미적분학이 원조라고 주장했습니다. 라이프니츠의 주장은 제기되지도 못했으며, 본인을 대변하기 위한 증거 제출도 허락되지 않았습니다.

이 독일 과학자는, 당시 연로했고 논쟁에 지쳐있었는데, 연구에서 벗어나 있을 수 있는 시간이 거의 없었습니다. 또한 40년 전에 일어났던 사건을 기억할 수도 없었기 때문에 여하튼 방어할 수 있는 것들을 많이 제시하지 못했을 것입니다. 음, 당시에는 진실보다 명성이 더 중요했습니다. 그리고 뉴턴은 매우 도덕성이 높은 인물이라는 명성을 지니고 있었습니다. 또한 영국에서뿐만 아니라 유럽 대부분의 지역에서도 당대의 저명한 과학자로 여겨지고 있었습니다. 그는 화폐 개혁에 대한 공헌으로 앤 여왕으로부터 기사 작위를 받았는데, 이로써 영국에 팽배했던 화폐 위조 범죄가 종식될 수 있었습니다. 라이프니츠 또한 당시 과학계의 스타였지만, 뉴턴과는 비교가 되지 못했습니다. 라이프니츠는 독일의 여러 귀족들에 의해 고용되어 법률가, 외교관, 그리고 역사가로서 일을 했습니다. 실제로 그는 대부분의 과학 연구를 여가 시간에 했습니다. 이러한 논란은 그의 명성에 심각한 타격을 입혔고, 1716년에 그가 사망하자 문제는 끝을 맺지 못했습니다.

사실들을 주의 깊게 조사해 보면 두 사람 모두 동시에 같은 것을 연구하고 있었다는 점이 드러납니다. 흥미롭게도 뉴턴의 주장이 라이프니츠의 주장보다 입증하기가 더 힘듭니다. 자, 어, 라이프니츠는 자신의 미적분학 이론을 발전시킨 과정에 대한 많은 노트를 남겼는데, 이로써 수학 및 역사 학자들이 매우 손쉽게 그 발전 과정을 추적할 수 있습니다. 그의 노트를 보면 대부분의 아이디어가 뉴턴의 방법과는 전혀 다른 방식으로 전개되었다는 점이 명백합니다. 문제는 우리가 뉴턴의 방법에 대해 많이 알지 못한다는 점입니다. 그가 어떻게 결론에 도달했는지를 보여 주는 증거가 거의 없고, 그의 아이디어는 미적분학에 관한 출판물에서만 드러나 있을 뿐입니다. 이러한 점은 라이프니츠를 옹호해 주는 것처럼 보이나, 뉴턴이 라이프니츠의 아이디어를 이용했다

는 증거는 전혀 존재하지 않습니다.

뉴턴의 미적분학은, 어, 18세기 대부분 동안 특히 영국에서 진정한 미적분학으로 간주되었습니다. 논란에 대한 차후의 조사를 통해 두 사람 모두 각각의 연구로 동일한 결론에 도달했다는 점이 드러났습니다. 이러한 문제가 중요하지 않은 것처럼 보일 수도 있겠지만, 과학자의 명성은 자신의 이론이 받아들여지는가 혹은 그렇지 않는가의 문제와 깊이 관련될 수 있다는 점을 여러분들이 생각해 보았으면 합니다. 이 말이 어떤 의미를 나타내는지에 대한 한 가지 예를 들도록 하겠습니다.

Lecture • Geology

p.135

교수: 고대 이후로 가장 흔히 사용되어 온 금속 중 하나는 구리입니다. 고대 사람들은 구리를 채굴하여 여러 가지 금속 도구와 금속 무기를 만드는데 사용했습니다. 특히 구리와 주석을 섞어 만드는 합금인 청동을 생산하기 위해 이를 활용했습니다. 과거에는 대부분의 구리가 지표면 근처의 매장지에서 채굴되었습니다. 이러한 점은 오늘날에도 사실인데, 대부분의 구리는 노천 광산에서 나오고 있습니다. 하지만 때때로 지하 깊은 곳으로부터 채굴되기도 합니다. 구리 광석을 캐내는데 이용되는 채굴 방식은 구리 광석이 어디에 위치해 있는가에 따라 달라집니다. 구리 광석이 비교적 지표면 가까운 곳에 위치한 경우에는 노천 채굴이 이루어집니다. 반면에 구리 광석이 지하 깊은 곳에 위치해 있을 때에는 터널을 파서 구리를 채굴해야 하죠. 일반적으로 노천 채굴이 비용이 더 적게 들고 보다 쉽게 광석을 캐낼 수 있기 때문에 선호되고 있습니다. 오, 어, 또한 광부들에게도 훨씬 더 안전한데, 광부들은 지하 터널에서 목숨을 잃을 위험을 겪지 않아도 됩니다.

구리의 노천 채굴에 대해 잠시 말씀을 드리도록 하겠습니다. 노천 구리 광산에서 구리를 덮고 있는 흙과 암석은 통칭하여 상부 퇴적물이라고 부릅니다. 광부들이 구리 광석에 접근할 수 있도록 상부 퇴적물은 다이너마이트로 폭파되거나 토공 기계 등으로 제거되어야 합니다. 때때로 상부 퇴적물 암석의 질이 우수한 경우에는 건설 및 기타 목적으로 사용하기 위해 이를 판매할 수도 있습니다. 이로써 광업 회사는 약간의 이윤을 얻게 됩니다. 많은 경우, 광맥은 지표면 근처에서 시작되어 지하 깊은 곳으로 이어집니다. 이러한 경우에는 광부들이 계속해서 폭파와 굴착 작업을 합니다. 땅 속으로 깊이 내려갈수록 노천 광산이 확대됩니다.

광부들은 가능하면 안전하게 광석을 캐낼 수 있도록 노천 광산을 보다 크게 만듭니다. 이로써 일부 광산들은, 음, 막대한 크기를 갖게 됩니다. 여러분의 책을 보세요. 95페이지에 노천 광산의 그림이 있는 것으로 알고 있는데… 모두들 보고 있나요…? 그래요. 좋습니다. 다양한 층들을 확실히 볼 수 있을 것입니다, 그렇죠? 각각의 층은 벤치라고 불립니다. 계단이 더 깊이 내려갈수록 벤치는 평지처럼 보이는데, 다음 벤치에 이르면 — 수직이지는 않지만 — 급경사가 나타납니다. 벤치 간의 급경사는 배터라고 알려져 있습니다. 궁금해 하실 것 같아 말씀을 드리면, 배터가 완전히 수직이지 않은 이유는 그렇게 해야 낙석의 위험이 감소하기 때문입니다. 어쨌든, 광산이 계단, 혹은, 어, 테라스처럼 보이는 방식에 주목해 주세요.

노천 광산의 또 다른 중요한 측면은 바닥에서 꼭대기까지 이어진 도로에 있습니다. 이러한 도로들은 일부 벤치에 지어지며, 종종 올라갈수록 우회하는 형태를 띱니다. 이러한 도로는 거대한 트럭으로 광산에서 광석을 빼내는 데 사용됩니다. 또한 광산의 바닥까지 기계와 물품들을 운반하기 위해서도 사용되죠. 광산이 최대한도로 가동될 때, 이러한 트럭들은 쉬지 않고 밤낮으로 이곳을 오르내립니다. 그래서, 어, 트럭이 광석을 싣고 표면에 도달하면 광석은 광산 근처에서 처리되거나, 아니면 트럭이나 철도에 의해 가공 처리 공장으로 보내집니다. 구리 주위의 암석이 제거되어 상업적 용도로 사용이 가능하게 되는 시점이 바로 그러한 처리 과정이 진행되는 때입니다.

학생: 땅에서 구리를 모두 캐내면 어떻게 되나요?

교수: 광석을 모두 캐내거나 광산 운영의 경제성이 사라지면 광산은 폐쇄됩니다. 남게 되는 것은 커다란 구덩이죠. 그러면 학생의 다음 질문을 제가 맞춰보도록 할게요: 구덩이는 어떻게 되나요? 많은 경우 광산 회사는 해당 지역을 지방 정부에게 임대하는데, 지방 정부는 구덩이를 쓰레기 매립장으로 사용합니다. 좋아요, 음, 여러분 중 다수가 노천 광산의 환경적 영향에 대해 궁금해 할 것 같군요. 과거 광산 회사들은 자신들이 환경에 끼치는 피해에 대해 거의 신경을 쓰지 않았다는 점은 사실이나, 오늘날에도 그런 것은 결코 아닙니다. 광산을 만들기 전에 광범위한 환경 연구가 진행됩니다. 특히 지하수면에 관한 연구가 강조되기 때문에 광산에 의해 지하수가 오염되지는 않습니다.

오늘날 노천 광산에 있어서 정말로 문제가 되는 것은 자연 경관에 거대하고 흉측한 상처를 남긴다는 점입니다. 일부 지역 주민들은 기업들이 채굴을 중단하면 광산에 흙을 채워서 그 부지에 나무를 심어야 한다고 주장합니다. 이는 최소한 해당 지역이 복구되는데 도움을 줍니다. 또 다른 중요한 문제는 상부 퇴적물 및 기타 사용되지 않은 물질들과 관련이 있습니다. 상부 퇴적물이 제거되면, 판매가 되지 않는 이상, 이들은 보통 구덩이 근처에 쌓입니다. 눈살을 찌푸리게 만드는 것이 되어 버리죠. 또한 광산은 폐석을 처리해야 합니다. 아, 폐석은 구리 광석을 처리하는 과정에서 생기는 폐기물입니다. 폐석은 종종 화학 물질로 오염이 되기 때문에 적절히 보관되지 않으면 지역 내 수계를 유독 물질로 오염시킵니다. 실제로 알래스카의 페블 광산에서 일어났던 일입니다. 그리고 그것이 우리가 다음으로 살펴봐야 할 내용이죠. 이 광산이 일으킨 문제들이 많았습니다.

Actual Test 07

Conversation

p.142

교수: 오늘 오후에 사무실에 들러 줘서 고마워요, Jeff. 왜 여기로 오라고 했는지 알고 있을 것이라고 생각해요.

학생: 음, 실은, Kimble 교수님, 저는 정말로 잘 모르겠어요. 제 말은, 어, 제 중간고사 성적도 좋았고, 과제는 모두 제출했고, 이번 학기의 모든 수업에 출석을 했죠. 제가 잘못한 것이 있나요?

교수: 흠… 학생이 잘못을 했다고는 말하고 싶지 않지만, 과제 수행에 있어서 확실히 잘못된 것이 있어요. 아직 제출하지 않은 것도 하나 있고요.

학생: 그런가요? 하-하-하지만 과제는 다 했는걸요. 다른 학생들과 함께 모두 제출한 것으로 기억하고 있어요.

교수: 아니에요, Jeff, 과제가 아니에요. 학생이 제출한 보고서는 모두 가지고 있어요. 저는 학생의 기말 보고서를 말하고 있는 것이에요.

학생: 하지만, 그것은 기한이, 어, 3주나 남았잖아요, 그렇죠?

교수: 맞아요. 하지만 지난 주말까지 보고서 계획안을 제출하기로 되어 있었어요. 학생을 제외하고는 수업 내 모든 학생들로부터 계획안을 받았어요. 혹시, 어, 지금 계획안을 가지고 있나요?

학생: 그것을 제출하기로 되어 있었다고요?

교수: 네. 네, 그래요.

학생: 오… 죄송해요. 제가 완전히 잘못 이해했네요. 무엇에 관해 쓸 것인지를 결정하지 못한 학생들만 계획안을 써서 제출해야 한다고 생각했어요. 저는 이미 제가 쓸 주제를 알고 있었기 때문에 계획서를 제출할 필요가 없다고 생각했죠.

교수: 아시다시피, 다른 대부분의 학생들의 말은 믿지 않겠지만, 사실 학생 말은 믿어요, Jeff. 모든 것이 다 오해 때문인 것으로 들리는군요.

학생: 네, 교수님. 그러면 계획안을 작성해서 내일 교수님께 가져다 드리면 될까요? 어, 실은, 이미 보고서의 절반은 써 놓았어요. 제가 하고자 하는 것에 잘못된 것이 없기를 바라요.

교수: Jeff, 이례적이기는 하지만 제게 아이디어가 하나 있어요. 학생의 계획에 관해서 지금 제게 말을 하는 것이 어떨까요? 그러면 학생이 제대로 하고 있는지, 아니면 잘못하고 있는지를 제가 알려 줄 수 있을 거예요. 그리고 그렇게 하면 계획안을 작성하지 않아도 되고요.

학생: 알겠어요. 좋아요.

교수: 그러면 말을 해 보세요.

학생: 음, 저는 제 과제로 아스펜 시의 역사를 검토해 보기로 결정했어요.

교수: 아스펜이요? 호화로운 스키 리조트를 말하는 건가요?

학생: 맞아요. 보세요, 음, 그 도시가 처음부터 그런 곳은 아니었어요. 본래 탄광 도시였죠. 제 생각에는 일종의 신흥 도시였어요. 그 후 여러 가지 이유로 경제가 붕괴되어서 사실상 유령 도시가 되어버렸죠.

교수: 좋아요. 그러면 어떤 측면을 살펴볼 건가요?

학생: 아시겠지만, 아스펜은 현재 부유하고 유명한 사람들이 모여드는 도시에요. 제가 하고자 하는 것은 어떻게 그 도시가, 음… 이렇게 이야기해야 할 것 같은데, 정체성을 변화시킬 수 있었는지를 살펴보는 것이에요. 그곳이 어떻게 해서 텅 비고 아무도 살지 않은 상황에서 벗어날 수 있었는지를 조사해 보려고 해요.

교수: 좋아요. 마음에 드는군요. 그곳의 시행정 담당관들이 내린 결정과, 아스펜이 겪은 부흥을 결코 겪지 못했던 시에서 내린 결정들을 비교하고 싶을 수도 있겠어요.

학생: 아, 좋은 아이디어네요. 조언에 감사를 드립니다. 잊지 않고 그에 대한 조사를 해 볼게요.

교수: 잘 되었군요. 좋아요. 이번 문제는 해결되었다고 말하고 싶군요, 그렇죠?

학생: 그럼요. 정말 고맙습니다, Kimble 교수님.

WORD REMINDER

drop by ~에 들르다　**by any chance** 혹시라도, 만일　**unorthodox** 정통적이 아닌, 특이한　**ritzy** 호화로운, 화려한　**boomtown** 신흥 도시　**virtual** 사실상의, 거의 ~와 다름없는　**identity** 정체(성)　**city manager** 시행정 담당관　**compare** 비교하다　**revival** 회복, 부활

Lecture · History

p.144

교수: 열차는 일종의 운송 수단으로, 여러분 중 다수는 탑승해 보지 못했을 것으로 생각합니다. 만약 탑승해 보셨다면 한두 번 정도만 타 보셨을 것 같습니다. 하지만 미국에서, 열차는 과거에 매우 중요한 운송 수단이었습니다. 특히 1800년대에 그러했죠. 미국의 철도 역사에 관한 짧은 영상을 보여 드릴 텐데, 하지만 그렇게 하기에 앞서 먼저 여러분들과 몇 가지 사실들을 살펴보고자 합니다. 그러니 제가, 어, 제가 1800년대 철도에 관한 몇 가지 중요한 점을 이야기하는 동안 잠시 인내심을 가져 주시기 바랍니다.

사실 원시적인 형태의 철도는 16세기 유럽에서도 존재했습니다. 하지만 산업 혁명이 시작된 후에 개발된 철도와는 전혀 다른 것이었죠. 대신, 이러한 원시적인 형태의 철도는 주로 광산 주변에서 사용되었고, 나무 트랙을 따라 사람이나 말에 의해 끌어졌습니다. 하지만 1700년대 증기 기관이 완성되자 필연적으로 철도에 증기 기관이 사용되었고, 열차가 만들어졌습니다. 그렇게 되기까지 어느 정도의 시간이 걸리기는 했지만, 1800년대 초에는 미국에도 철도가 도입되었습니다.

존 스티븐스 대령이 북미에서 최초로 철도 부설 허가를 받은 때가 바로 1815년이었습니다. 하지만 스티븐스 대령은 행동이 다소 느렸기 때문에 1832년이 되어서야 철도의 선로를 완성시켰습니다. 그러는 동안 다른 사람들 역시 철도 산업에 뛰어들었습니다. 1827년에 설립된 발티모어 오하이오 철도는 미국 철도 산업의 진정한 시작으로 평가받고 있습니다. 이는 화물 및 승객을 수송하는 운수업체로 승인을 받은 미국 최초의 철도 회사였습니다.

하지만 발티모어 오하이오 철도가 미국에서 유일한 철도 회사는 아니었습니다. 실제로 수많은 철도 회사들이 미 전역에서 빠르게 세워지기 시작했습니다. 보다 유명한 것 중 하나는 사우스캐롤라이나 운하 철도 회사였는데, 이 회사는 1830년 성탄절에 승객들을 태우기 시작했습니다. 당시 6마일의 트랙만을 가지고 있었지만, 이는 미국에서 가장 길게 운행되던 철도 선로였습니다.

철도 선로 건설은 1830년대에 진정한 호황을 맞이했습니다. 생각해 보세요. 미국은 커다란 나라입니다. 많은 사람들이 그러한 점을 깨닫고 있지 못하지만 미국은 거대합니다. 그리고 1830년대 무렵 사람들은 미대륙 전역으로 퍼져 나가고 있었고, 미시시피 강을 지나 서쪽으로 이주하고 있었습니다. 걸어서 가는 것, 말을 타고 가는 것, 마차를 타고 가는 것, 혹은 기차를 타고 가는 것 중에서 최선의 선택은 분명했습니다. 또한 육지에서는 그 어떤 것보다 열차가 훨씬 더 많은 짐을 실을 수 있다는 점도 사람들이 알게 되었습니다. 이는, 1840년경, 최초의 미 철도 회사가 설립된지 단 14년 만에 미시시피 강 동부 지역에 2,800마일 이상의 철도 선로가 존재하게 되었던 이유입니다. 1850년 무렵에는 그 수치가 9,000마일 이상으로 증가하게 되었습니다. 하지만 그 중 많은 부분이 미 북동부에 집중되어 있었고, 나머지는 남동부 및 중서부 지방에 집중되어있었다는 점을 주목해 주세요.

이처럼 철로가 엄청나게 증가함으로써 미국의 통합에 도움이 되었었습니다. 사람들은 기차를 타고 미시시피 강 서쪽까지 미 동부의 여러 지역을 빠르

게 이동할 수 있었습니다. 또한 철도는 농업의 확장을 가능하게 만들었는데, 특히 중서부 지방에서 그러했습니다. 위스콘신, 미네소타, 그리고 기타 지방의 농부들이 곡식과 동물들을 가지고 와서 더 동쪽에 있는 시장으로 보냈기 때문에, 일리노이 주의 시카고는 중요한 교통 중심지가 되었습니다.

또한 두 가지 이유로 1860년대가 철도 역사상 중요한 시기였다는 점도 말씀드려야겠군요. 먼저, 여러분들도 틀림없이 알고 있으리라고 생각하는데, 1861년부터 1865년까지 남북 전쟁이 일어났습니다. 철도가 중요한 역할을 담당했던 최초의 전쟁이었죠. 북부에서는 남부보다 선로의 마일 수가 더 높았는데, 이로써 북부에서 군대와 장비를 이동시키는 것이 훨씬 더 수월했습니다. 이는 북부 연합의 승리에 주요한 요인이 되었습니다. 1860년대에 있었던 또 다른 중요한 사건은 1862년 대서양과 태평양을 연결시키는 대륙 횡단 철도의 건설이 시작되었다는 점이었습니다. 이 철도는 1869년 5월 10일 유타 주의 프로먼터리 포인트에서 마지막 못질이 이루어지기 전까지 완공되지 못했습니다. 그럼에도 불구하고 미국은 마침내 통일되었으며, 그렇게 만든 것은 바로 철도였습니다.

철도는 이후 19세기에도 계속 확장되었습니다. 1900년대 무렵에는 미국 전역에 5개의 대륙 횡단 철도뿐만 아니라 약 193,000마일에 이르는 철도 노선이 존재하게 되었습니다. 철도 운영 업체들은 표준 철도의 폭에 관한 합의를 이루었는데, 이로써 철도들이 서로 연결될 수 있었다는 점도 마찬가지로 중요했습니다. 1800년대는 미국 철도의 진정한 황금기였습니다. 좋아요. 충분히 이야기를 한 것 같군요. 편하게 앉아서 미국 철도의 역사에 관한 영상을 보도록 하겠습니다. 그리고 누군가가 질문을 하기에 앞서, 그래요, 여러분들이 이러한 내용을 잘 알 수 있기를 바라기 때문에 시청하는 동안 필기를 잘 해 두세요.

> **WORD REMINDER**
>
> incredibly 믿을 수 없을 정도로, 굉장히   highlight 가장 흥미로운 부분, 하이라이트   steam engine 증기 기관   inevitable 불가피한, 필연적인   grant 주다, 수여하다   charter 인가, 허가; 허가하다; 전세 내다   slow off the mark 행동이 둔한, 머리 회전이 느린   in the meantime 그 사이에, 그러는 동안   common carrier 일반 운수업자, 철도 회사   veritable 진정한   boom 호황, 붐   stagecoach 역마차   bring together 묶다, 합치다   hub 중심지, 중추   crucial 중요한, 중대한   transcontinental 대륙 횡단의   spike 못   golden age 황금기, 전성기

PART 2

Conversation
p.148

학생: Jessie 선생님, 선생님께서 저와 잠시 이야기를 나누고 싶어하신다고 Stewart가 말하더군요.

오케스트라 지휘자: 네, Kelly, 맞아요.

학생: 음, 알겠습니다. 제가 도와 드릴 일이라도 있나요? 약 15분 후에는 도서관에서 모이는 스터디 그룹에 참여해야 하거든요.

오케스트라 지휘자: 걱정 말아요, Kelly. 이 일로 학생의 시간을 많이 뺏지는 않을 거예요. 스터디 모임에는 늦지 않을 것이고요. 어쨌든, Kelly, 지난 며칠 동안 연습 시간에 학생의 집중력이 떨어지는 것 같아 보였다고 생각했어요. 이렇게 이야기해서 미안하지만 최근 학생의 연주는 정말로 기대에 못미치고 있어요. 학생에게 일어나고 있는, 제가 알아야 할 문제라도 있나요?

학생: 어… 실은, 그래요. 아시겠지만, 어, 저는, 음… 음, 오케스트라를 그만두려고 생각하고 있었어요.

오케스트라 지휘자: 그만둔다고요? 아마 진심은 아니겠죠, 그런가요? 도대체 왜 그만두려는 것이죠?

학생: 제 성적 때문이에요. 아시다시피, 음, 이번 학기에 성적을 유지하는데 많은 어려움이 있었어요. 첫 2년 동안은 최소한 학기마다 3.50점의 평점을 받았기 때문에 항상 장학생 명단에 제 이름이 올라갔죠. 하지만 이번 학기의 중간고사 성적은 그만큼 좋지가 않았어요. 그리고 많은 수업에서 학업에 뒤쳐지기 시작했고요. 모두들 3학년 때의 화학 공학이 정말로 힘들다고 하는데, 그리고, 음, 그 사람들의 말이 모두 맞는 것 같아요. 그리고 제 성적이 떨어진다면 내년에 제가 4학년이 될 때 괜찮은 직장을 얻기가 힘들어질 거예요.

오케스트라 지휘자: 그러면 학업에 집중하기 위해 오케스트라를 그만둔다는 생각을 하고 있는 건가요?

학생: 네, 선생님. 제 말은, 우리가 매주 평일에 하루 두 시간 연습을 하는데, 제게는 오케스트라에 전념할 수 있는 시간이 많지가 않아요. 정말로 유감이지만, 학업에 집중을 해야만 해서요.

오케스트라 지휘자: 타협안과 같은 것을 생각해 보는 것은 어떨까요?

학생: 어떻게요?

오케스트라 지휘자: 이렇게 해 보죠… 이번 주는 연습에 참가하지 말고 쉬세요. 그러면 4일 동안은 여기에 있을 필요가 없는데, 그렇게 하면 수업 내용을 따라가고, 과제를 하고, 그리고 성적을 높이는데 시간을 사용할 수 있을 거예요.

학생: 좋아요. 하지만 다음 주에는 어떻게 되나요? 매일 연습에 참여해야 하나요?

오케스트라 지휘자: 아니요, 저는 그렇게 생각하지 않아요. 매일 오는 대신 일주일에 3일이나 4일만 연습하러 오는 것은 어떨까요? 매주 사나흘 정도의 연습만으로도 다음 달에 공연하게 될 겨울 연주회를 준비하는데 충분할 거예요. 이 아이디어에 대해 어떻게 생각하나요?

학생: 흠… 그럴 수도 있을 것 같아요. 그렇게 한번 해 봐야겠어요.

오케스트라 지휘자: 잘 되었군요. 하지만 잊지 말고 저를 위해 한 가지는 해 주세요, Kelly.

학생: 어떤 일이죠?

오케스트라 지휘자: 먼저 해야 할 것들을 신경 쓰세요. 오케스트라에 속해 있는 것이 감당하기 힘들면 그만두고 학업에 전념한다고 해도 전적으로 이해할 수 있어요. 이곳에 함께 있었던 때를 그리워하겠지만, 절대적으로 학생의 성적이 우선시되어야 하죠.

학생: 그렇게 말씀해 주셔서 감사합니다. 선생님으로부터 그런 말을 들으니 기쁘네요. 저는 자신보다 다른 사람들의 행복을 먼저 생각해 주는 사람을 존경해요.

> **WORD REMINDER**
>
> take up (시간 등을) 차지하다   distracted (정신이) 산만한, 집중력이 떨어진   up to par 보통 정도는 되는, 기대에 부응하는   keep up 유지하다   fall behind 뒤쳐지다, 뒤떨어지다   dedicate 헌신하다   compromise 타협   welfare 복지, 행복

Lecture • Environmental Science
p.150

교수: 아시겠지만, 여름이 다가옴에 따라 이곳 주변 날씨가 꽤 더워지기 시작했습니다. 온도가 상승하면 저는 이곳 도시를 벗어나 시골로 가는 것을 좋아합니다. 제가 그렇게 하는 이유 중 하나는 시골 지방의 기온이 도시 중심지

의 기온보다 몇 도 정도 더 낮은 경향을 보이기 때문이죠. 여러분 중에 그러한 점을 알고 있는 사람이 있는지 궁금하군요. Heather?

학생: 제 가족은 이곳에서 한두 시간 떨어져 있는 농장에서 살고 있습니다. 도시와 시골 지역 간에 온도 차이가 존재한다는 점은 확실히 알고 있어요. 이곳 캠퍼스보다 농장이 훨씬 더 시원할 수 있죠.

교수: 제가 드리는 말씀이 바로 그것입니다. 여러분. 이러한 현상에 대한 명칭이 있습니다. 우리는 그것을 도시 열섬이라고 부릅니다. 도시의 온도를 시골의 온도보다 더 높게 만드는 여러 가지 요인이 존재합니다. 실제로 일부 시골 지방은 인근 도시 지역보다 섭씨 5도에서 9도 정도 더 시원할 수 있습니다. 상당히 큰 차이죠, 그렇지 않나요? 음, 왜 이런 일이 발생하는지 말씀드리도록 하겠습니다.

시골 지역을 생각해 보세요. 그러한 장소들은 주로 들판과 산림 지역으로, 건물, 도로, 인도, 그리고 기타 인공적인 구조물들이 거의 없습니다. 낮 동안 태양이 시골 지방에 햇빛을 비춥니다. 지면 근처에 흡수되는 태양 에너지는 식물과 토양 내에 있는 수분을 증발시킵니다. 이러한 수분이 증발되면 냉각 효과가 발생합니다. 게다가 시골 지역에서 바람이 불 때 바람을 방해하는 구조물들이 많지 않습니다. 따라서 바람은 방해를 받지 않습니다. 왜 이러한 점이 중요할까요? 음, 바람이 불면 공기가 순환됩니다. 이로써 뜨거운 공기와 차가운 공기가 — 혹은 선선한 공기가 — 서로 섞이게 되죠. 그 결과 뜨거운 공기는 냉각되어 기온이 낮아집니다. 아시겠지만, 인공 구조물이 결여되어 있고, 많은 식물이 존재하며, 바람이 순환한다는 사실이 합쳐짐으로써 시골 지방의 기온이 낮아지는 것입니다.

하지만 도시 지역은 어떨까요…? 먼저 도시 지역에는 시골 지역보다 식물이 훨씬 더 적게 있습니다. 물론 도시에 한두 개의 공원이 있을 수도 있지만, 일반적으로 도시에 그처럼 많은 나무 및 수풀이 존재하는 것은 아닙니다. 따라서 도시에서는 도시를 냉각시켜 줄 수분의 증발 현상이 거의 일어나지 않습니다. 또한 이러한 점도 생각해 보세요: 시골 지역에 비가 내리면 빗물이 토양에 흡수됩니다. 이후 이러한 수분은 태양 광선에 의해 증발될 수 있습니다. 하지만 도시에 내리는 비는 어떻게 될까요? 비가 지면으로 흡수되지 않습니다. 어찌되었던 지면은 보통 포장이 되어있으니까요, 그렇죠? 대신 빗물은 도시의 배수 시스템에 의해 처리되는데, 따라서 차후 증발에 의해 일어날 수 있는 냉각 효과가 차단됩니다.

도시에는 식물이 거의 없습니다. 하지만 무엇이 많을까요…? 음, 하나는 건물입니다. 도로, 인도, 주차장, 그리고 기타 인공 구조물 또한 많습니다. 햇빛이 비출 때 이 모든 것들이 태양의 열을 흡수합니다. 이러한 구조물들은 여러 물질들 중에서 벽돌, 콘크리트, 타르, 그리고 아스팔트로 만들어져 있다는 점을 기억하세요. 도시에 사는 사람들에게는 안타까운 일인데, 이러한 물질들은 뛰어난 열 전도체입니다. 이는 낮 동안 이러한 물질들이 많은 양의 열을 흡수하고 이를 보유하게 된다는 점을 의미합니다. 무더운 날 콘크리트 바닥을 만져보면 제가 무슨 말을 하고 있는지 알 수 있을 것입니다. 이러한 구조물들은 열을 보유하기 때문에 심지어 밤에도 온기를 지닙니다. 이로써 도시의 온도가 상승하게 되는 것이죠.

또한 도시 중심부에서 운행 중인 수많은 차량들에 대해서도 생각을 해야 합니다. 자동차, 트럭, 버스, 열차, 지하철, 그리고 엔진으로 작동되는 기타 운송 수단들이 도시 전체에서 운행되고 있습니다. 이러한 장비들은 열을 발생시키는데, 이 중 많은 열이 대기로 유입됩니다. 따라서 도시 지역의 온도가 상승하게 됩니다. 마지막으로, 시골 지역에서 방해를 받지 않고 부는 바람에 대해 제가 언급했던 점을 기억하시나요…? 좋아요, 우리 주변에 대해 생각해 봅시다. 우리는 높은 건물에 둘러싸여 있습니다. 이곳에서는 바람이 많이 불지 않는데, 이는 공기가 잘 순환되지 않는다는 점을 의미합니다. 따라서 바람

에 의해 차가운 공기가 들어와 뜨거운 공기를 분산시키지 못하기 때문에 도시에는 뜨거운 공기가 남게 됩니다.

도시 열섬이 여름에만 일어나는 현상은 아닙니다. 일년 내내 그리고 밤낮으로 일어나죠. 도시와 외딴 시골 간의 기온 차이는 통상 조용하고 화창한 저녁에 가장 크게 나타납니다. 그러한 이유는 시골 지역이 도시 지역보다 밤에 훨씬 더 빠르게 냉각되기 때문입니다. 따라서 해가 진 후 3시간에서 5시간 정도가 최대 열섬 효과라고 알려진 시기에 해당합니다. 이때 두 지역 간의 온도 차이가 가장 큽니다.

도시 열섬은 지역 및 그곳 주민들에게 심각한 부작용을 가져다 줄 수 있습니다. 사람들이 열사병을 겪을 수도 있고, 몇몇 사람들은, 특히 노년층인 경우, 여름의 극한 더위 때문에 사망하기도 합니다. 또한 여름에는 에어컨을 가동하기 위해 보다 많은 에너지를 사용합니다. 그리고 공기가 순환하지 않으면 대기 오염이 심각해집니다. 다행히도 도시 열섬 효과를 경감시키는 일은 가능합니다. 그렇게 할 수 있는 몇 가지 방법에 대해 말씀을 드리죠.

WORD REMINDER

phenomenon 현상   urban heat island 도시 열섬   dramatic 극적인   sidewalk 인도   manmade 인공의   evaporate 증발하다   cooling effect 냉각 효과   obstruct 방해하다   circulate 순환하다   moisture 습기, 수분   sun's ray 태양 광선   pave (도로 등을) 포장하다   drainage system 배수 시스템, 배수 장치   preclude 불가능하게 만들다   conductor 전도체   motorized 엔진이 있는   conveyance 운송 (수단)   disperse 흩어지다, 흩뜨리다   outlying 외진, 동떨어진   adverse effect 부작용, 역효과   resident 거주자, 주민   heatstroke 열사병

PART 3

Conversation

p.154

학생: 안녕하세요, Chambers 학생처장님. 저와 만나기 위해 시간을 내 주셔서 감사합니다.

학생처장: 천만에요, Janet. 편하게 앉아서 캠퍼스를 위한 학생의 원대한 계획을 얘기해 볼래요?

학생: 고맙습니다, 처장님… 본론으로 들어가죠. 저는 캠퍼스가 여러 가지 방면에서 더 좋게 보일 수 있다고 생각하고, 그렇게 하기 위해 도움을 줄 수 있는 자원 봉사자들을 모집하고 싶어요.

학생처장: 매우 의욕적이군요.

학생: 음, 저는 학교와 캠퍼스를 매우 좋아하지만 개선의 여지가 있어요. 그리고 제가 도움이 되고 싶어요.

학생처장: 정확히 어떤 점이 개선되어야 한다고 생각하나요?

학생: 몇 가지가 있어요. 무엇보다 캠퍼스 주변에 쓰레기가 너무 많아요. 제 말은, 어디를 가더라도 거의 항상 바닥에 떨어져 있는 쓰레기를 볼 수가 있죠.

학생처장: 그래요, 자, 어, 관리부에서 담당하는 일이군요. 몇몇 관리자들이 일을 그다지 열심히 하고 있지 않을 수도 있지만, 학생들이 무료로 쓰레기를 줍겠다고 하면 관리부 직원들이 크게 기뻐할 것 같지는 않아요.

학생: 정말인가요? 왜 그렇죠?

학생처장: 치워야 할 쓰레기가 없으면 그들이 일자리를 잃게 될 테니까요.

학생: 아… 그렇군요.

학생처장: 또 다른 아이디어가 있나요?

학생: 네, 처장님. 있어요. 캠퍼스 주변에 아름답게 꾸밀 수 있는 장소가 몇 군데 있다고 생각해요.

학생처장: 아름답게 꾸민다고요?

학생: 네. 예를 들어 학생 회관 주변 지역은 상당히 단조롭고 지루해요. 콘크리트로 가득할 뿐이죠. 우리가, 흠… 학생들로 하여금 그곳에 미술 작품을 전시하게 하거나 재능이 있는 미대 학생들로 하여금 콘크리트 벽에 벽화를 그리도록 할 수 있는지 궁금해요. 그렇게 하면 캠퍼스를 아름답게 꾸미는데 정말로 도움이 될 것이라고 생각해요.

학생처장: 흠… 가능할 것 같군요. 그에 대해 메모를 해서 Terry Sommers에게 연락을 할게요. 그와 같은 일이 실현 가능한지 그가 알려 줄 거예요.

학생: 정말 고맙습니다.

학생처장: 또 있나요?

학생: 지금으로서는 한 가지가 더 있어요. 캠퍼스 동쪽 끝에 있는 Granite 호수 주변 지역도 꽤 지루해요. 호숫가에 아무것도 없죠. 사람들이 식사를 할 수 있는 피크닉 테이블이 있어야 하고, 잔디를 더 자주 깎아야 해요. 그래서 약간만 더 좋아지면 많은 학생들이 그곳에 가는 것을 좋아할 거예요.

학생처장: 흠… 일리가 있는 것 같군요. 며칠 전에 저도 호수에 가 보았는데, 두어 개의 비슷한 생각을 했어요. 좋아요, 어, 제가 하려는 바를 알려 줄게요. 제가 학생이 생각하고 있는 프로젝트 중 어떤 것도 직접 승인할 수는 없지만, 학생의 아이디어는 마음에 들어요. 그래서 학생이 Janet Anderson 씨와 만날 수 있는 자리를 마련할게요. 이곳 부총장님 중 한 분이시죠. 그분께 학생의 아이디어를 말씀하세요. 하지만 제가 충고를 한 마디 할게요.

학생: 네, 처장님?

학생처장: 그분과 이야기할 때에는 준비가 더 잘 되어 있어야 해요. 학생의 아이디어와 학생이 문제라고 생각하는 점을 해결하기 위한 제안이 적혀 있는 두 가지 프린트물을 가지고 있어야 해요. Anderson 씨는 매우 바쁘기 때문에 그분께 학생의 아이디어를 알릴 수 있는 시간은 10분 정도일 거예요. 학생이 자신의 시간을 낭비하고 있다고 생각하시면 즉시 학생과의 대화를 중단하실 것이고요. 알겠죠?

학생: 완전히 이해했어요. 고맙습니다.

학생처장: 좋아요. 미팅이 준비되면 연락할게요.

WORD REMINDER

set aside 따로 떼어 두다   custodian 관리인   beautify 아름답게 꾸미다, 미화하다   mural 벽화   presentable 남 앞에 내놓을 만한   authorize 권한을 부여하다, 승인하다   contemplate 숙고하다

Lecture • Musicology   p.156

교수: 가장 흔한 악기 중 하나가 바이올린인데, 바이올린은 몇 가지 형태로 존재하며 다양한 장르의 음악에서 사용됩니다. 물론 대부분의 오케스트라에서도 중요한 악기로 사용되고요. 하지만 여러 종류의 민속 음악에서도 사용되며, 종종 미국의 컨트리 음악 밴드의 일부분을 차지하기도 하는데, 여기에서의 바이올린은 피들이라고 알려져 있습니다. 오늘은 우선 바이올린의 역사, 바이올린의 다양한 부분, 그리고 몇몇 유명한 바이올린 제작자들에 관해 이야기를 하려고 합니다.

바이올린의 정확한 기원은 알려져 있지 않지만, 과거의, 어, 즉 류트와 리라라는 현악기로부터 발전했을 가능성이 높습니다. 실제로 바이올린과 같은 현악기를 제작하는 사람들은 '루시아'라고 불리고 있기 때문에, 이 둘 사이에 관련성이 있을 수 있습니다. 자, 현악기를 연주하기 위해 활을 쓰는 것은 중앙 아시아에서 유래되었다고 생각되는데, 그 이유는 이 지역에 기원을 둔 음악을 연주하기 위해 활을 필요로 하는 현악기들이 상당수 존재하기 때문입니다. 시간이 지나면서 이러한 악기들이 서쪽으로 퍼져나가 중동 및 동유럽에 이르게 되었습니다. 주로 현재의 그리스와 터키 지방에 해당되는 비잔틴 제국에서 리라는 19세기에 매우 인기가 높은 현악기였습니다. 몸통은 비어 있었고, 형태는 타원형이었으며, 음악가가 리라를 수직 방향으로 잡은 상태에서 활로 현을 그어 연주가 되었는데, 이는 첼로가 연주되는 것과 거의 동일한 방식입니다. 스크린에 리라의 사진이 있습니다… 현대의 바이올린과 거의 흡사하다는 점에 주목해 주세요.

하지만 우리가 알고 있는 바이올린은 비잔틴 제국에서 유래한 것이 아닙니다. 대신 16세기 중반 베니스와 제노바의 항구 도시 근처의 북부 이탈리아에 그 기원을 두고 있습니다. 베니스와 제노바는 당시 이탈리아에서 가장 부유하고 가장 강력한 도시 국가였습니다. 이 국가들은 중동 지역 및 오토만 제국과 광범위한 무역 관계를 맺고 있었는데, 1400년대 중반 이들이 비잔틴 제국 자리에 들어서게 되었습니다. 바이올린은 이러한 경로로 서방에 유입되었을 가능성이 있고, 바이올린이 리라로부터 개량된 것일 수도 있습니다. 그건 그렇고, 알려져 있는 바이올린 중 가장 오래된 것은 그 연대가 1560년까지 거슬러 올라갑니다. 여하튼, 1500년대 말 바이올린은 서유럽에서 잘 알려져 있었습니다. 시간이 지나면서 바이올린에 개량이 이루어졌지만, 바이올린의 기본적인 형태나 스타일은 본질적으로 1500년대부터 거의 같은 상태로 남아 있었습니다.

좋아요, 어, 바이올린의 그림을 살펴보고 그 부분들을 검토해 보기로 하죠. 여기 스크린 위쪽을 봐 주세요… 바이올린은 두 개의 주요 부분으로 이루어져 있습니다: 몸통과… 목입니다. 목에서 주요한 부분은 지판인데, 지판은 바이올린 연주자가 손가락을 눌러 4개 현의 음 높이를 변화시키는 부분입니다. 여기 목의 끝 부분에는… 장식이 들어가 있는 소용돌이 무늬의 부분이 있습니다. 또한 줄감개집도 있습니다. 여기에서 여러분들은 4개의 줄감개를 보실 수 있는데, 이들은 현의 장력을 조절하고 음의 높낮이를 변화시킵니다. 몸통은 모래시계 형태를 띠고 있다는 점에 주목해 주세요. 윗부분은 우퍼 바우트라고 부릅니다. 철자는 B – O – U – T이고요. 아랫부분은, 어, 짐작하시겠지만, 로우어 바우트입니다. 여기 중간의 좁은 부분은… 허리입니다. 바이올린의 몸통은 속이 비어 있으며 몸통에는 두 개의 S자 모양의 폭이 좁은 구멍이 있는데, 이들은 F홀이라고 불립니다. 몸통에서 주요한 부분 중 하나는 줄받침입니다. 보이시나요…? 이곳에서는 몸통 위쪽으로 현들이 아치 형태를 띠고 있습니다. 현은 줄걸이에 의해 몸통에 연결되는데, 음, 줄걸이는 끝에 있는 검정색 부분입니다. 줄걸이 옆에는 턱받침이 있는데, 이것은 바이올리니스트가 자신의 턱을 올려 놓는 곳이죠. 자, 바이올린의 재료는… 네?

학생: 음, 방해해서 죄송하지만, 활은 어떤가요?

교수: 아, 그래요. 제 잘못이군요. 중요한 부분을 잊을 뻔 했네요. 활은 길이가 약 75센티미터이고 무게는 매우 가볍습니다. 활은 나무와 말털로 만든 줄로 이루어져 있습니다. 끝에는, 어, 활털 조이개라고 불리는 줄개가 있는데, 이것이 말털의 장력을 조절해 줍니다. 바로 여기에서 활털 조이개를 보실 수 있습니다…

구성 요소에 대해 말씀드리면, 바이올린은 나무로 만들어집니다. 나무의 종류에 따라 음질이 바뀌죠. 다른 요인들, 예컨대 나무의 두께와 사용된 광택제의 품질 또한 소리에 영향을 미칠 수 있습니다. 연식이 오래될수록 음질이 더 좋기 때문에 바이올린의 연식도 하나의 요인이 됩니다. 당연하게도, 가장 오래된 바이올린들이 가장 우수한 것으로 여겨지고 있습니다. 초기의 모든 바이올린은 북부 이탈리아에서 제작되었고, 최상급의 바이올린들은 이러

한 지역에서 나온 것들입니다. 아마도 가장 유명한 바이올린 제작자는 안토니오 스트라디바리였을 것입니다. 그는 17세기 후반과 18세기 초반에 살면서 작업을 했습니다. 그의 바이올린은 정교함과 변치 않는 품질로 귀중히 여겨지고 있으며, 오늘날 수백만 달러의 가격으로 판매가 되고 있습니다. 그 중 하나를 만져 보고 싶지 않으신가요?

Lecture • Astronomy

p.159

교수: 좋습니다. 모두들 과제를 제출했나요…? 그런가요…? 좋아요. 다음 주 월요일까지 돌려 드리도록 하겠습니다. 여러분 중 다수가 이전에 제출했던 과제보다 더 뛰어난 것이기를 정말로 바랍니다. 자, 오늘 수업을 시작해야 할 것 같군요. 역사에 관한 간단한 이야기로 시작해 보겠습니다. 1801년 1월 1일, 천문학자 쥬제페 피아치가 세레스를 발견했습니다. 세레스는 화성과 목성 사이에서 발견되었는데, 이곳은 대부분의 사람들이 행성이 있을 것이라고 예상했던 바로 그 지점이었습니다. 이러한 점 때문에 처음에는 세레스가 행성으로 분류되었습니다. 하지만 이후 6년에 걸쳐, 거의 같은 지역에서 세레스와 유사한 천체가 세 개 더 발견되었습니다. 여기에는 베스타가 포함되어 있었는데, 베스타는 1807년 독일 출신 천문학자인 하인리히 올베르스에 의해 발견되었습니다.

여러분도 짐작할 수 있듯이 이러한 사실은 많은 논쟁을 불러 일으켰는데, 그 이유는 이러한 천체들이 기존의 행성의 개념에 적합하지 않는다는 점을 대부분의 천문학자들이 깨달았기 때문이었습니다. 그러한 천체들은 너무나 작아서 육안으로는 볼 수 없고 망원경으로만 관찰할 수 있었기 때문이었죠. 1802년 세 번째 천체인 팔라스가 발견된 후 윌리엄 허셜이 "소행성"이라는 용어를 고안해 냈습니다. 그럼에도 불구하고 많은 천문학자들이 이러한 천체들을 계속해서 행성이라고 불렀으며, 1820년대에 태양계 내에서 11개의, 어, 행성들이 확인되었습니다. 1851년에는 총 15개의 천체가 존재했는데, 이들은 화성과 목성 사이에서 태양 주위를 돌고 있는 것으로 밝혀졌습니다. 마침내 그 후 천문학자들은 이러한 천체들이 새로운 종류의 천체를 나타낸다는 점을 깨달았고, 이들을 소행성으로 부르기 시작했습니다. 분명 천문학자들은, 어, 허셜이 반 세기 전에 제안했던 명칭을 받아드린 것이었죠. 오늘날, 이러한 우주 공간은 총칭해서 소행성대로 알려져 있습니다. 약 십만 개의, 직경 6마일 정도의 소행성들이 발견되었습니다. 이 중 직경이 약 590마일에 이르는 세레스가 가장 크고, 직경이 330마일에 이르는 베스타가 세 번째로 큽니다.

학생: Martinez 교수님, 저는 세레스가 왜성인 것으로 알고 있었는데. 제가 잘못 알고 있는 건가요?

교수: 전혀 잘못 알고 있는 것이 아니에요, Paula. 생각나게 해 줘서 고마워요. 2006년 국제 천문학 연합이 천체에 대한 새로운 용어를 만들어 냈다는 점을 말씀드려야 할 것 같군요: 바로 왜성입니다. 이는 명왕성이 행성에서 왜성으로 강등되면서 만들어졌는데, 세레스는 왜성의 지위로 승격되었다고 말해야 할 것 같습니다. 세레스는, 그건 그렇고, 우리 태양계에서 몇 안 되는

왜성 중에서 가장 작은 왜성입니다.

자, 세레스와 베스타 모두 몇 가지 이유로 천문학자들의 호기심을 자극하고 있습니다. 실제로 너무나 흥미로워서 이들을 가까이에서 탐사하기 위해 NASA의 인공위성인 돈 호가 보내졌습니다. 돈은 2011년 여름에 베스타 주위를 돌기 시작했습니다. 약 1년 동안 머문 다음 그곳을 떠나 세레스로 갈 예정인데, 이곳에는 약 2015년에 도착하게 될 것입니다. 돈 호의 임무의 중 하나는 이들 두 천체의 성분을 알아내는 것이었습니다. 자, 어, 지구에서의 연구에 따르면, 행성의 형성과 관련된 조건 및 과정에 대한 단서를 제공해 줄 수도 있는 성분이 세레스와 베스타에 있다는 점이 밝혀졌습니다.

세레스의 외부는 두꺼운 얼음 층 위에 존재하는 먼지로 덮여 있는 것으로 보입니다. 이러한 얼음은 깊이가 60마일에 이를 수도 있으며, 공모양의 암석 주위를 감싸고 있다고 생각됩니다. 매우 흥미롭게도 세레스에는 철 성분의 핵이 없을 가능성이 높습니다. 세레스에 관한 또 다른 흥미로운 점은, 태양계에서 커다랗고 얼음으로 이루어져 있고 지하수가 존재할 수 있도록 충분한 온기를 제공하는 내부 열기를 가지고 있을지도 모르는 모든 천체 중에서, 세레스가 태양과 가장 가까이에 있다는 점입니다. 이것이 왜 중요할까요? 음, 달보다 먼 곳으로 유인 우주선을 보내는 것을 고려한다면 태양계를 통과하는 동안 자원에 접근해야 할 필요성이 생기게 될 것입니다. 우리가 사용할 수 있기를 바라는 양보다 더 많은 양의 물이 세레스에 있을 가능성이 꽤 높습니다. 태양계 내에서의 세레스의 위치를 생각해 볼 때 세레스는 태양계의 바깥쪽, 즉 목성, 토성, 천왕성, 해왕성으로 향하는 유인 우주선에게 이상적인 경유지가 될 것입니다. 오, 그리고 그곳에 액체 상태의 물이 있다면, 세레스에 — 얼마나 멀리 떨어져 있는가에 상관없이 — 생명이 존재할 가능성은 항상 존재합니다. 극히 원시적인 형태의 생명체일 수도 있겠지만, 어, 어디에선가 생명체가 존재한다는 점을 밝혀낸다면 역사상 중대한 사건이 될 것입니다.

자, 베스타는 어떨까요? 음, 베스타는 세레스와 상당히 다릅니다. 거대한 크기와 중력이 갖는 효과 때문에 세레스는 비교적 둥근 형태를 띠고 있는 반면, 베스타는 불규칙한 형태를 띱니다. 그리고 베스타는 매우 건조한데, 이는 세레스와 크게 다른 점입니다. 베스타는 또한 철 성분의 내핵을 가지고 있습니다. 돈 호가 그곳으로 보내진 이유 중 하나는 베스타와 세레스가 왜 그렇게 다른지를 알아내기 위한 것이었습니다. 또 다른 흥미로운 점은 천문학자들이 지구에서 발견된 운석 중 20개당 하나는 베스타에서 온 것으로 추측하고 있다는 점입니다. 왜 그런 일이 발생하는지는 저도 모릅니다. 사람들은 돈 호의 임무로 그러한 미스터리 또한 밝혀지기를 희망하고 있었습니다.

TOEFL MAP

ACTUAL TEST

New TOEFL® Edition

Listening 2